Woodbourne Library
Washington-Centerville Public Library
Centerville, Ohio
DISCARD

D1029222

NEW CLASSICISTS

# ROBERT ADAM
The Search for a Modern Classicism

# NEW CLASSICISTS

# ROBERT ADAM
## The Search for a Modern Classicism
by Richard John

FOREWORD BY H.R.H. THE PRINCE OF WALES

images
Publishing

Published in Australia in 2010 by
The Images Publishing Group Pty Ltd
ABN 89 059 734 431
6 Bastow Place, Mulgrave, Victoria 3170, Australia
Tel: +61 3 9561 5544  Fax: +61 3 9561 4860
books@imagespublishing.com
www.imagespublishing.com

Copyright © The Images Publishing Group Pty Ltd 2010
The Images Publishing Group Reference Number: 562

All rights reserved. Apart from any fair dealing for the purposes of private study, research, criticism
or review as permitted under the Copyright Act, no part of this publication may be reproduced,
stored in a retrieval system or transmitted in any form by any means, electronic, mechanical,
photocopying, recording or otherwise, without the written permission of the publisher.

National Library of Australia Cataloguing-in-Publication entry
Author:          John, Richard.
Title:           Robert Adam: the search for a modern classicism / Richard John.
ISBN:            9781920744540 (hbk.)
Series:          New classicists.
Notes:           Includes index.
                 Bibliography.
Subjects:        Adam, Robert, 1948-
                 Architects – Great Britain.
                 Architecture, Modern – 20th century – Great Britain.
                 Classicism in architecture – Great Britain.
Dewey Number:    720.92

Coordinating editor: Robyn Beaver

Designed by The Graphic Image Studio Pty Ltd, Mulgrave, Australia
www.tgis.com.au

Pre-publishing services by United Graphic Pte Ltd, Singapore
Printed on 140 gsm Gold East matt art paper by Everbest Printing Co. Ltd., in Hong Kong/China

IMAGES has included on its website a page for special notices in relation to this and our other
publications. Please visit www.imagespublishing.com.

# CONTENTS

Nigel Anderson      Paul Hanvey      Hugh Petter      Robert Adam      George Saumarez Smith

CLARENCE HOUSE

'Inspiration does exist but it must find you working'.

Pablo Picasso

When Robert Adam was studying architecture in London in the late 1960's the idea of taking an interest in 'traditional architecture' was not exactly encouraged but, clearly, something fascinated him about it. Perhaps it was being part of the continuity of the culture and language of building that had been refined over millennia and the peculiar fact that this knowledge was so close to extinction?

It was in keeping this flame alive that Robert found himself studying in Rome as a scholar at the British School and being inspired as much by the cultural and social elements of tradition as by the buildings themselves. Those early seeds saw the growth of a quest that some 35 years later has led to the formation of the largest practice of traditional architecture and urbanism in Europe.

Core to the practice is social and environmental sustainability and it is within this spirit that the firm is carefully structured around a lineage of directors varying in discipline and age so that, as Robert finds more time for disseminating his ideas, the practice can continue to grow and develop with new blood and inspiration.

I have often said, and will carrying on doing so, that architects ought to have acquired a basic "grammar" that is related to the fundamental structure and proportions of Nature before they move on to more complicated narratives in building and that, over their lifetime, they should first learn, then practise and finally teach. I only hope Robert can find time in his busy schedule to inspire others with what he has learned and practised so that, once again, a creative and truly living tradition in architecture becomes the spirit of the age and the heritage of tomorrow.

*Bust of Robert Adam by Alexander Stoddart*

# PREFACE

Robert Adam has practised architecture in Winchester since 1977. In 1986 he co-founded Winchester Design, a firm that has been known as Robert Adam Architects since 2000 and in 2010 became known as ADAM Architecture. In an unusual move for an eponymous architectural practice, Adam has been joined by four fellow directors. Their names, and the years in which they joined the firm and were appointed director, are as follows: Nigel Anderson (1988, 1991), Paul Hanvey (1982, 1996), Hugh Petter (1987, 1997), and George Saumarez Smith (2003, 2004). Three of these are architects, the fourth, Paul Hanvey, is the technical director of the practice.

Adam talks about the involvement of these fellow directors as the realisation of what he calls the *schola* principle. S*chola* in Latin means the disciples of a teacher, though in fact all four of them had completed their training and worked in other practices before joining the firm. It is important, also, not to confuse the term with the art historical concept of the 'school' of an artist, because there are very clear stylistic differences between the work of each of the four design directors and it is unlikely that the designs of one could be confused with those of another. The 'schola' concept is, rather, a visionary approach to the expansion of the practice to ensure its continued vitality through the infusion of new blood. The work of the other directors is noted in what follows but the principal subject is the work of Robert Adam. Each director has a body of work that could be studied in its own right. The practice is unique both in the wide talent among the directors, all designing in the same tradition but with an individual character, and in its size. At more than 90 strong in 2008, with offices in both London and Winchester, the firm is currently the largest wholly traditional firm in Europe and possibly in the world.

# CHAPTER 1

# INTRODUCTION

*'Throw away Respect, Tradition, Forme, and Ceremonious dutie.'*

William Shakespeare, *Richard II*, III. ii. 173

By the mid 1960s the orthodoxy of the International Style was being challenged in Britain by a generation of architectural practitioners still in their thirties. Two diverse reactions to the slick uniformity of corporate Modernism can be identified. On the one hand, a fetish was made of technology by architects such as Jim Stirling, whose engineering faculty building at Leicester University was completed in 1963, and by Archigram, the self-consciously avant garde group based at the Architectural Association. While the members of Archigram had no actual buildings to their name, they nevertheless proved hugely influential through a stream of pop-culture manifestos and polemical projects. These drew for inspiration on the imagery of contemporary science fiction and the futuristic fantasies of Buckminster Fuller. Thus they produced visions of modular cities, such as Peter Cook's 'The Plug-in City' (1964), and mobile robot-like habitations, as in Ron Herron's 'The Walking City' (1964).

A quite different response to the banality of the International Style can be seen in the New Brutalism of Peter and Alison Smithson. Moving away from the restrained idiom of their Hunstanton school (1949–54), they enthusiastically embraced the language of *béton brut* first in their Economist building in St James's (1959–64) and then, with much less success, in the large public housing project of Robin Hood Gardens in Poplar (1966–72). This was how the architectural scene looked in Britain when, in 1967, the auspiciously named Robert Adam enrolled in the architecture school at the Regent Street Polytechnic in London.[1]

Adam, a doctor's son who had studied English, History and Art at 'A level', did not find the Polytechnic the most congenial of learning environments. During his third year at the school he lived with a group of 'normal middle-class people', as he later described them, who were lawyers or wine merchants. Their grounded pragmatism provided a refreshing counterbalance to his pretentious and utopian classmates whom his flat-mates saw as being 'completely bonkers'. His tutors at the Polytechnic included the now-fashionable Rick Mather, an Oregonian expatriate who had studied at the Architectural Association after moving to London in 1963. In general the tutors there were not supportive of his interest in tradition, though the arch-Corbusian Bernard Lamb said: 'I don't like what you're doing, but you're the only person that is and I think it's very important.'

---

1   The Regent Street Polytechnic merged with the Holborn College of Law, Languages and Commerce in 1971 to form the Polytechnic of Central London, which was renamed the University of Westminster in 1992.

Adam wrote his dissertation on the subject of probability theory, entitling it 'Chaos and The Enigma of the Environment'. For this he was awarded the Bannister Fletcher dissertation prize in 1972. Ostensibly it was about the mathematics of chance and philosophies of perception and began with a Borges-inspired short story about the philosopher Oakeshott witnessing a fatal car accident. Its main thrust, however, was rather an attempt to explain why the most satisfying human environments have not been specifically designed for certain activities, that is, where 'form follows function', but have grown up haphazardly over time, so that they come to fulfil very different requirements from those originally intended.

Though 'Chaos' featured prominently in the title, the substance of the text did not touch at all on the mathematical 'chaos theory' which was to become such a fad in architectural theory in the 1990s[2]; in fact 'chaos' would not even be coined as a term in mathematics until 1975.[3] Adam's attempt to yoke mathematics with analysis of the built environment was inspired in part by an essay published by Christopher Alexander in 1965, 'A City is Not a Tree'.[4] Another recently published work that clearly influenced Adam, particularly in the short final section of his dissertation where he attempted to transfer some of his theoretical concepts into the realm of actual architecture, was Robert Venturi's book, *Complexity and Contradiction in Architecture*.[5]

Mainly as a result of the success of his highly original dissertation, Adam won a special Rome Scholarship offered by the Architects Registration Council of the United Kingdom (ARCUK), and spent 1973–74 at the British School in Rome studying the urban morphology of the city, focusing specifically on the period from late antiquity to the early Middle Ages. He was fascinated by the continuity that he found in Roman architecture from the fully canonical classicism of the Imperial period, through the early Christian use of antique *spolia*, to the archaising forms of Romanesque architecture. The language was always classical, but there had been a gradual transformation. In turn the Romanesque style of the eleventh and twelfth centuries heralded the Renaissance revival of classicism and to such an extent that art historians even described it as 'proto-renaissance'. In Adam's eyes Rome provided the perfect example of a tradition continuously evolving over some twenty centuries, from the second century BC through to the flowering of the Baroque in the Seicento.

His studies of later Roman architecture were to provide him with invaluable precedents when later, wishing to work in a simple brick idiom but anxious to avoid the banalities of the neo-vernacular, he adopted the bold and simple typologies of late antiquity for projects such as Sheridan House, an office building in Winchester, and the new public library at Bordon in Hampshire.

During his time at the British School, Adam researched and wrote a number of essays on Roman topics, concentrating on the buildings and urbanism of the Campus Martius, the low-lying marshy area in the bend of the Tiber which during the Republican era had been a military exercise ground, but later became a locus for imperial iconography from Augustus through to the Antonines. What fascinated Adam more than anything else was the relationship between politics and architecture, and he sought to trace how the

2   E.g. Charles Jencks, *The Architecture of the Jumping Universe*, Academy, London and New York 1995.

3   It was first used in the context of mathematics by T.Y. Li and J.A. Yorke in their article 'Period Three Implies Chaos', *American Mathematics Monthly*, 82 (1975), p. 985.

4   Christopher Alexander, 'A City is Not a Tree', *Architectural Forum*, vol. 122, no. 1, April 1965, pp. 58–62 (Part I), vol. 122, no. 2, May 1965, pp. 58–62 (Part II).

5   Robert Venturi, *Complexity and Contradiction in Architecture*, New York, 1966.

early emperors developed the site to achieve particular political goals through architectural symbolism and urban iconography. This caused Adam to ponder the way in which buildings can be a vehicle for meaning: 'A building has no meaning whatever. It is a vessel which can have meaning put into it – and just as easily tipped out again. Any interpretation or symbolism that I will use is modern. It may relate to old things but it cannot be anything but modern.'[6] Later he concluded that 'it has been necessary to impose a meaning on the buildings. This meaning was not an inherent quality of the buildings themselves, it is just a way of understanding them, and therefore understanding the direct relationship between political, social and economic realities, ideas and buildings.'[7] Embodied in this line of thought is a crucial idea: that the meanings associated with buildings or styles are not fixed, but are fluid and dependent on context, thus changing from century to century and place to place. This concept would prove valuable in the following decade as Adam developed his arguments to defend classicism from that old chestnut of Modernists, that classical architecture was somehow fascist because of its associations with the Third Reich.[8]

A second essay traced the decline of Rome during the third century until the new imperial capital was established in Constantinople. He paid particular attention to the rapid transformation of Rome under Constantine, with the construction of his triumphal arch, the completion of Maxentius' basilica next to the Sacred Way, and the creation of the first Christian basilicas, a newly invented typology often incorporating *spolia*, elements plundered from earlier structures. Finally, he attempted a spatial analysis of the Campus Martius as it exists today, following its complex and haphazard transformation during the Middle Ages and Renaissance. He took special delight in the urban ambiguities that he discovered there: 'I am excited and interested in muddled surroundings, I like to be surprised and meet the unexpected, I enjoy the challenge of being lost and finding hidden places. I do not want to know exactly what lies around the next corner … I do not like clear and explicit statements – I find them rather boring … I think that variety, change and difference are a good thing.'[9]

While in Rome he met Quinlan Terry who had returned there for a visit having been a Rome scholar four years earlier. A comparison of their differing attitudes to the city is instructive. Following in the great tradition of architects from Palladio in the 16th century to John Russell Pope in the 20th, Terry had spent his time in Rome almost exclusively in making measured drawings of antique and renaissance buildings, providing him with a mother lode of architectural details that he continues to mine for his projects to this day. By contrast, Adam, while he certainly kept a sketchbook during his time in Rome, used his sojourn at the British School primarily to engage in original historical research and to investigate the fundamental relationship between architecture and urbanism on the one hand, and politics and society on the other. These different approaches to the fountainhead of classicism may be seen reflected in their bodies of work. Terry, eleven years Adam's senior, has practised with a quasi-religious conviction in a focused neo-Georgian mode, occasionally adopting slight regional variations where appropriate; for instance, turning to Schinkel for inspiration for a house in Frankfurt, and essaying, most convincingly, an American Colonial idiom for a row of shops in Williamsburg, Virginia. On the other hand, as will become apparent, Adam in his work has drawn fully on the entire classical tradition from Ancient Greece and Rome up to the neo-Baroque of Edwardian Britain and the Beaux-Arts skyscrapers of the American Renaissance. In addition to this wide-ranging exploration of the varied idioms

6  Robert Adam, *Rome: The Image of Empire*, unpublished essay, p. 37.

7  ibid., p. 50.

8  Robert Adam, 'In Defence of Historicism', *RIBA Journal*, December 1981, pp. 39–43.

9  Robert Adam, *Campus Martius Rome: Spatial Analysis*, unpublished essay, p. 1.

of classicism, he has also unhesitatingly engaged through his buildings the most pressing issues of technology and society as a whole. The one area of practice where Adam and Terry are perhaps closest is urbanism: both have drawn on their experiences of Italian cities to design townscapes of great richness in Britain and America.

## THE RADIANCE OF THE PAST

In 1980, the year of the *Strada Novissima* exhibition at the Venice Biennale, Adam wrote an essay entitled 'The Radiance of the Past', which was published in a much abbreviated form three years later in the *Architects Journal*.[10] The title is taken from Petrarch's epic poem about the Roman general Scipio Africanus, the *Africa*. At the very end of the epic, Petrarch addresses the poem itself, lamenting the current state of letters and predicting that, 'This sleep of forgetfulness will not last forever. After the darkness has been dispelled, our grandsons will be able to walk back into the pure radiance of the past.'[11] This passage, generally taken to be a harbinger of the rebirth of antique culture in the Italian Renaissance, was cited by Adam in his title to indicate the significance he attached to the recent reappearance of historic forms in British architecture. Perhaps the most prominent example of this new phenomenon was Terry Farrell's shop for Clifton Nurseries built in 1980–81 on a parcel of vacant land in the heart of Covent Garden and designed to occupy the site only temporarily while the Royal Opera House made preparations to build its planned extension. This ephemeral structure was, in essence, a greenhouse masquerading as an archaic Doric temple, though Farrell had wittily designed some of the squat columns to be constructed out of *treillage* giving an ironic post-modern twist to the supposed solidity of the primitive Doric forms.

Adam's essay, concerned as it was with revivals and revivalism, represented a marked maturation in his contributions as a theorist. Previously, he had sometimes seemed to struggle to make solid connections between his researches in fields such as probability theory, political history and early Christian theology, and the actual practice of architecture. In 'The Radiance of the Past', however, he was dealing directly with a contemporary architectural issue, and every time he cited an example from the history of literature or art it was specifically used to bolster his central argument. In making his points he was clearly motivated by a focused polemical intent; again and again he addressed the attacks being made on the emerging architectural 'historicism' from an unimpeachable philosophical high ground and dispatched them one by one as fallacious.

He began by identifying the crucial element in a revival as being the designer's *intent*; it didn't matter if references to historic buildings 'occur several times or once … [are] done well or badly … [are] done wholly or partially, it is still a revival.'[12] He illustrated this with a range of examples drawn from the tenth to the eighteenth centuries, including Michelozzo, Vignola, Palladio and Hawksmoor. He then dealt with the criticism that an architectural revival is mere mimicry, 'contemptible enslavement to the past' in Le Corbusier's words,[13] pointing out that the history of western architecture is mostly composed of periods of revivalism, which are more often inventive or erroneous than dry or pedantic. The difference between 'survival' and 'revival' was clarified, and he established that even a lapse of only a few decades was sufficient

---

10   *Architects Journal*, 16 November 1983, pp. 71–3.

11   'non omnes veniet Letheus in annos / Iste sopor! Poterunt discussis forte tenebris / Ad purum priscumque inbar remeare nepotes.' Petrarch, *Africa*, IX, 455–7 (ed. Festa, p. 278). For the context of this passage see Theodore E. Mommsen, 'Petrarch's Conception of the "Dark Ages" ', *Speculum*, vol. 17, no. 2, pp. 226–242.

12   Robert Adam, *The Radiance of the Past*, unpublished essay, p. 2.

13   Le Corbusier, *Towards a New Architecture*, London, 1923, p. 97.

to draw a distinction between one and the other. This was a crucial point because fewer than thirty years had passed since classicism had been taught in British schools of architecture, and the survival of the classical tradition through the 1950s in actual buildings was evident from prominent buildings such as Bracken House (1955–59), Sir Albert Richardson's headquarters for *The Financial Times*.

In order to illuminate the phenomenon of revival in the late 20th century Adam examined in depth some of the characteristics of revivals in previous eras. First he considered those inevitable anachronisms in the depictions of historical events which are painfully obvious to later viewers, but were invisible to their creators. One excellent example he gave was the range of different costumes seen in representations of classical figures from the Middle Ages to the present, so that Julius Caesar can often be seen wearing medieval armour in manuscript illuminations. In architecture these anachronisms can, in time, take on a validity of their own: Palladio's use of porticos for private houses, for example, was erroneously based on his belief that, 'the ancients made use of [porticoes] in their [public] buildings … it is very likely that they took the idea and the reasons for it from private buildings or houses.' Adam observed that Palladio 'made porticos on houses fashionable and it is a practice that continues as a consequence of his error'.[14]

While Palladio's reinterpretation of the temple façade as a domestic type was a result of his erroneous understanding of ancient buildings, many architectural reinterpretations were quite conscious variations on the original theme. Adam cited the relationship between the Propylaea in Athens built by Mnesikles in the fifth century B.C. and the Greater Propylaea at Eleusis of the first century B.C. whose designer copied the central section of the Athenian propylon for specific symbolic reasons. Alberti's use of the Roman triumphal arch motif at Sant'Andrea, Mantua, Sansovino's elaborate Doric order on the Biblioteca Marciana, Venice and even Hawksmoor's defence of Castle Howard as following ancient precedent all served to illustrate his notion of 'progressive reinterpretation'. Adam noted that the power of architectural symbolism was such that even the most abstracted forms could carry a heavy freight of meaning, so that 'the only stylistic condition that Mies van der Rohe placed on his chosen contributors to the 1927 Stuttgart exhibition' was to abjure pitched roofs.[15]

Adam's profound studies of Roman architecture and its influence allowed him to identify an even more subtle phenomenon, erroneous revivals of revivals. Here a designer was looking back, not to what he thought was the origin of a motif or style, but rather to one of its later revivals. Brunelleschi was clearly inspired by the Romanesque buildings of Tuscany, such as the Florentine baptistery and San Miniato al Monte; but, in common with all his contemporaries, he had believed that the baptistery was an Ancient Roman temple of Mars and so mistakenly thought that he was reviving authentic Roman architecture. In this case the Russian doll-like nesting of revivals went even further because, as Adam pointed out, it is likely that much Romanesque architecture developed directly from the Ottonian revival of classicism, and so was based not on genuine antique buildings but, rather, was dependent on the classicising Carolingian revival of only two centuries earlier.

While advocates for the modern movement had often tried to suggest the motive for revival is simply nostalgia, in fact there was generally a range of different reasons. At the base of all of them, Adam maintained, was a 'deep-rooted reverence or respect for the revived style' and this was apparent in

---

14   Robert Adam, *The Radiance of the Past*, unpublished essay, p. 22.

15   ibid., p. 27.

attitudes to Ancient Rome in the Renaissance, and to Ancient Greece in the eighteenth and nineteenth centuries. He emphasised that this reverence did not deny a designer the opportunity to be original; in fact, in many cases, the revival of past forms was acknowledged as consciously innovative, whether in the purity of Bramante's *all'antica* work or in the austerity of Wilkins' Grecian houses. Adam concluded with a forceful call to arms: 'Revivalism has been a complex and extraordinarily persistent architectural phenomenon … [It] has provided Western architecture with a visual vocabulary of remarkable richness, constantly regenerating itself from common sources … It would be extraordinary to claim that a break of only about thirty years in this evolutionary process should negate either its validity or the significance of its imagery. Turning technology into a master rather than a slave hardly seems to be a satisfactory substitute.'[16]

Within a year of the publication of the article based on 'The Radiance of the Past', the tone of the public debate about the revival of traditional architecture was transformed by a single incident: the speech given by HRH The Prince of Wales at the Mansion House on 30 May 1984. The occasion was doubly significant: the presentation of the Royal Gold Medal to the Indian architect, Charles Correa, and the 150th anniversary of the Royal Institute of British Architects. The Prince used the opportunity to attack the proposal to erect a tower designed by Mies van der Rohe on a site adjacent to the Mansion House describing it as 'a tragedy if the character and skyline of our capital city were to be further ruined and St Paul's dwarfed by yet another giant glass stump, better suited to downtown Chicago than the City of London.'[17] He also meted out harsh criticism of the proposed extension to the National Gallery in Trafalgar Square designed by Ahrends, Burton and Koralek, famously saying that it was 'like a monstrous carbuncle on the face of a much-loved and elegant friend.' Almost immediately it was as though lines had been drawn in the sand between the architectural establishment, whose members through education and force of habit advocated a Modernist approach, often in a self-consciously 'high-tech' idiom, and a small handful of practitioners who espoused a revival of traditional forms, materials and techniques.

The new combative tone of the debate is evident from Adam's article 'The Paradox of Imitation and Originality', which appeared four years later in *Architectural Design*.[18] This magazine, published by Dr Andreas Papadakis, functioned almost as a house journal for post-modernism and the new classicism throughout the late 1970s and 1980s with a roster of guest editors that included luminaries of the movements such as Charles Jencks and Demetri Porphyrios. In this piece, illustrated by his recently completed house in Salisbury Cathedral Close, Adam lamented the illogical suppositions and undefined assumptions that were bandied around in the discussion because 'in the emotional atmosphere of current architectural sectarianism this lack of clear thinking can close the minds of credulous students and practitioners alike.'[19] He focused on the word 'pastiche' and the phrase 'of its time', particular favourites of Modernists engaged in the counter-offensive following the Prince's speech. He showed that borrowings from past styles, disparagingly referred to as 'pastiches', were a marked characteristic of all architectural periods from Ancient Rome onwards, and that to suggest that this type of emulation was artistically invalid would eliminate most of Western architecture from serious consideration.

16  Robert Adam, 'Radiance of the Past', *Architects Journal*, 16 November 1983, p. 73.

17  http://www.princeofwales.gov.uk/speeches/architecture_30051984.html, accessed August 2006.

18  Robert Adam, 'The Paradox of Imitation and Originality', *Architectural Design*, vol. 58 (1988), nos. 9–10, pp. 18–19.

19  ibid., p. 18.

The phrases 'of its time' or 'of our time' were often used as code words for Modernism through the implication that any building that was not Modernist could not be 'of our time'. Here Adam was emphatic: 'Any building erected today, regardless of what it looks like, expresses some aspect of modern society and is, in this sense at least, a building "of our time".'[20] The issue, which he correctly identified, was that Modernists wanted desperately to avoid their buildings being judged from the point of view of style or aesthetics, and therefore their arguments were pitched beyond the notion of personal taste or judgment, appealing instead to some higher authority like the *zeitgeist* or to some spurious moral code such as 'truth to materials'. David Watkin had kicked away Modernism's philosophical crutches as long ago as 1977 in his essay 'Morality and Architecture', but still, more than a decade later, these tired incantations were being repeated. It is even more ironic that today, when much of what passes for Modernism is an exercise in historical revival, the same hollow arguments continue to be echoed.

20  ibid., p. 19.

*Opposite: The first new house to be built in Salisbury Cathedral Close for more than 50 years. A combination of orthodox classical design and an Arts and Crafts vernacular mostly expressed with brick detailing and colouring.*

*Left: River façade*

Later the same year, now wearing his professional journalist's hat for perhaps the last time, Adam reviewed *Architectural Design*'s 'Academy Forum'. The topic for debate at this public symposium was *The Vision of Britain*, the 1988 BBC television programme promoting The Prince of Wales's views on traditional architecture and urbanism. In his review of the event Adam voiced a concern that had never previously been heard from the traditionalists' camp: 'I was … distressed to see the classicism I love presented solely in the frozen form put forward by [Quinlan] Terry.'[21] This unexpected point of view did, however, have a precedent in Adam's writings. In the mid 1970s he had decried the increasing prevalence of the so-called 'neo-vernacular' that was, to his mind, Modernism watered down and made palatable to the planners through the addition of mansard roofs, bay windows and brick sills.[22] One might not have expected an advocate of traditional architecture to have attacked this new style of 'neo-vernacular', appearing as it did to weaken the stranglehold of Brutalism or the International Style, but to Adam this 'conservitecture', as he dubbed it, had few positive attributes, being rooted instead in 'pessimism and disenchantment'.[23] Again in the late 1980s, Adam avoided engaging ideological High Modernism as the enemy, seeing that battle perhaps as tilting at windmills; instead he preferred to keep his powder dry for skirmishes that were closer to his heart, fending off those tendencies which he saw as threatening an authentic revival of the classical tradition: on the one hand the meaningless ahistorical pastiche of the neo-vernacular and, on the other, what he believed to be a paralysing neo-Georgianism.[24]

21   Robert Adam, 'The Academy Forum: A Personal View', *Architectural Design*, vol. 58 (1988), nos. 11–12, p. 17.

22   Robert Adam, 'The Inevitable Destruction', *Architectural Review*, November 1975, p. 280.

23   ibid.

24   John Martin Robinson has, interestingly, identified a Modernist streak in Terry's approach. See his review of Professor Watkin's Radical Classicism: The Architecture of Quinlan Terry: 'An evangelical architect', *Apollo*, vol. 164 (2006), no. 536 p. 114.

NEW HOUSE
IN
SALISBURY
CATHEDRAL CLOSE
FOR
Mʀ & Mʀˢ BRISBANE

ROBERT ADAM
ARCHITECT
MCMLXXXIII

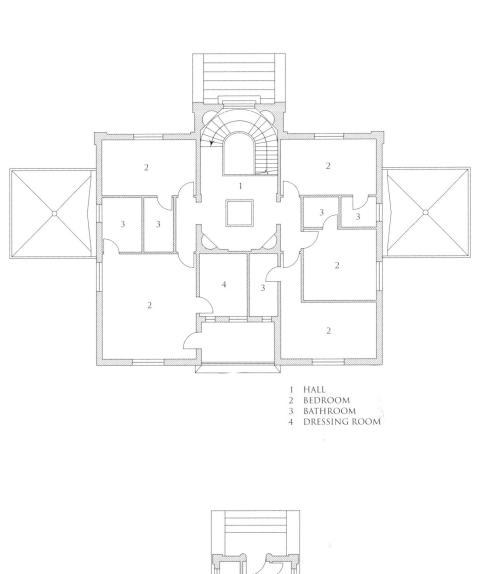

1 HALL
2 BEDROOM
3 BATHROOM
4 DRESSING ROOM

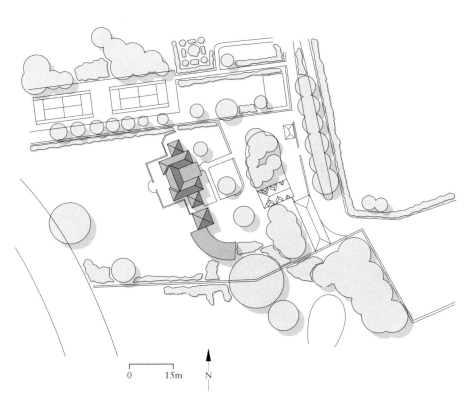

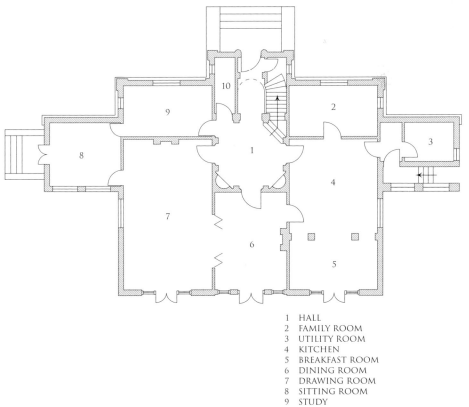

1 HALL
2 FAMILY ROOM
3 UTILITY ROOM
4 KITCHEN
5 BREAKFAST ROOM
6 DINING ROOM
7 DRAWING ROOM
8 SITTING ROOM
9 STUDY
10 WC

0 5m

N

**Opposite:** *Pen and ink drawing by Robert Adam. This drawing contains a number of clues about the design. The architect gestures to the house with his client, Ross Brisbane, behind him. In the distance, the 18th-century Robert Adam converses with Sir Edwin Lutyens. Scattered fragments mixed with measuring instruments show the use of square proportioning on the design and a tablet on the ground shows how this proportion relates to the gothic architecture of the cathedral. The drawing on the portfolio at the architect's feet sets out the proportioning system. The fragments are overgrown with ivy indicating antiquity and a broken column shows the interruption of the classical tradition with nettles, representing modernism, growing in the break.*

**Clockwise from above:** *New house in Salisbury Cathedral Close. Site plan.*

*First floor plan*

*Ground floor plan*

0 15m

N

Over the following two decades, from the late eighties to the present, Adam sought to develop an intellectual framework for his belief in the enduring validity of tradition through lectures and articles, polemical projects and buildings, and a book.[25] The projects, buildings and book will be discussed in subsequent chapters, but to appreciate fully Adam's particular contribution to the revival of interest in classicism, it is worth taking a moment here to compare his activities over this period with those of his close contemporaries in the movement. In 1987, John Simpson organised an exhibition at the Building Centre in London, which he boldly entitled 'Real Architecture'.[26] While projects by more than thirty architects and designers were included in the show, one can identify six practitioners who have been most prominent in the classical movement in Britain during the twenty years since the exhibition: Quinlan Terry (b. 1937), Julian Bicknell (b. 1945), Leon Krier (b. 1946), Robert Adam (b. 1948), Demetri Porphyrios (b. 1953), and John Simpson (b. 1954).

The involvement of these six leaders of the movement in education has been equally varied. Krier and Porphyrios were both Thomas Jefferson Professors at the University of Virginia in the early 1980s, and from the 1990s through the present decade have regularly held visiting chairs at Yale University including the Davenport, Bishop and Saarinen Professorships. Bicknell, who studied architecture at Cambridge, had been a tutor at the Royal College of Art before entering practice, and was director of its Projects Office from 1973–79. In the mid 1990s Porphyrios and Bicknell were the regular studio tutors for the postgraduate program of the Prince of Wales's Institute of Architecture, with Simpson also occasionally teaching at the school. Adam also taught briefly at the Prince of Wales's Institute of Architecture where he joined Hugh Petter who had helped to set up and run the pioneering Foundation Course. Adam has himself recently become more involved in education having been appointed a visiting studio professor at the University of Strathclyde when a new postgraduate urban design course was set up there in September 2006.

Quinlan Terry has been less involved in architectural education,[27] but he has written a few important polemical essays. As already noted, Adam has written many articles promoting his views on traditional architecture and urbanism and, in 1990, published an invaluable handbook on classicism, *Classical Architecture,* which is discussed in detail here, in Chapter 9. Of the six leaders of the movement in Britain to emerge from the exhibition *Real Architecture*, Porphyrios has contributed significantly to the theoretical debate about classicism through his writing and editing, and Krier has been and continues to be particularly influential. While the written output of these classicists has been minimal since the early 1990s, Adam has continued to research and develop the theoretical base of the movement. He has published a number of papers on tradition and collective memory, heritage and, most recently, has emerged as the leading expert on the effects of globalisation on architecture. His seminal paper on the subject was published in the *Architectural Review* in February 2008.

There is one area in particular in which Adam's achievements have most clearly set himself apart from the other five: his engagement with the wider architectural profession and public committees or 'quangos'.[28]

---

25  He had noted the need for such a theoretical base to underpin the movement as far back as 1981: 'Historicism now needs the development of a firm theoretical base to heighten the consciousness of its existing scattered exponents and to structure its future', Robert Adam, 'In Defence of Historicism', *RIBA Journal*, December 1981, p. 43.

26  Charles Knevitt, 'Architecture: Looking back to the future', *The Times*, 24 March 1987.

27  In 1988 Adam had drawn attention to this lack of engagement in teaching, which he saw as a particular failing of Terry's, noting that 'as the best-known practitioner, he continues to eschew educating and attracting young architects'; Robert Adam, 'The Academy Forum: A Personal View', *Architectural Design*, vol. 58 (1988), nos. 11–12, p. 17.

28  On the proliferation of quangos (quasi-autonomous non-governmental organisations) in the UK – there are now 2566 – and their wasteful cost and inefficacy see Maurice Chittenden and Yuba Bessaoud, 'Pay £180bn: you've been quangoed', *The Sunday Times*, September 3, 2006.

While Krier, Porphyrios and Bicknell all served on either the academic board or the board of trustees of the Prince of Wales's Institute of Architecture from 1992–98, none has engaged with the Royal Institute of British Architects (RIBA). Adam, by contrast, has devoted a vast amount of time in the last fifteen years to serving on its committees and filling various important offices. In particular, he is the only member of the traditional architecture fraternity in the UK to actively engage with the wider profession. Adam has been an assessor for the RIBA architecture awards on and off for a total of twelve years since 1989. While he found this interesting, he often felt that, as awards were rarely if ever given to traditional buildings and he was prepared to consider modernist buildings on their own terms, he was only a tame representative of the traditional community, sanitising the award process and giving more than he received. In 1995 he was appointed a member of the RIBA's Planning and Urban Design Group and also chaired the RIBA President's Special Working Party. He was elected twice by the membership to serve as one of the sixty RIBA council members from 1999–2005 and was Honorary Secretary of the RIBA in 2001–03.

From 1999–2004, Adam served specifically to represent the traditionalist viewpoint as part of a panel of thirty experts on the Design Review Committee of the Commission for Architecture and the Built Environment (CABE) when it was first founded; Porphyrios has now taken his place on the same committee. Quinlan Terry had previously been a commissioner on the quango that CABE replaced, the Royal Fine Art Commission, though he stepped down in 1997 after only one three-year term, perhaps because he felt, as is so often the case in these situations, that he was there merely as a token classicist. From 1996–2001 Adam was a member of the panel advising on conservation issues in London for English Heritage, the government agency for building conservation.

In addition to working with existing organisations of the architectural establishment, Adam has also been active in setting up new organisations: in 1995 he founded the Popular Housing Forum, which later merged with a former RIBA interest group to form the non-profit company, Design for Homes. In 2000 he established the International Network for Traditional Building, Architecture & Urbanism (INTBAU) which, under the leadership of its secretary Dr Matthew Hardy, has grown apace with chapters in Canada, Germany, India, Iran, Nigeria, Romania and the USA. While he was Honorary Secretary of the RIBA he established the Traditional Architecture Group as a 'linked society' – a special role within the RIBA – as he was sure that, once such an organisation was set up, it could not politically be disbanded and would keep traditional architecture represented in the RIBA. Reflecting the increasing role of masterplanning and urbanism in his practice, Robert Adam has also founded, with the help of others, the Council for European Urbanism (2003) and the Academy of Urbanism (2006).[29] In these cases, as in INTBAU, he was the draftsman of their core statements of principles, initiating the text and coordinating the responses of the founding committees. Through his tireless committee work and the establishment of these new organisations, traditional architecture is now firmly established as part of the UK architectural scene. Adam is now confident that traditional architecture and urbanism will continue to be recognised, if not actively supported, by the profession. He hopes that it will develop further to take a more prominent place as a significant participant in the improvement of the built environment and as a major challenge to the orthodoxy of modernism.

---

29   On the controversy aroused by this organisation see Helen Crump, 'Gough quits urban group over awards: Architect says academy favours places "conceived in the distant past"' *Building Design*, 13 July 2007, p. 3.

CHAPTER 2

# POLEMICAL BUILDINGS
# AND PROJECTS

*'The sale of a Deputy-Acting-Vice-Resident-Engineer,*
*Bought like a bullock, hoof and hide,*
*By the Little Tin Gods on the Mountain Side'*

Rudyard Kipling, *Public Waste*, 1886

Adam developed and promulgated his own intellectual underpinning for a modern classicism through two complementary routes: writing and designing. In the latter case, particularly earlier in his career, these projects were never intended to be built but were instead consciously polemical designs: their primary purpose was to challenge the architectural status quo. One can trace the tradition of such polemical projects at least as far back as Revolutionary France, when both Étienne-Louis Boullée and Claude-Nicolas Ledoux drew projects that were never intended to be built, but rather put forward an entirely new architectural aesthetic based on the simplest geometrical solids. Freed from the confines of practical economics and the pragmatics of building, such designs could be powerful exercises in pure form. While Adam's concerns were quite different – in particular he focused on how to incorporate the latest technology into the classical tradition and on how to apply that tradition to the commercial skyscraper – the means were essentially the same.

## TIN GODS

Adam delivered a paper entitled 'Tin Gods' to the Royal Institute of British Architects in February 1988. An extract was published in *Building Design,* and then an expanded version was appeared as an essay in *Architectural Design* in the following year.[1] Adam vigorously attacked some of the profound misunderstandings that surrounded technology and its relationship to society and culture. It was described in *The Guardian* by Martin Pawley as 'the first truly original scholarly dissertation by a practicing architect' to be delivered to the RIBA.[2]

Adam primarily focused on exposing the myth that technology, is, in and of itself, a propulsive force which takes culture forward. He argued that history demonstrated that technology was the tool of society rather than its master, and that it was absolutely the decision of the marketplace whether a certain technological innovation was in fact adopted or not. He illustrated how the application of technology was tightly controlled by the market through a number of examples from the car industry, including the Ford motor company's development of the bodywork for the Sierra model. He observed that it took six years and cost $800 million for prototypes and testing, an expenditure that could only be predicated on a huge number

---

1   Robert Adam, 'Spurious Linkage', *Building Design*, 4 March 1988, pp. 32–33; Robert Adam, 'Tin Gods', *Architectural Design*, vol. 59 (1989), nos. 9/10, pp. VII–XVI.

2   Martin Pawley, 'The Hi-Tech Fogey', *The Guardian*, 22 February 1988.

of unit sales. And, by 1993, when the model was discontinued, some 2.7 million Sierras had indeed been manufactured. He drew a stark contrast with the process of preparation for the construction of the Lloyds building where only £250,000 was spent on the creation and testing of prototypes of its innovative system of cladding. Adam was prescient in highlighting the gross inadequacy of this sum because in 1995, just nine years after the building's completion, £12 million had to be spent repairing the rust which had corroded most of the vertical water and waste pipes concealed beneath the stainless steel skin of the building. Since the corrosion had in part been caused by the flawed and inadequately tested design of the cladding, the architects, the Richard Rogers Partnership, together with Bovis and Arup Associates, were forced to foot the repair bill.[3] The comparison drawn between this building and the manufacture of motor cars has an additional irony: the Lloyds building must be unique in having a 'dent removal' team permanently on hand to take out the 'dings' that are constantly being left in the steel panels by service crews.[4]

Adam pointed out that the masonry arch was known about but hardly used in architecture for some 1200 years before the Romans embraced it and that plastic replacements for household china, though first manufactured more than three decades ago, had never caught on for everyday use, despite their clear practical advantages. This latter example provided Adam with an illustration of a skeuomorph that is an artefact which retains the form derived from its earliest technology of manufacture, even after the methods and materials of production have changed. A good example would be the presence of rivet-like painted markings on ancient ceramics which reflect their origins in gold and silver vessels. It has even been hypothesised that the painted Athenian ceramics – the so-called Attic vases – which today we value so highly, both in artistic and commercial terms, are nothing more than cheap copies of lost silver (black-figure) and gold (red-figure) originals.[5] This notion of the skeuomorph, borrowed as it was from archaeology and anthropology, became a crucial concept for Adam at this period as he sought to validate the classical tradition in the late 20th century. He argued that the forms of Greco-Roman architecture, and in particular the Doric order, were the result of transferring selectively the details of timber construction into masonry. The ancient Roman architect and author Vitruvius had indeed recorded this origin myth for the Doric order in his *De architectura libri decem*, the only architectural treatise to survive from antiquity. In his talk Adam expanded this notion of the skeuomorph to all technological changes where the earliest form is retained. For example, ceramic tableware, though now manufactured by dust-pressing rather than being turned on a wheel, still imitates the forms that originally resulted from that initial process of manufacture. Similarly, he pointed to the widespread adoption of Stephenson's railway gauge of 4 foot 8 ½ inches, even though there were technical disadvantages compared to Brunel's proposed 7-foot gauge. Adam emphasised the fact that Stephenson had adopted his gauge from the horse-drawn railway at Killingworth colliery, and compared this survival to the way in which computer keyboards had followed the QWERTY layout of early mechanical typewriters that had specifically been designed to minimise the binding of the keys when typing at high speeds. We now describe such survivals not as technological skeuomorphs but as examples of 'path dependence', a similar concept increasingly used by economic historians to explain how certain procedures become 'locked in' despite the seemingly obvious advantages of a different method.[6]

3  Pauline Springett and Julia Finch, 'Rogers pays for Lloyd's pipes', *The Guardian*, 8 July 1998, p. 3.

4  Angella Johnson, 'Lloyd's Threatens Legal Action to Stop the Rot', *The Guardian*, 5 October 1995, p. 4.

5  On this theory see Michael Vickers and David Gill, *Artful Crafts: Ancient Greek Silverware and Pottery*, Oxford 1994.

6  See S.J. Liebowitz and S.E. Margolis, 'The Fable of the Keys', *Journal of Law & Economics*, vol. XXXIII (1990), pp. 1–25; and P. Garrouste and S. Ioannides (eds), *Evolution and Path Dependence in Economic Ideas: Past and Present*, Cheltenham 2001.

Using these examples Adam made two particularly powerful points in his paper: first that 'new technology helps you do what you *want, better* and *cheaper* – and that's all.' Therefore one should not impose a self-consciously high-tech aesthetic on the spurious grounds of morality or by reference to the false religion of technology. Secondly, and here Adam hoped he was providing a source of inspiration to supplant the former fallacy, 'artefacts carry with them the history of their evolution both in their technological development and in our use and perception of them – the skeuomorph principle.'[7] Thus he was arguing that though we may have adopted new materials and new techniques of construction, we should still adhere to the old forms, in just the same way that an Athenian potter might copy the shape and decoration of an older metal vessel as he worked in the new medium of painted ceramic.

In the same year as his acclaimed RIBA paper, Adam began to engage the Modernist establishment through polemical designs as well through his writings. Without any specific client or site in mind, he designed a 30-storey tower entirely within the classical idiom. The overall articulation was based on a series of stacked giant orders: Doric, Ionic, Corinthian and Composite, each corresponding to five or six floors, with, at the top, a tetrastyle pavilion fronted by a statue of Apollo. The giant orders were used with great restraint, being more often implicit than explicit. Thus the lower five stories were grouped together as a kind of banded and rusticated base, with the notional Doric order which united them being indicated only by the overhanging mutulary cornice. The corners of the next section, the Ionic, were emphasised by implied pilasters, the existence of which was signalled by their capitals and bases. This kind of ambiguity between wall and pilaster in the rendering of an order was characteristic of the Italian mannerists, though it also could be seen in the nuanced work of Raymond Erith, who had died only 15 years previously. At the centre of this Ionic section the order manifested itself fully in the form of columns framing a rather over-wide glazed opening. This feature was repeated on the Corinthian section above, though it was here flanked by seven-storey octagonal towers capped by small Lutyens-inspired domes. The central bays of the next section, the Composite, were arranged as a triumphal arch, though the precedent chosen was unusual: the side elevations of the arch dedicated to Augustus at Orange in the south of France, where the central arch breaks through the entablature of the order into the attic above to create a powerful vertical emphasis. This same motif had been used by Nicholas Hawksmoor at Christchurch, Spitalfields, and also by C.R. Cockerell at the Ashmolean Museum, Oxford, a building that Adam was later to extend with his addition of the Sackler Library. If shown standing alone the Apollo Tower might have seemed like a mere creative indulgence, but the polemical intent of the design was made explicit by the two buildings that Adam drew as its neighbours to give it a hypothetical urban context. On one side he depicted a Modernist skyscraper with a rectangular grid of windows and spandrels articulated only by applied I-beams in the manner of Mies van der Rohe; on the other side he showed a circular tower entirely clad in a reflecting glass curtain wall of extreme banality. The message was clear. The monotony of these two types, which had come to dominate the design of tall buildings during the post-war period, was not inevitable. Instead one could have a building which took its cues from the Anglo-American tradition of the 1920s and 1930s, and which, through the use of a confident Beaux-Arts classicism, could both respect the scale of a human being and yet also respond to the forms and materials of the surrounding city.

A more public opportunity to offer a vision for the future direction of high-rise architecture was provided in the competition held by BBC2's *Late Show* to tackle the infamous tangle of elevated highways near Birmingham known popularly as 'Spaghetti Junction'. Five designers were invited to submit projects intended to improve the monstrous interchange. Adam observed that while motorway flyovers were a recent phenomenon, the problem

7   Robert Adam, 'Tin Gods', *Architectural Design*, vol. 59 (1989), nos. 9–10, p. XVI.

APOLLO TOWER
ROBERT ADAM
MCMLXXXVIII

*Apollo Tower. An imaginary tower of glass and stone with complex façades contrasting with the bland designs on either side.*

*Clockwise from above: Spaghetti Junction Towers.* One of a number of designs prepared for a BBC 2 television programme by different architects for the notorious motorway intersection outside Birmingham, nicknamed Spaghetti Junction. The linked towers are designed as a gateway to the city sitting in the wasteland created between the flyovers. A screen photograph of a specially created fly-through.

*Spaghetti Junction Central Tower.* A round tower with car parking on the lower floors and an illuminated roof based on the Mausoleum of Halicarnassus.

*Spaghetti Junction Square Tower.* A giant Doric tower with inset ascending Doric, Ionic and Corinthian columns. The lower floors are car parking and lift the occupied floors well above the road level.

FACING AWAY FROM MOTORWAYS
ELEVATION OF SQUARE TOWERS

ELEVATION OF CENTRAL TOWER

of how to deal with massive infrastructure was not itself new: the Romans had embellished their vast aqueducts and viaducts, and the Victorians their great bridges and tunnels. Therefore he decided that, rather than the expected response of trying to bury it or build over it, the best approach was to celebrate the junction as a gateway to Birmingham. Assisted by Nigel Anderson, one of the future directors, and Rod Maclennan, Adam designed three towers, one circular, the others square, linked by high bridges, so that they straddled the entire intersection. He proposed that they should be office buildings, but in order to achieve the monumental scale necessary he drew on the precedent of ancient Greek and Roman commemorative structures, so that the square towers are massive Doric pylons, carrying aloft glazed belvederes in the form of peripteral temples. The sides facing away from the motorways are fenestrated in the manner of the steel-framed buildings of the American Beaux-Arts, so that between the two giant Doric pilasters which rise the entire height of the tower, is a vertical band of glazing over which a sequence of stacked orders is superimposed. The taller circular tower echoes ancient funerary structures such as the tomb of King Mausolus of Halicarnassus, with its stepped top storey, and the imperial mausolea of ancient Rome, with their encircling cypresses. There is even a reminiscence of another of the Seven Wonders of the World: the Pharos or lighthouse at Alexandria, though since its fallen remains were not discovered until 1994, Adam was recollecting its Renaissance reconstructions.

Another opportunity for a polemical project to further the debate about the role of technology and new materials in traditional architecture came with the invitation to submit designs for a folly to sit in the grounds of Scotney Castle, one of the most self-consciously romantic landscapes in England. Scotney was laid out in the mid 1830s by Edward Hussey and Anthony Salvin as a picturesque landscape inspired by the theoretical writings of Richard Payne Knight and Uvedale Price. This garden thus seemed a particularly appropriate choice as the setting for a theoretical statement in the form of a folly. The garden building as a type had traditionally been the arena for architectural experimentation in 18th-century England, for instance, the first complete example of a Greek revival building was James 'Athenian' Stuart's Doric Temple (1758) in the park of Hagley Hall, Worcestershire.[8] The proposed new structure was intended to be a retreat for a poet, and four architectural firms were invited to submit projects. Adam chose to reprise the theme of Apollo, in this case appropriately enough because of the association with the arts and creativity, and so designed his poet's pavilion in the form of a colossal kneeling statue of the god. The head was an entirely glazed steel-framed structure which radiated spikes in a sort of punk sunburst and housed a sun lounge complete with deckchair and cat. The body of the colossus was made of reconstituted stone except for a breastplate and codpiece of bronze, and, at its midriff, a large lunette window that illuminated the poet's bedroom. While it has to be conceded that this habitable statue did indeed have a certain shock factor, so that it vastly outshone the other traditionally oriented entry, a humdrum circular tower from the firm of Birds Portchmouth Russum, it was not really recognisable as an architectural statement. Rather it belonged to that obscure tradition of the anthropomorphic fantasy, as practised by such architects as Deinocrates of Rhodes, Wendel Dietterlin, and Jean-Jacques Lequeu.

## THAMES RIVERSIDE MARKERS

The United Kingdom's National Lottery was set up in 1993 by John Major's government primarily to raise capital funds for architectural projects in preparation for the new millennium. Many of these were not ultimately built, either because they did not gain Lottery funding, or because they failed to attract the necessary matching

8   For the competing claim to this title of the Shepherds' Monument at Shugborough, also by Stuart, see Eileen Harris, 'Cracking the Poussin Code', *Apollo*, vol.163 (2006), no. 531, pp. 26–31.

Perspective View

Section

**Left:** *Bradstone Folly, Kent. One of a series of follies designed by different architects for Scotney Castle in Tunbridge Wells, Kent and funded by the cast stone manufacturer, Bradstone. This is the house for a philosopher, designed as a giant figure of the god Apollo. The materials of the folly become lighter as the rooms ascend to the head of the giant, starting with Bradstone, ascending to brick, then copper and finally glass.*

**Above:** *Section*

*Left:* Thames riverside markers. One of a series of columns marking key points on the river Thames, designed for the Millennium. Each marker would have a shelter and information point.

*Below:* Ten different columns of similar proportion and detail but individually designed to signify the history of each location

BELL HILL HAMPTON

CAST METAL TORPEDO COLUMN FOR THORNEYCROFT MTB WORKS. HORSESHOE LAMP FOR HURST PARK RACECOURSE

QUEENS PROMENADE

BRICK CHIMNEY COLUMN FROM HAMPTON COURT. OCTAGON DOME LAMP FROM HAMPTON COURT

KINGSTON WATERFRONT

STACKED OARS COLUMN IN CAST METAL. CORONATION CROWN LAMP

TEDDINGTON LOCK

COILED ROPE COLUMN IN CAST METAL. FLAME LAMP FOR CANDLE FACTORY

RADNOR GARDENS TWICKENHAM

GOTHICK COLUMN FOR STRAWBERRY HILL. RUGBY BALL LAMP.

THAMES MARKERS
HAMPTON
TO KEW
ROBERT ADAM ARCHT.
JANUARY 1996

KEW BRIDGE

CARVED TREE TRUNK COLUMN. CLOCK LAMP FOR TOMPION'S SETTING OUT AT KEW GARDENS.

BRENTFORD

BASKETWORK COLUMN IN CAST METAL FOR BASKET MAKING. BARGE LAMP FOR GRAND UNION CANAL

ISLEWORTH

STAINLESS STEEL OBELISK IN COLUMN FOR OLD MERIDIAN. LAMP FROM OBELISK POINT.

RICHMOND RIVERSIDE

CARVED VERMICULATED RUSTICATION FROM LOST HORSE FOUNTAIN IN GEORGE STREET. LAMP FROM RICHMOND PALACE DOME.

ORLEANS GARDENS

CARVED ORLEANS OCTAGON COLUMN. LAMP FROM RAILING AT HAM

CAST STAINLESS STEEL CAPITAL AS PLAITED ROPE.

CAST STAINLESS STEEL BASE AS LIFEBELT

29

funds. During the first years of the Lottery, applications for grants were frequently characterised by the lack of an orthodox function or building programme; instead they were often related to a generic marking of the millennium or to some broad celebration of national or local heritage. One such project was the proposal in 1996 from Richmond Borough Council for a series of riverside markers designed by Robert Adam to be placed along the Thames from Hampton to Kew. In some cases, such as at Teddington Lock, these markers would be associated with pavilions housing public amenities. Adam designed ten column markers for particular sites, and another ten generic markers that could be placed anywhere along the river. The location-specific markers all featured the same cast stainless steel capital and base; the former imitating a ring of plaited rope, the latter a lifebelt. Most unusually, what varied from location to location was the form of the shaft and the shape of the finial lamp on top. The series of markers demonstrated Adam's remarkable ability to generate a whole sequence of variations on a theme, much in the same way as he would often provide a client with as many as ten different proposals for a single project.[9] It also illustrated the almost infinite capacity of the classical orders to be bearers of meaning. In antiquity the variations mostly occurred in the form of the capital, and whereas the original significance of the three Greek orders is now a matter of speculation, we can, for instance, be fairly confident that the so-called Pergamene order with its palm frond capital was originally intended as a mark of the patronage of the Attalid kings.[10] Two examples will suffice to show both Adam's fertility of invention and the specificity of reference: at Brentford he designed a column shaft with a surface that imitated basketwork to commemorate the basket weaving traditions of the area, and at Twickenham he proposed a shaft composed of clustered gothic colonettes in reference to Horace Walpole's neo-medieval fantasy of Strawberry Hill. Adam also took the opportunity in this project to show how the classical orders could be abstracted and re-imagined in steel to create a stripped industrial idiom. The shallow curved roof of his pavilion at Teddington Lock was supported by an elegant metal colonnade which, with its attenuated cylindrical columns and the elongated volutes of their capitals, owed much to mid 19th-century experiments with cast iron.

## MILLENNIUM GARDEN PAVILION, HAMPSHIRE

While the project for the Thames markers came to naught, Adam was given an extraordinary opportunity to pursue his interest in the application of new materials and technologies to classicism when Lord Sainsbury of Preston Candover commissioned him to design a pavilion for the park of his 18th-century house in Hampshire. Lord Sainsbury had overseen the flotation of his family's grocery business on the stock exchange in 1973 and which under his chairmanship until his retirement in 1992, had become the United Kingdom's largest supermarket chain. Adam had previously worked for him in 1989, designing a modest but elegant brick house in the village of Preston Candover. This had combined an Arts and Crafts idiom of tall chimneys, broad roof and deep eaves, with the simple classical details of a Tuscan colonnade and acanthus-carved brackets. These disparate elements were all brought together with the kind of lightness of touch that one associates with an accomplished Edwardian such as Herbert Baker.

For the pavilion, built to mark the new millennium, Adam essayed a much bolder idiom. It was set on a gentle rise, a little above the house, with views across the valley. The basic form, a domed open tholos or circular temple, has plenty of precedents for its use as a belvedere set in parkland. It was perhaps most perfectly realised by Leo von Klenze in his Monopteros in the Englischer Garten in Munich (1836). Here, however,

---

9   For example, the different proposals for a garden pavilion at Shalden Park, and the numerous variations on 'a country house with a rotunda for Mr Collins' designed as part of a limited competition.

10   For instance as found on the interior colonnade of the upper story of the Stoa of Attalos in the Athenian Agora.

**Clockwise from left:** *Millennium garden pavilion, Hampshire. A garden pavilion to mark the turn of the millennium on a private estate in Hampshire. The brief was for a classical structure but of a distinctly modern design. The classical columns support a dome which, through innovative engineering, appears to float above the columns.*

*The dome is held up with stainless steel finials, like stamens, rising out of stainless steel balls that are contained within column capitals made of bronze leaves*

*View from the pavilion back to the main house*

Adam completely transformed this prototype. Working closely with the engineer Tony Hunt, Adam made it a structural *tour de force,* so that, until one is quite close, it appears that the dome is hovering just above the circle of six limestone columns. Only the upper two-thirds of the columns are fluted, just as in a Hellenistic stoa, to indicate the secular nature of the structure and to preserve the arrises from damage. The abstracted Corinthian capitals consist of three ranks of plain bronze leaves, furled, half unfurled and fully open. These were individually cast by a local foundry and bolted to a steel core from which thin steel pins rise to support the ring beam at the base of the dome. The dome itself consists of a spiralling aluminium lattice sheathed in thin copper plates which are lacquered on the inside so that mysteriously they seem to glow.

The dome's stability under lateral wind loading is ensured by tensioned cables, which run diagonally to complement the compression support provided by the pins, thus creating what Buckminster Fuller called a tensegrity structure. All of this occurs in the zone of the entablature normally occupied by the architrave and frieze. Thus their omission, and therefore the effect of the floating dome, is not a mere whim of the architect indulging in fancy tricks, but rather the logical result of translating the load-bearing members of classicism into a new technology. The tholos sits on a larger oval platform of the same stone as the columns, paved in a radiating pattern and enclosed at its rear by a low flint and stone wall with a wooden bench. Set at the very centre of the pavement is a circle of black slate and, a little further out, a ring of the same material divided into 20 parts, corresponding to each of the centuries of our era. These were carved by Gary Breeze with an inscription that pays homage to those who 'contributed greatly to our nation's history, heritage and culture' and the encircling list begins with Boadicea and ends with Baroness Thatcher.

## LINCOLN CENTER, NEW YORK

The Millennium Pavilion was an exquisite exercise in updating the classical language through the use of materials and technologies that were not available to previous generations of practitioners. At the same time as he was striving to innovate within the tradition at this small scale, Adam was also contemplating the same task on a

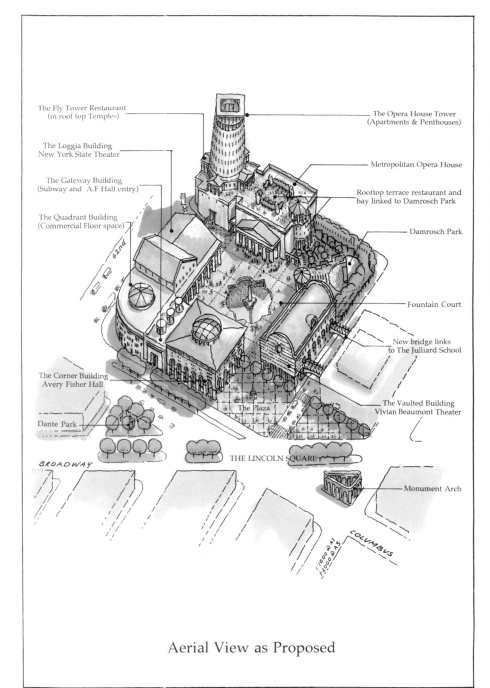

The Fly Tower Restaurant
(in roof top Temples)

The Loggia Building
New York State Theater

The Gateway Building
(Subway and A.F Hall entry)

The Quadrant Building
(Commercial Floor space)

The Corner Building
Avery Fisher Hall

Dante Park

The Opera House Tower
(Apartments & Penthouses)

Metropolitan Opera House

Rooftop terrace restaurant and
bay linked to Damrosch Park

Damrosch Park

Fountain Court

New bridge links
to The Julliard School

The Vaulted Building
Vivian Beaumont Theater

Monument Arch

BROADWAY

THE LINCOLN SQUARE

COLUMBUS

Aerial View as Proposed

View from Fountain Court

*Opposite: Apartment Tower, Reading. A project for an apartment building at the entry to the town of Reading.*

*Left: Lincoln Centre, New York. A scheme designed for the* City Journal *for the rebuilding of the Lincoln Centre. One of a series designed by different architects. The buildings have been rearranged to create a series of varied public spaces within the urban block and to enhance the small park at the intersection of Broadway and Columbus Avenue. The buildings are varied to express their different functions and to create a sense of place. An apartment tower has been included in the southwest corner to generate revenue.*

*Above: View into the inner court*

much larger canvas: a 12-storey mixed-use tower for Reading. This project, designed for Donfield Homes in 1999, remains unexecuted, but it was soon followed by two polemical projects and a research article exploring the same theme of classicism and the skyscraper. All were commissioned by Myron Magnet, the editor of the Manhattan Institute's quarterly publication of urban affairs, the *City Journal*. Dr Magnet is perhaps best known as the author of *The Dream and the Nightmare: The Sixties' Legacy to the Underclass* (1993), which President George W. Bush once described as the most important book he had read after the Bible.[11]

In 2000, the management of New York's Lincoln Center reported that 1.5 billion dollars was required for the restoration of the arts complex despite it being less than 40 years old. Magnet's response was to urge that the complex should not be restored, but torn down and replaced. To stimulate the debate about the nature

11 www.manhattan-institute.org/html/magnet.htm, accessed November 2006.

VIEW FROM PUBLIC PARK and W 30th STREET

*Above:* Lower East Side redevelopment, New York. *A group of classical towers designed for the* City Journal *for a proposed redevelopment of the area. The towers are, clockwise from the top right, by Franck Lohsen McCrery, Thomas Gordon Smith, Peter Pennoyer, Robert Adam, Richard Sammons and John Simpson.*

*Right:* Robert Adam's tower, *a simple and commercial design, facing onto a scheduled new park. It develops the traditional tower design theme of a column with a base, shaft and capital and a lower self-contained 'palace' design at street level.*

of its replacement he cleverly approached three architectural firms and asked them to draw up proposals for the site for publication in the *City Journal*. Only one firm was American, Franck Lohsen McCrery, a very recently established outfit of young classically trained graduates of the University of Notre Dame, the other two were British architects, Quinlan Terry and Robert Adam. Terry emphasised in his proposal that all the buildings would be constructed in load-bearing Indiana limestone, though he seemed to have little interest otherwise in introducing any kind of innovation in the project: he offered no variation on the existing layout of the buildings of the centre, and even used the identical basilican form for three of the five buildings in his sketches. Franck Lohsen McCrery had clearly invested considerable time in its well thought-out designs, though the idiom it embraced, the etiolated classicism of Washington's Federal Triangle, perhaps reflected the firm's District of Columbia location (and its hoped-for clientele there) rather than the vigour of New York's indigenous architecture. Adam, by contrast produced a scheme that transformed the site completely. He rejected the existing relationship of the complex's central square with Broadway as a banal and hollow gesture, and instead enclosed the space with buildings, moving Avery-Fisher Hall to the Columbus Avenue edge of the site. Stylistically his proposed buildings owed much to the simplified classicism of Ledoux's utopian schemes, so that none of the structures were completely articulated using the orders though they all had arcades or attached porticos for shelter. For Americans who grew up with Post-Modernism, however, the idiom of his proposal might have been a little too reminiscent of Michael Graves's work of the late 1980s to seem very original. Compared to the schemes of the other two firms, Adam's design was distinctive in two specific ways: first, it consciously introduced variety to the buildings, giving the complex more of the vibrant feel of a traditional organic city than a master-planned ghetto of high culture. Secondly, it proposed a dynamic mix of uses, including shops, restaurants and a 17-storey residential tower in the form of giant column placed on top of the opera house's fly tower. These two aspects reflect Adam's long-standing interest in the messy vitality of real cities, going back to his studies of the Campus Martius and his student thesis.

Adam's inclusion of a tower clearly piqued Myron Magnet's interest; the following year he commissioned him to write a research article on that uniquely American contribution to the catalogue of building types, the skyscraper. Here Adam traced the development of the form, from the coining of the term in the 1880s through to its climax in Cass Gilbert's stately United States Court Building of 1936. He lamented the amnesia that seemed to have affected the new traditionalists, who had mostly left Modernism's grip on the tall building unchallenged. Despite this critique, he ended on a note of optimism by discussing recent examples of tall classical buildings by Robert A.M. Stern and Demetri Porphyrios and his own unbuilt work.

The rich seam of material that Adam brought to light in this article proved fruitful, because in 2005 Myron Magnet, inspired by its content, commissioned a series of skyscraper projects from six architectural firms – four American and two British – again including Adam. For his site, on Eleventh Avenue at 33rd Street, Adam further developed the basic *parti* of the defunct Reading project, though now at a very different scale. He argued pragmatically that it made the most sense to keep the form fairly simple and restrained, in order that it appear financially viable. Even so, with its polished marble columns, copper stepped roof, and gold capitals and finial, the result was extravagant indeed by comparison to the Donfield Homes project of six years earlier.

## BROOK HOUSE, BASINGSTOKE

It seemed possible that Adam might realise one of his tower designs. Brook House is a 14-storey octagonal apartment building to replace a disused office building in the southern English town of Basingstoke, most notable for its 1960s expansion to accommodate population overspill from London. The tower is based on the principles he had examined when writing on tall buildings for *City Journal*. It has a prominent roof – particularly suitable for its landmark position at the end of long vistas in the approach to the central business district of Basingstoke – an architecturally developed base to respond to the street scene and a plain treatment for the floors between. The key to the design was the division of the composition into three parts horizontally: two lower wings onto the side streets and an octagonal centre tower, the tower differentiated from the wings with recessed balconies. Central Basingstoke is not a high-value area and so the design is simple and economic. The proposal was, however, rejected by town officials as not 'contemporary' enough for the 'forward looking' town, in spite of the fact it had been supported by the government design review body CABE (see Chapter 1). The developer was to take the decision to a government inspector for a final decision but the 2008 recession resulted in the cancellation of the project and its substitution with a conversion of the crumbling 1960s office block on the site.

At the time of writing the recession has resulted in the cancellation of many such large projects on marginal sites and the attraction of the prominent symbolic – or iconic – building seems to be increasingly associated with the profligacy of the 15-year boom. It may be that Adam's work on the traditional office block will remain in the realms of the polemic but it is to be hoped that a future economic recovery will yet enable this important work to be turned into reality.

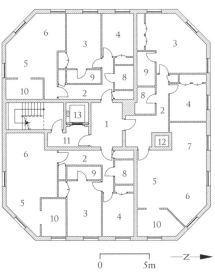

1   LOBBY
2   HALL
3   BEDROOM 1
4   BEDROOM 2
5   DINING
6   LIVING
7   SITTING
8   BATHROOM
9   ENSUITE
10  KITCHEN
11  FIRE FIGHTING LOBBY
12  AOV
13  LIFT 1

*Above: Brook House, Basingstoke. A design for a brick-clad apartment block on a principal entry route to the centre of the town of Basingstoke. It uses the column base, shaft and capital principle of traditional tower design. The central tower is separated from the lower flanking buildings with balconies.*

*Right: Typical floor plan, tower*

Tower of the Orders. A pen and ink drawing prepared for the Royal Academy Summer Exhibition in London. The drawing shows a street populated with classical architects from history and focusing on a tower with the three principal classical orders – Doric, Ionic and Corinthian – stacked one on another. Robert Adam is in the foreground with the ceramic artist, David Birch, examining one of the terracotta Hart's Tongue Fern designs for the capitals illustrated (a fern grows under the arch). Facing them is Quinlan Terry with Raymond Erith behind him. In the centre is Sir Edwin Lutyens. To his right are John Belcher and John James Joas and behind them is C.R. Cockerell. Looking back into the building on the right is Sir John Soane. In the centre behind Lutyens is the 18th-century Robert Adam and, to the right of Lutyens, Sir John Vanburgh talks to Nicholas Hawksmoor. In the background are a group of renaissance architects and in the far background Roman architects. On this street all the architects can talk to one another notwithstanding their separation in time. Also on the street is the naked figure of truth and a peacock symbolising incorruptibility. In the disk at the top left is a quotation from the Roman architect and author, Vitruvius, 'Derived from the true things of nature.'

CHAPTER 3

# COMMERCIAL DEVELOPMENTS

*'He and I had an office so tiny that an inch smaller and it would have been adultery.'*
Dorothy Parker (1893–1967)

In comparison with the fields of residential and institutional architecture, commercial development during the last quarter century has almost completely shunned the serious practitioners of classical and traditional architecture. Quinlan Terry's picturesque Richmond Riverside was deservedly successful in the late 1980s, but the following decade saw an unhappy outcome for the most ambitious classical proposal of modern times – the Simpson/Farrell/Beeby plan for Paternoster Square adjacent to St Paul's Cathedral.

During Margaret Thatcher's premiership manufacturing declined sharply and the service economy began a period of phenomenal growth, resulting in two office-building booms, first in the mid 1980s and again in the late 1990s. During these boom times developers have, from a stylistic point of view, mostly adhered to what they had done since the 1970s: in areas of historic sensitivity they were forced to use an anodyne neo-vernacular in order to get planning permission, but everywhere else they opted for a watered-down Modernism that was cheaper to build and therefore more profitable. [1] Robert Adam is unique amongst the present generation of classical architects in having first made his name in the national press with commercial projects in traditional and classical idioms rather than other building types.

Sheridan House in Winchester, completed in 1984, provides four floors of open-plan office space, two shops, and even incorporates vehicular access to a rear alley and parking area. The simplicity of its front on historic Jewry Street belies the intricate complexity of the plan behind. From the street it appears as two buildings, one wide, consisting of three bays, and the other narrow, of just a single bay that replaced an historic building which collapsed during construction. Each of the bays of the wide section was based on a large semicircular brick relieving arch, rising through two storeys. The triple-bay façade drew on Adam's studies of Romanesque architecture, with three giant arches each framing a trio of smaller arches that light the first floor rather like the triforium of an early medieval basilica, such as San Ambrogio, Milan, or like the clerestory windows of the Basilica of Constantine in Rome. The second floor is slipped in discreetly below the eaves like a low loggia or gallery, with a band of windows interrupted only by slender brick piers that establish the link with the system of arcuated supports below. Most unusually for a relatively small provincial office building it was written up in the national press, perhaps because it so clearly punched above its weight in architectural terms and yet, at the same time, fitted in so admirably with its sensitive context. It received a Civic Trust commendation in 1984.

---

1  Richard Pommer, 'Architecture and the Collective Consumer', *Assemblage*, no. 8 (1989), pp. 124–131.

**Above:** *Sheridan House. A new office building with ground-floor shops in the city centre of Winchester. The arcaded street façade fits into a varied historic street while making a distinctive contribution. There is extensive accommodation to the rear. The right-hand arch gives access both to car parking and the office entrance.*

**Left:** *The name of the building spans one complete bay and is a terracotta and faïence panel with lettering designed by Richard Kindersley and manufactured by David Birch of the London Pottery*

# DOGMERSFIELD PARK, HAMPSHIRE

The same year, Adam completed a very different kind of commission for an office building. The Amdahl Corporation had been set up in 1970 by the Norwegian–American computer architect and entrepreneur, Gene Amdahl, best known for the law of parallel computing that bears his name.[2] The firm, based in Sunnyvale, California, competed aggressively with IBM in the 1980s and early 1990s in the market for large servers for institutions and government agencies. In the early 1980s the company bought Dogmersfield Park, a country house in Hampshire that had recently been damaged by fire. The house had been built in 1728 for Martha Goodyer and her husband Ellis St John, and described without malice by Pevsner[3] as 'large, red brick and plain'. The 13-bay *corps de logis* survived, but the two retreating wings that had framed a rear courtyard had been destroyed in the fire. Amdahl commissioned Gebler Tooth Architects to add a new east wing to the surviving block, which would more than double the available space. Though the plans they produced for the open office floors were deemed acceptable, their subdued neo-vernacular elevations did not find favour. Adam was hired as a design consultant to clothe Gebler's plans and was required to follow the floor-to-ceiling heights and the window spacing of the 18th-century house. Rather than devise an extension that would be submissive to the original house – a difficult task considering its extreme reticence – he took the opposite tack and produced a marvelously vigorous essay in a muscular Baroque idiom. Though the style differed, the materials followed the cue of the main house: stock brick with stucco parapets and mouldings.

Adam worked with Nigel Anderson and came up with a tripartite composition focused on a central pavilion dominated by a wide stucco pediment over a portico in antis. The giant order was not of round columns, but rather square pillars, which are unconventionally tapered and built of roofing tiles in the manner of Roman bricks. This refinement, though uncanonical, gives the pillars a powerful presence, making them seem to bow under the weight they bear and recall those used by Inigo Jones at St Paul's, Covent Garden, in the 1630s. The broad tympanum is penetrated from below by an aedicule of freestanding stucco columns framed by a stucco relieving arch. The raking cornice of the pediment breaks back above as if responding to the vigorous thrust from the arch underneath. The same contrasting forms are also found locked in conflict on the end pavilions where deep projecting pediments seem to have been broken open from below, this time by thermal windows. In spite of the powerful sense of an overarching composition, the front is not strictly symmetrical; the southern pavilion has a shallow semicircular portico that is absent from the northern end. This asymmetry in the façade reflects the irregularity of the plan: though most of the interiors are open-plan offices, in response to the needs of the programme the service and circulation core is located at the southern end of the wing.

The bold aplomb with which Adam handled the classical language at Dogmersfield had not been seen in British architecture for many decades. Such a confident swagger had probably not been exhibited in an office building since the heady optimism of the Edwardian era. While the label Baroque has sometimes been a byword for architectural dishonesty, suggesting theatrical effects and false façades, at Dogmersfield Adam made no attempt to hide the truth of its date: the windows are simple punched openings filled with plate glass. These expanses of glass, unencumbered by the *politesse* of glazing bars, made explicit the absolute modernity of the building and served to demarcate it clearly from the routine neo-Georgianism of conventional suburban development.

---

2 Gene Amdahl, 'Validity of the Single Processor Approach to Achieving Large-Scale Computing Capabilities', *AFIPS Conference Proceedings*, vol. 30 (1967), pp. 483–485.

3 Nikolaus Pevsner and David Lloyd, *The Buildings of England, Hampshire and the Isle of Wight*, 1967, p. 192.

*Above:* Dogmersfield Park, Hampshire. The new building is divided into bays with a broken pediment and giant columns made of tiles in the centre of the long façade.

*Left:* The broad tympanum is penetrated by an aedicule of free-standing stucco columns framed by a relieving arch

DOGMERSFIELD PARK

TRIVMPHAL ARCH
END PAVILION
FOR NEW BVILDING
ROBERT ADAM·ARCHITECT
MCMLXXXV·····SCALE

*Above:* After a fire, Dogmersfield Park was converted to a corporate headquarters. Robert Adam's extension on the left is a deliberate contrast with the 18th-century original while in the same classical language. The building is now a hotel.

*Left:* The composition is based on a simplified version of a Roman triumphal arch with Tuscan Order, with brick rusticated piers supporting a large cornice and smaller Order inset. The windows are single panes and the lack of divisions increases the apparent scale of the building. A pen-and-ink stipple drawing by Adam.

This was Adam's first recognisably classical project to receive national attention, and it was immediately apparent that he was using classicism in total seriousness, rather than in a half-hearted or jocular fashion; it was evidently not intended to be a parody of an historical style, as so often had been the case in post-Modernism.[4] Adam confidently set forth his claim in an interview: 'This is a further development of classicism … Just because I used certain formal principles rooted in the past with bold forms and bold effects, there is no need to reproduce smaller elements like glazing bars.'[5] The quality of Adam's design has ensured that his wing has outlived the short-term use of the building. Following a change in the company's fortunes in the 1990s Amdahl sold the property and Dogmersfield Park found a new use, this time for conversion into a luxury country house hotel, which opened in 2005. Two new wings were added to the south and west in precisely the restrained brick vernacular that had been eschewed by Adam, suggesting that after only a brief period of vision and foresight, the British planning system has again retreated into the safe haven of mediocrity.

## PATERNOSTER SQUARE, LONDON

Adam's most ambitious office project before the present decade was his contribution to the highly controversial Paternoster Square scheme masterplanned by John Simpson, Terry Farrell and Thomas Beeby. Since, in hindsight, this project can be seen to play a crucial role in Adam's development of a new classicism, it is worth examining in detail even though it has remained unbuilt.

In the 1960s the area to the north of Sir Christopher Wren's masterpiece, St Paul's Cathedral, had been extensively redeveloped according to a post-blitz masterplan by Lord Holford. He wiped away the fine grain of medieval lanes and alleys, originally occupied by the makers of rosaries and latterly filled with booksellers, in order to replace them with a sequence of bleak plazas dominated by a repetitive series of office blocks designed by Trehearne and Norman, Preston and Partners. Though they were in fact clad in Portland stone, these grim buildings aged so poorly that while they had never been much loved, by the mid 1980s they were actively reviled.

In 1986 the site was purchased by Mountleigh Estates, which immediately announced its intention of redeveloping it with buildings better suited to the needs of computer technology. It invited proposals from seven firms including such well-known high-tech and Modernist practitioners as James Stirling, Arup Associates, Arato Isozaki, Norman Foster and Richard Rogers. The winners of this limited competition were Arup Associates and Richard Rogers, though the latter resigned after being offered only a minor role in the scheme. Remembering the debacle over the Ahrends, Burton and Koralek proposal for the National Gallery – a competition-winning design that came to naught after being publicly attacked by HRH The Prince of Wales as a 'monstrous carbuncle' – Stuart Lipton, the project director for the development, showed the Prince the competition designs privately in the hope of defusing a potential time bomb. His ploy backfired. The Prince, who was 'deeply depressed' on seeing the proposals, launched a scathing attack on both the process and the entries of the closed competition in a speech given at the Mansion House in 1987.[6] He memorably began his tirade by pointing out that 'You have, ladies and gentlemen, to give this much to the *Luftwaffe*: when it knocked down our buildings, it didn't replace them with anything more offensive

4   On this phenomenon see Linda Hutcheon, 'The Politics of Postmodernism: Parody and History', Cultural Critique No. 5, Modernity and Modernism, *Postmodernity and Postmodernism*, Winter 1986–1987, pp. 179–207.

5   Quoted by Martin Pawley, 'The Future is a Classic Cover Up', *The Guardian*, 10 September 1984, p. 11.

6   'Speech Given at Mansion House: HRH The Prince of Wales', *APT Bulletin*, vol. 20 (1988), no. 3, pp. 3–8.

than rubble.' He urged that the site be reconsidered, making a plea instead for the reconstruction of 'the medieval street plan of pre-war Paternoster' with buildings of 'the kinds of materials Wren might have used – soft red brick and stone dressings perhaps, and the ornament and details of classical architecture, but on a scale humble enough not to compete with the monumentality of St. Paul's.'[7]

In the wake of the Prince's speech, the *Evening Standard* promoted an alternative masterplan by John Simpson, putting it on show in a popular exhibition and finally announcing that they would submit this counterproposal for outline planning permission. Unsurprisingly, Mountleigh sold the site on, though Arup Associates continued to work on the project and finally presented a fully developed scheme in November 1988. Within a year the by-now highly controversial site had changed hands again, now being bought by a consortium of American, Japanese and British developers called Paternoster Associates. In place of Arup, they commissioned a new masterplan from three architects, two British and one American: John Simpson, Terry Farrell and Thomas Beeby. In addition to these three, individual buildings were also to be designed by Demetri Porphyrios, Julian Bicknell, Allan Greenberg and Robert Adam. In 1993 planning permission was finally granted for this new classical scheme, but the moment had passed. During the seven years since the site was first sold for development, London had seen an office building boom of unprecedented scale. Now with rising interest rates and predictions of economic recession, there was a vast surplus of office space with perhaps as much as 40 million square feet lying empty in the capital. When interest in the site revived at the end of the 1990s, the Prince of Wales's commitment to classicism had waned and he gave his blessing instead to a new masterplan by Sir William Whitfield, which now involved some of the key players in the neo-Modernist revival such as Eric Parry.

Though it was not built, Adam's scheme for 2B Paternoster Square is of considerable interest both for illuminating his own development as a classicist, but also as a thematic basis for later buildings, including 198–202 Piccadilly, completed in 2007. While Dogmersfield had acknowledged its modernity through the use of plate glass for the windows, it had achieved its primary aesthetic impact through the plastic modelling of the wall mass, an essentially Baroque characteristic.[8] This sculptural approach to a classical building came as a revelation in the mid 1980s, and continues to this day to exert a powerful effect on the viewer. Up until then, the revived classicism had primarily been the style used for its iconographical associations or as a sop to contextualism. The potency of Dogmersfield can be judged by comparison with a contemporaneous building that has also been described as Baroque – Quinlan Terry's Howard Building at Downing College, Cambridge.[9] Here, the interest in the Baroque aesthetic is indicated by the over-elaboration of surfaces and the whimsical play of detail. In the Howard building the order is immured and the wall remains almost static – its plane only edges forward in the central bay. The overall effect, despite Terry's self-declared interest in the Baroque, is rather one of effete Mannerism. Adam, on the other hand, is concerned at Dogmersfield with much more fundamental principles of the Baroque – the rhythmic composition of pavilions, the advance and recession of the façade, the duelling of elements in the elevation and ultimately, with the expression of the solid mass of the wall as a sculptural entity. This is a 'Baroque' that stretches the boundaries of purely chronological definition: going back before Vanbrugh, and even

7   ibid., p. 8.

8   For a basic understanding of these characteristics, see Heinrich Wolfflin, *Renaissance Und Barock. Eine Untersuchung Uber Wesen Und Entstehung Des Barockstils in Italien*, Munich 1888; translated by Kathrin Simon as Renaissance and Baroque, Ithaca, NY, 1966.

9   See Quinlan and Francis Terry LLP Architects website; Public Buildings; Howard Building, Downing College.

PATERNOSTER SQUARE BUILDING
BUILDING GROUP TWO

MCMXC

*The unbuilt Paternoster Square scheme with work by all the leading classicists of the 1980s. Robert Adam's building is on the left, filling the north side of the main square. The north side of the main square in stone and London Stock Brick. The symbolic decorative scheme is shown on the drawing: 12 free-standing columns for the apostles (four paired as the evangelists) and an upward progression from the pagan to the Christian, including reference to early representations of Christ as the Sun God (including his four-horse chariot).*

*An unbuilt complex of commercial buildings proposed for the grounds of the historic house, Stoke Park,*
*in Buckinghamshire. The original house is by James Wyatt and is now a golf club. The illustration shows*
*the architect in conversation with the Regency architect John Soane and the ancient Greek architect,*
*Iktinos, as a demonstration of how the modern can converse with the historic in classical architecture.*

beyond Cortona, to ancient Rome, to the moulding of space that occurs in the concrete architecture of the baths and imperial basilicas.[10] Yet, for all the kinetic feeling it generates – one derives a sense of movement empathetically from this style – seeing it applied to a steel-framed building involves the suspension of disbelief. Those massive piers and deep recesses do not reflect the statics of masonry masses, but are merely the undulations of a thin curtain wall. The aesthetic of an ancient load-bearing architecture is being created through late 20th-century building technology, and though not a falsehood – the candid adoption of plate glass makes sure of that – this plastic idiom does not fully realise the potential of this new marriage of style and technology, of classicism and the steel-reinforced frame.

The cognitive leap that embraces these two seeming antitheses and brings them together can be seen for the first time in Adam's design for 2B Paternoster Square. The result represents genuine progress within the classical language. Adam had begun experimenting with the integration of the curtain wall with classicism in 1988 in his polemical design for a skyscraper, the Apollo Tower. Even though the project lacked the constraints of a real programme and client, the result was not wholly successful. The wide central bays framed by the main order and filled with a glass curtain wall contrast too markedly with the pierced masonry masses of the flanking corner towers to form a stylistically coherent whole. Adam explored the issue further in the following year with an ambitious scheme for three low-rise office blocks in the grounds of a late 18th-century house, Stoke Park. Here, however, the glazed areas were restricted to the stacked Doric and Ionic colonnades that linked the corner pavilions of the blocks, rather than the basic forms of the buildings themselves. Adam hinted at his personal sense of urgency to modernise the classical tradition in his presentation perspective drawing (1990) for the project that showed him deep in conversation with James Wyatt, the original architect of the house, and Iktinos, the architect of the Parthenon.

The theme of combining the technology of the curtain wall with the trabeated language of classicism is evident again in another polemical scheme, the towers for Spaghetti Junction prepared for the BBC in 1990. Again, the sketchy nature of the proposal only allows for a cursory exploration of the issue. Finally, in 2B Paternoster Square, we see a complete and coherent solution to the problem: how can one apply an architectural language first developed nearly 3000 years ago as an expression of the compressive forces in monumental masonry to the lightweight and slender structures of a steel reinforced frame and plate glass? The question, in only a slightly different form, has been posed before. Karl Friedrich Schinkel addressed it in the early 19th century when he tried to apply the lessons he had learned from his studies of English factory architecture to the monuments of royal Berlin. A century later, in early 20th-century America, the same issue arose in the early history of the skyscraper. Though the architects of the Chicago School had seemed content with a more utilitarian approach to tall buildings, perhaps as a result of the rapid reconstruction of the 'Loop' following the great fire of 1871, in Manhattan architects such as Stanford White sought to give a more completely classical form to their steel-framed buildings, such as the Gorham building of 1905.

Adam's design for Paternoster Square was seven storeys tall with a main façade more than 100 feet long. He used a system of tripartite subdivisions to provide a strong compositional structure to this large-scale elevation. In height it was divided into three main zones: at the ground, two retail floors were united by massive, blocked pilasters in polychromatic stone. These divided the width of the building into five large bays, each of which was broken down into three smaller bays by a framework of slim metal colonnettes.

---

10  On the application of the stylistic term Baroque to ancient architecture see Margaret Lyttelton, *Baroque Architecture in Classical Antiquity*, Ithaca, NY, 1974.

Above these, squat pilasters and an emphatic entablature formed the base for the three storeys of the middle zone. This was treated as a conventional masonry wall pierced by windows; the three-bay pavilions at either end were rusticated and projected slightly to frame the nine-bay central section. At the corners of each of these two projecting *avant-corps*, an implied giant Ionic order was hinted at through the placement of angled volutes under the entablature. The square pillars implied by these fragments of an Ionic capital were also given a taper, just like the muscular pillars at Dogmersfield. The effect here at Paternoster was much more dramatic, as the taper gave the outer walls of the building a pronounced batter, making the transition from the massive pilasters of the lowest zone below to the slender columns of the highest zone above. This upper zone, consisting of two storeys articulated by a double-height Corinthian order, abandoned the traditional relationship of solid to void found in masonry buildings, and adopted instead the kind of rational trabeated grid that Schinkel used in his Neues Schauspielhaus (1819–21) in Berlin.

Perhaps this project would have suffered compromises if it had actually been built. But, as it stands, as a two-dimensional drawing of an elevation, it is a perfect illustration of how the classical tradition can be used to control and articulate a large and complex façade, in this case seven storeys high and fifteen bays wide. Every detail elegantly contributes to the sense of hierarchy and lucidity of the design. Even the slight batter given to the sides of the building, completely unnecessary in a steel-framed building from a structural point of view, acknowledges the masonry origins of the language and gives the structure the necessary sense of presence for it to stand in the shadow of a monument such as St Paul's.

The new-found appreciation of the spare structural logic of classicism apparent in Adam's scheme for Paternoster transformed his work and helped set it apart from all those interpretations of the language that were constrained by a fixation with its roots in the mere physics of loadbearing. Adam himself became acutely aware of the innovation in his style and within a few years was even referring to this particular idiom on his drawings as a new style: 'Trabeated Rationalism'.[11] The sense of an underlying system of posts and lintels – not the monotonous repetitive grid of Mies van der Rohe, but rather a nuanced and inflected skeleton of trabeation – holds out the hope for a new direction for classicism in the 21st century. The traditional patterns of window and wall, dependent on the performance of materials, on the tensile limits of stone or the compressive constraints of wood, no longer need govern the use of classicism. The benefits of technology – central heating, air conditioning and double glazing – need no longer be seen to require the stylistic precepts of Modernism, now that the fallacy of the *zeitgeist* has been exposed. For, in a northern clime, the shade of a *salone* by Palladio can be replaced by a luminous drawing room by Alexander 'Greek' Thomson. This transformation is apparent not just in Adam's Wakeham, Solar House in West Sussex, where such environmental concerns were paramount, but also in his office and retail development at Union Court, Richmond and in a range of residential projects including Delaford Park and the new country house in Hampshire.

Union Court was an exemplary exercise in urban regeneration in a complex urban setting. The site consisted of a small neglected urban court with an adjacent area that also faced onto Eton Street, one of the surrounding shopping streets. The odd plot shape for a free-standing office building in the court was exploited to differentiate the entrance to the building, which was designed as a copper-domed pavilion giving a strong focus and identity to the court. The remaining office building is a restrained brick design with shallow modulation to suggest pilasters and a brick cornice. The building onto Eton Street has offices

---

11   See the labels on the drawings for the scheme for Nyn Park in 2000.

*Clockwise from right:* Union Court. The inner square of a small mixed-use urban regeneration scheme in Richmond, outside London. The square is in the centre of an urban block and was very run down. To help regenerate it and create an individual character, the entrance to the office building was given a distinctive treatment.

The street façade onto Eton Street with shops with offices above. A study in understatement, the elevation is principally distinguished by its very simple recessed stone classical window surrounds.

Union Court ground floor plan

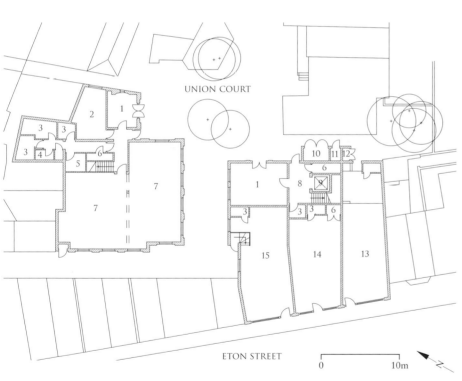

UNION COURT

ETON STREET

0          10m

| 1 | RECEPTION | 9 | LIFT |
| 2 | CONFERENCE ROOM | 10 | BIN STORE |
| 3 | WC | 11 | GAS |
| 4 | SHOWER | 12 | ELEC |
| 5 | KITCHEN | 13 | UNIT 1 |
| 6 | STORE | 14 | UNIT 2 |
| 7 | OFFICE | 15 | UNIT 3 |
| 8 | LOBBY | | |

over ground-floor shops and is detailed with great simplicity, the only feature being a shallow recessed window surround with stripped down classical details, set just behind the face of the brick. Adam believes that this is a demonstration of how a classical building can be both modest and a sophisticated design; its extreme modesty making it almost invisible in its wider setting but with refined design details available for any passerby who might take an interest.

Several ideas from the Paternoster project re-emerged in the commission for a substantial new office building on a highly visible site in the heart of the West End in 2001. 198–202 Piccadilly occupies an important location of extreme sensitivity, between a church by Sir Christopher Wren, St James', and an icon of early Modernism in Britain, Simpson's store (now a Waterstones bookshop). The latter, appropriately enough for our discussion, was an early attempt to create a shop front unencumbered by supports by using a Vierendeel transfer structure. Adam's new office building, completed in 2007, houses 70,000 square feet of offices, 30,000 square feet of retail space and has elevations facing three separate streets: Piccadilly, Church Place and Jermyn Street. On the last two façades the amount of ornament is pared down in relation to the urban context and on Church Place, brick is mostly used rather than Portland stone in deference to the church of St James'. The main elevation, on Piccadilly, consists of nine bays, divided into three larger units. This tripartite division is emphasised on the first two floors by the use of massive Doric piers with subdivisions provided by bronze pilasters and spandrels to create large shop windows for the retail units. The next two floors are united by a series of shallow Corinthian pilasters carrying a plain architrave and simplified cornice, the frieze being completely elided. Here the nine-bay rhythm is restored, but the sense is very much of a stripped, superficial system tautly stretched over the façade. The syncopated beat in triple time of the ground floor articulation emerges again on the fourth floor with the upper part of an order of giant pilasters appearing from underneath the entablature of the third floor. These giant pilasters feature anthropomorphic capitals sculpted by the important Scottish classical sculptor Alexander Stoddart (part of a long association between the practice and Stoddart). The capitals are based on personifications relevant to such an ambitious project including, for instance, Audax, 'Daring'. The entablature of this order features a deep cornice, scaled to the whole building, and corresponding approximately to the height of its neighbours. Above this the building steps back, first to a series of three deliberately overscaled dormer windows, again emphasizing the syncopation below, and then, out of sight from the street, to a glazed roof pavilion housing two further floors of offices. The corner between Piccadilly and Church Place is prominently marked by an octagonal tower, which carries aloft an austere Doric tholos. The realisation on site was overseen by Paul Hanvey, director of ADAM Architecture, who is primarily a project manager, an essential contributor when, as here, the logistics are fraught with potential complications.

Hanvey joined the firm at the age of 26 as an architectural technician. He originally trained in the office of Robert Potter FRIBA FSA, an architect specialising in historic preservation, who was responsible for numerous restoration projects in Oxford, including Duke Humphrey's Library and the late 13th-century Muniment Room at Merton College.[12]

After planning permission was won at the first presentation to the locally elected committee (a rare achievement for such a prominent project), Hanvey managed this project for four years, coordinating the details and specifications and developing specific construction techniques. One particular concern was to

---

12   See Robert Potter, 'The Repair of Oxford's Historic Buildings, with Special Reference to the Divinity School and Duke Humphrey's Library', *Monumentum*, 1971, VI, pp. 23–31.

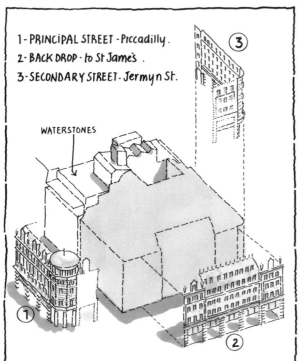

1 - PRINCIPAL STREET - Piccadilly.
2 - BACK DROP - to St James's.
3 - SECONDARY STREET - Jermyn St.

WATERSTONES

*Previous page:* Piccadilly is one the world's most famous streets and the Piccadilly façade has a complex decorative treatment based on an ascending series of classical orders. The outer corner of the building is a landmark that can been seen from a long distance as St James' Church next door is set back and surrounded by lower buildings.

*Above:* The full building can be seen from the west end of Piccadilly revealing a two-storey glazed temple structure set back on a roof terrace

*Left:* The design is one unified building with a continuous façade that varies according to the different street settings

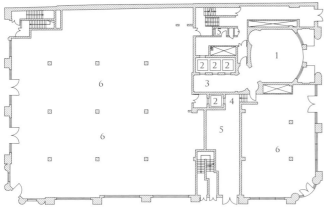

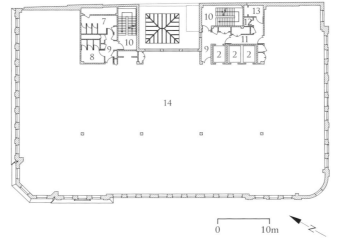

*Clockwise from top left: The Jermyn Street façade has a much simpler treatment with much of the decoration removed but with the essential architectural elements marked out with shallow recesses and restrained details*

*The top of the corner tower has a colonnade of granite columns with glass behind, creating an office with spectacular views down Piccadilly to Hyde Park Corner. The roof-top building is supported on narrow steel columns in front of a glass wall. The columns have specially designed stainless steel capitals.*

*The detail on the Jermyn Street entrance shows the rustication to the ground floor*

*A treatment of the corner between Jermyn Street and Church Place is a restrained version of the corner tower on Piccadilly*

*Typical floor plan*

*Ground floor plan*

0    10m

| 1 | OFFICE ENTRANCE | 9 | LOBBY |
|---|---|---|---|
| 2 | LIFT | 10 | STAIR |
| 3 | LIFT LOBBY | 11 | CORRIDOR |
| 4 | GOODS | 12 | SHOWER |
| 5 | REFUSE | 13 | DISABLED WC |
| 6 | RETAIL | 14 | OFFICE |
| 7 | MALE TOILETS | 15 | WC |
| 8 | FEMALE TOILETS | | |

ensure that the precast concrete panels, which hang from the building's steel frame, were manufactured to the highest tolerances possible in order to minimise the expansion joints. The visibility of these joints, which immediately indicate that a building is not constructed from traditional load-bearing masonry, is further reduced by spraying the mastic joints with a stone coating, a process specially developed by Hanvey and Adam. In order to maintain the quality of the building while keeping within its £20-million budget, Hanvey travelled to China to select the granite cladding and oversaw the production of the bronze ornaments.

The many difficulties of the location, ranging from its topography to its historical sensitivity, have resulted in a building that is complex in the extreme. Yet every nuance of programme and context has been addressed in the elevations and the result is a rich and multi-layered composition, passing from one street front to the next. The diagrammatic simplicity of the single façade of 2B Paternoster Square has, unsurprisingly, been left behind here; but the underlying sense of clarity which Adam developed in that unbuilt project remains supremely evident in his lucid solution to the challenges of a large office building in a complex urban setting.

*A new mixed-use building for a prominent corner site in the old city of Beirut. Robert Adam cooperated with Beirut architect and friend Fadlallah Dagher after his firm Dagher Hanna & Partners Architects had won a competition for the development of the site. The building houses shops, offices and apartments. The design specifically develops a Middle Eastern classicism with modern materials. The prominent corner is a memory of the Bab Idris gate of the city, which was said to have sat on the site and which marked the line of the rising sun on the day of the city's foundation.*

# CHAPTER 4
# PRIVATE RESIDENCES

*'ARCHITECT, n. One who drafts a plan of your house, and plans a draft of your money; who estimates the whole cost, and himself costs the whole estimate.'*

Ambrose Bierce, *The Cynic's Word Book*, 1906

The private house is the one area of architectural activity where a traditional approach has remained the norm throughout the rise and fall of Modernism. During the middle decades of the 20th century even apparently ardent advocates of the avant garde in the public realm would often choose to live in a traditional home. In the 1930s, to cite one famous example, the Rockefeller family were early supporters of Modernism, publicly funding a building by Edward Durell Stone and Philip L. Goodwin for the new Museum of Modern Art in Manhattan. Privately, however, they lived in completely traditional houses which they built on their huge estate outside New York, Pocantico Hills. Even as late as the 1960s they were still commissioning classical residences for the estate such as Hillcrest, designed by Mott B. Schmidt for Marth Baird Rockefeller, the widow of John D. Rockefeller, Jr.[1] It was the slow steady stream of commissions for private houses of this kind that kept the most dedicated traditional architects in business through the heyday of Modernism in the 1950s and 1960s.

## CROOKED PIGHTLE, ROBERT ADAM'S OWN HOME IN HAMPSHIRE

For many young architects the dream client for a private house early in their careers takes the form of a parent or parent-in-law; it is generally less common for them to be in a position to build a house for themselves. One notable exception was Philip Johnson, whose Glass House in New Canaan, Connecticut, of 1949 established him at the forefront of the American architectural avant garde in his early 40s. In the classical fold, several contemporary American architects established their reputations by building houses for their families which made a very public demonstration of their commitment to classicism: for instance Thomas Gordon Smith and Duncan Stroik spring to mind.[2] Robert Adam's opportunity to build a house for his young family came in the late 1980s when he acquired a generously sized plot in a picturesque village about five miles northwest of Winchester. It was designed while Adam was working on his book,

---

1  Now the home of the Rockefeller Family Archives. On Schmidt's work see Mark Hewitt, *The Architecture of Mott B. Schmidt*, New York 1991.

2  On Smith's two houses for his family, see the present author's *Thomas Gordon Smith and the Rebirth of Classical Architecture*, London 2001. Gil Schafer, the former president of the Institute of Classical Architecture, similarly demonstrated his facility with the classical tradition by building a weekend house in a Greek Revival idiom for himself in Dutchess County, New York.

*Classical Architecture*, and though his initial ideas for a house were in the vein of a Richardsonian Romanesque style, the form rapidly evolved into a classicised Arts and Crafts idiom, the vernacular materials of which belie the layered complexity of the design.

The brick façade is divided into five bays, the central three bays of which advance to form a projecting block framed by quoins. On closer inspection of the details, however, the presence of bases and capitals made from moulded brick reveals that these corner quoins are in fact blocked pilasters of a giant order. One can tell that this order is clearly Doric even though it has been abstracted and its frieze omitted, because there are regularly spaced mutules in the deep soffit of the overhanging eaves. On the rear façade this giant order reasserts itself, again creating a tripartite composition, though now the central bay features a counterpoint: a subsidiary order which articulates the central three bays. This secondary order is again abstracted, with two simple brick pilasters supporting the archivolt of a thermal window, but the sophisticated entablature is fully realised in cut stone. Appropriately enough for a garden front here the pulvinated frieze is represented as rough-hewn blocks of flint, reading like a horizontal course of rustication, a conceit suggested by Palladio in his account of the Tuscan order in the *Quattro libri*.[3] By contrast the frieze above the entrance door at the front is delicately carved in a swag representing the fruits of Hampshire; its naturalism is such that a close examination causes the viewer to recoil on seeing a worm burrowing into an apple. Any suggestion that this is an exercise in neo-Georgianism, as might have been expected from a new classical house built in the 1980s, is vigorously resisted by both the casement windows at the front and the oriels at the back; its Arts and Crafts heritage is further reinforced by the emphatic pitch of the clay tile roof. Some of the moulded terracotta and brick details used so successfully at Bordon library are here reprised, including panels of *opus reticulatum* work under the windows.[4]

A long and narrow vestibule establishes a strong central axis. It leads directly to the literal and metaphorical heart of the house: a double-height living hall, a perfect cube. Some premonition of this noble space is given to the visitor by the central block that projects from the main façade; its presence is made explicit, however, on the garden front through the arrangement of the giant order which frames the French windows and a lunette above. These windows open onto the garden terrace; opposite them, on the other side of the room, the space is overlooked by a timber balcony. This balcony outwardly resembles the minstrel's gallery of a medieval hall, but serves the essential purpose of providing the main transverse circulation for the bedroom floor. It is supported by a pair of giant elm consoles on either side of the entrance door and has as its centrepiece a wrought-iron panel of anthemia by the blacksmith Richard Bent. The focus of the room is a carved stone chimneypiece, the breast of which is emphasised as it rises to the ceiling by a bold bracketed cornice. This cornice is scaled as if it was part of a giant interior order, corresponding notionally to the exterior blocked pilasters. Opposite the hearth sits a custom-made refectory table which, with the flagstones of the floor, helps create the feel of an English manor house. There are also, of course, plenty of precedents for such a powerful volume at the heart of a house in the classical tradition including the double-height *saloni* of Palladio's villas and the *atria* of ancient Roman houses.

On either side of the central axis of the vestibule and hall subsidiary spaces are disposed: to the left, starting with a 'back door' cleverly hidden in the re-entrant corner of the projecting central block, one finds a mud room and then the kitchen. To the right of the hall, one finds a cloakroom, the stairs, a study and a sitting room. The first floor exhibits a similar lucidity of plan with the bedrooms for the two children, Jamie and

---

3   Andrea Palladio, *I Quattro libri dell'architettura* …, Venice 1570, pp. 18 and 21.

4   For Adam's Bordon Library see chapter eight.

**Above:** *Crooked Pightle House, Robert Adam's own house in Hampshire.*
*Entrance façade.*

**Opposite:** *Garden façade*

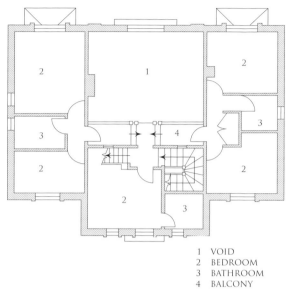

1 VOID
2 BEDROOM
3 BATHROOM
4 BALCONY

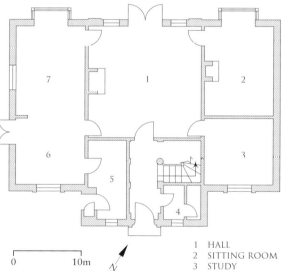

0     10m    N

1 HALL
2 SITTING ROOM
3 STUDY
4 WC
5 UTILITY
6 FAMILY ROOM
7 KITCHEN

**Opposite, clockwise from top left:** *Entrance hall. The central column is painted with a spiral wreath of bay leaves.*

*Family sitting room, decorated in Pompeian style by Robert Adam*

*Central hall chimneypiece*

*Festoon over front door. Carved with the fruits of the county used for brewing – hops, barley and* apples – to symbolise hospitality. A worm crawls out of a central apple as a reminder of mortality.

**Clockwise from above:** *Central hall. In the manner of a medieval hall or a Roman atrium, this 6-cubic-metre room sits at the centre of the house and is the principal reception room.*

*First floor plan*

*Ground floor plan*

Charlotte, on one side of the volume of the hall, and the master suite on the other. The guest bedroom, which lies above the vestibule, is also given a sense of privacy by being set back from the balcony of the living hall, behind the stairs leading to the attic.

In the garden, the robust practicality of the house gives way to refined poetry with an iconographic programme that leads us from Bacchus to Apollo, from a terrace of earthly pleasure to a grove of heavenly delights. Adam takes advantage of the natural topography of the site to create a series of stepped hemicycles, an effect that recalls the steeply raked seats of an anatomy theatre and conjures up memories of illustrations to Dante's *Divina Commedia*. The symbolism of the plants placed at different levels of the terraced bank reinforces this visual metaphor, from the underworld, represented by pennyroyal (*Mentha pulegium*), one rises up through memory, indicated by rosemary (*rosmarinus officianalis*), to the Olympian heights, suggested by laurel (*lauris nobilis*) the plant that the nymph Daphne turned into when caught by Apollo. At the top a little garden temple acts as a focus for a simple lawn. At the bottom, ritually placed on axis like a sacrificial altar to the Bacchic rites, one finds that modern locus of burnt offerings, a barbeque.

## NEW COTTAGE ORNÉE, HAMPSHIRE

Most of the houses designed for private clients by ADAM Architecture are classical, but there are some notable exceptions.[5] While Nigel Anderson's facility for the classical language is evident in houses such as a Palladian villa in Sussex and a Queen Anne House in Dorset, he has also tried his hand with great success at less familiar idioms, such as the Gothick style of the early 19th century. Anderson has produced a remarkably convincing essay in this style, creating a 'Cottage Ornée' of extreme subtlety.[6] Though it was replacing a rather unprepossessing red brick house, the site was highly sensitive since it was on the edge of a pretty village. The client therefore felt it important that though it would be of a decent size, the house should appear modest, even self-effacing. Anderson developed a picturesque cottage style, with Gothick tracery in the sash windows and carved bargeboards on the eaves, so that the house is commodious without appearing remotely grandiose. It cleverly combines a lightly-worn symmetry in the balanced façade presented to the road, with a happy informality on the sides and back, indicative of the casual living patterns of a modern family. The lime-render walls and slate roof will ensure that the house should age gracefully and in a very short time indeed it will surely seem as though it has always been there.

## RIVERSIDE COUNTRY HOUSE, DORSET

This picturesque approach was adopted on a much larger scale for a house near the river Piddle in Dorset. The site is a romantic landscaped park that survived from a previously demolished country house. The vistas to the east, south and west are all spectacular, including a sequence of lakes, a weir and copses of mature trees. Adam cleverly adopted an irregular 'butterfly' plan to take advantages of the variety of views, and broke down the composition of the house into a series of differentiated Italianate pavilions, very much following the precedent of John Nash's Cronkhill, a picturesque villa that was much favoured by the client. Each pavilion

---

5   One could also mention in this context Adam's Arts and Crafts Farmhouse in Hampshire, built of local materials, which incorporates a pre-existing barn.

6   This unusual idiom has also been used by Anderson at Poundbury.

*New Cottage Ornée, Hampshire. Nigel Anderson's essay in the Gothick or Cottage Ornée style showing the subtle and informal symmetry of the main south-facing garden façade.*

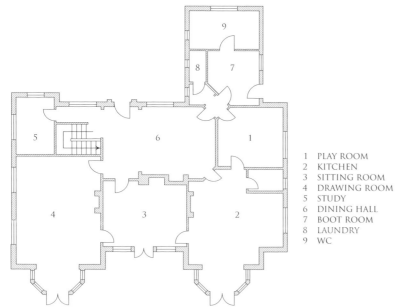

1 PLAY ROOM
2 KITCHEN
3 SITTING ROOM
4 DRAWING ROOM
5 STUDY
6 DINING HALL
7 BOOT ROOM
8 LAUNDRY
9 WC

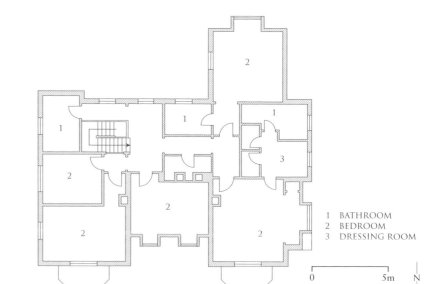

1 BATHROOM
2 BEDROOM
3 DRESSING ROOM

0          5m          N

**Opposite top:** *New Cottage Ornée, Hampshire, entrance façade. A lower eaves line gives the house a modest character within the context of its edge of village setting. The owner's coat of arms has been incorporated into the design over his study window to the right of the front door.*

**Opposite:** *Ground floor plan (left); first floor plan (right)*

**Above:** *Riverside country house, Dorset, river façade. Designed in a Regency manner but as a collection of buildings, each side faces one of the exceptional all-round views from the site.*

represents a different function and roof levels are stepped down as the building moves outwards and the major rooms become minor rooms. Adam worked closely with the interior designer Chester Jones to model the complex arrangement of rooms, dictated by the irregular plan, to create a rich but unexpectedly logical interior.

The external walls of the mostly single-storey house are mainly of render over a plinth of local stone, and the shallow-pitched roof with deeply overhanging eaves is of Welsh slate. At nodal points in the composition there are two vertical accents. On the garden front a stone octagon with a conical copper roof houses a study. On the entrance side, the main entrance is differentiated by a tall square stair tower containing a cantilevered stone stair that serves the only first-floor room, the master bedroom. Outside the family room, facing a weir in the river, a room-sized verandah with a shallow domed copper roof provides year-round shelter. It is supported by narrow columns with specially designed cast-iron capitals. Paul Hanvey worked closely on the meticulous detailing of the project.

The house is a remarkable picturesque composition from all viewpoints and is set against a much-improved landscape designed by the Belgian landscape architect, François Goffinet.

*Left:* Entrance façade. The front and back doors share the same façade. A cast-iron portico distinguishes the front door.

*Right:* Dining pergola

*Clockwise from left:* Riverside country house, Dorset, detail of river façade. The octagonal room is the library and the tower houses the staircase.

*Site plan*

*First floor plan*

*Ground floor plan*

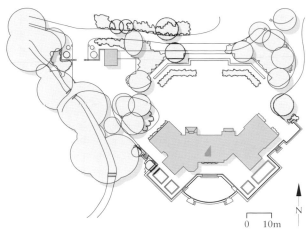

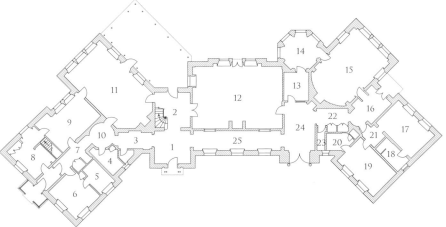

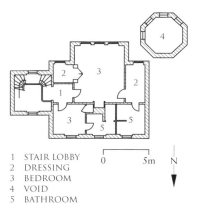

| 1 | ENTRANCE HALL | 14 | OCTAGON STUDY |
|---|---|---|---|
| 2 | STAIR HALL | 15 | BILLIARD ROOM |
| 3 | EAST HALL | 16 | TACKLE ROOM |
| 4 | LARDER | 17 | WEST BEDROOM A |
| 5 | EAST BATHROOM | 18 | WEST BATHROOM A |
| 6 | EAST BEDROOM | 19 | WEST BEDROOM B |
| 7 | EAST CORRIDOR | 20 | WEST BATHROOM B |
| 8 | UTILITY ROOM | 21 | LOBBY |
| 9 | KITCHEN | 22 | WEST HALL |
| 10 | ROTUNDA | 23 | WEST CLOAKROOM |
| 11 | DINING ROOM | 24 | SECONDARY |
| 12 | DRAWING ROOM | | ENTRANCE HALL |
| 13 | BAR | 25 | GALLERY |

| 1 | STAIR LOBBY |
|---|---|
| 2 | DRESSING |
| 3 | BEDROOM |
| 4 | VOID |
| 5 | BATHROOM |

# GEORGIAN HOUSE EXTENSION, HAMPSHIRE

George Saumarez Smith joined Robert Adam Architects in 2003, becoming a director in 2004. For the previous seven years he had worked for Quinlan Terry, in a practice that was originally founded in 1946 by Saumarez Smith's own grandfather, Raymond Erith. While working for Terry he had become expert in detailing traditional construction and preparing precise working drawings for contractors. He also spent this period studying Erith's superb work, filling a series of exquisite clothbound sketchbooks with studies of his buildings. Though Saumarez Smith's first major project for ADAM Architecture, the reworking of this Georgian House, is not a new residence built from scratch, it is so substantial, and so masterfully handled, that it justifies discussion in this context. The client has a large young family, and combines running a fund management group which he founded in 1991 with the more reclusive life of an author. His books, on business and history, include an acclaimed account of his great-grandfather's relationship with Winston Churchill.[7] His home is listed grade II* with a fine three-storey brick façade of 1760–80 constructed of blue headers and red dressings and capped by a parapet with stone copings.

Saumarez Smith's brief was to expand the house with a library, cellar, summerhouse and several new bedrooms. After much historical research, reconstructing the stages of the house's transformation, he made a number of proposals, each of which was carefully justified by reference to earlier structures that had been demolished in the 1930s. He proposed a single-storey addition over the drawing room, and a pendant wing on the west side, to create a new balanced garden façade symmetrically framed by the pedimented gables of the two additions. These are executed in lime render and contrast with the red brick of the garden façades of the new library and free-standing pool pavilion. The library, occupying the site of the demolished Victorian morning room, is tucked in behind the drawing room wing. Its three-bay bowed façade faces east with a central French window directed towards the pool house. While self-effacing externally, the interior of the library is a grand and noble space, with oak bookcases built into deep arched bays on either side. By giving it gently curving apsed ends, Saumarez Smith was ingeniously able to conceal a number of necessary service spaces and circulation routes in the 'poché' between the addition and the existing structure. This also serves to isolate the library acoustically from the noisy family areas of the house. The marble chimneypiece, inspired by austere models by Soane, features a series of carved floral paterae, one for each of the children of the house. The room's bracketed cornice, echoing the 18th-century one on the façade of the house, is derived from the Pantheon in Rome.

The last phase of the project, a summerhouse containing a swimming pool, is architecturally the most significant of the ensemble. Originally an 18th-century orangery stood on the site, though no records of its appearance survive. Taking his cue from surviving orangeries of that period, including the one by Hawksmoor at Kensington Palace, Saumarez Smith brilliantly reinterprets the north Italian classicism of Palladio and Sanmicheli using moulded and rubbed brick in a façade of five bays articulated by Doric pilasters. As with all canonical examples of the Roman Doric, the size of the bays is dependent on the spacing of the triglyphs of the frieze. The wider bays, framing sash windows or doors, have intercolumniations of three triglyphs each, and the narrower ones, at the corners, have only two triglyphs. Instead of glazed openings these narrower bays contain low relieving arches of rubbed brick, the central stone keystone of which supports the stone cill of a sunken relief panel above. The superimposition of these panels over the relieving arches makes them read like false mezzanine windows, giving a sense of monumental scale to the Doric pilasters. These unfenestrated end bays also serve to give depth and solidity to the wall. The rhythmic sense of the composition is enhanced by pairing the pilasters

7   Robert Lloyd George, *David and Winston*, London 2005; see also Robert Lloyd George, The East–West Pendulum, London 1992.

LANGTON HOUSE

A  New west wing, constructed 2004
B  New east wing, constructed 2004-5
   (incorporating ground floor of 1822 wing)

C  New library, constructed 2004-5
D  New summerhouse, constructed 2005
   (on footprint of 18ᵗʰ century orangery)

**Top:** *Georgian house extension in Hampshire, designed by George Saumarez Smith. The new wings are designed to give a strong sense of balance to the asymmetrical back of the house.*

**Above:** *Sketch showing the work carried out in phases including the new summerhouse*

*Left: Georgian house extension, Hampshire. The east wing incorporates the early 19th-century drawing room on the ground floor, with a new bedroom and bathroom above. To the right of the picture is the curved bay of the new library.*

*Below left: Interior of the new library. The cornice is based on the external cornice of the Pantheon in Rome.*

*Opposite, clockwise from top: Summerhouse in the grounds of a Georgian House in Hampshire designed by George Saumarez Smith. Main garden front of the new summerhouse. The building was designed as an 'apprentice piece' to test the skill of the bricklayers.*

*The Doric order used on the summerhouse is simplified to suit the use of bricks. This detail shows the variety in the use of the short and long ends of the bricks to produce different patterns.*

*The side of the new summerhouse showing the paired pilasters with side of the entrance doors. Beyond the wall on the left-hand side is the original walled garden.*

that frame the entrance bays on the short ends. The cornice and blocking course which help conceal the hipped slate roof, are both of Portland stone. In the drawings Saumarez Smith's attention to detail is apparent: here the mason is given the explicit instruction to randomly vary the width of the cornice blocks between 450 and 750 millimetres, and to ensure that they are set so that the natural bed is perpendicular to the ground, so-called 'edge-bedding'.[8] In the centre of the roof a small octagonal lantern rises to draw light down to the pool below.

In translating the refined details of Cinquecento classicism into an English vernacular context it was crucial that the working drawings specified exactly the size and placement of every last brick, especially because Saumarez Smith employed all the different types of brick bond in his design.[9] The handmade bricks, mostly in standard sizes but with three types of special moulded bricks, were supplied by the historic Swanage brickworks. The chief bricklayer who undertook this painstaking work was John Howell, assisted by Gary Kail, both of R.J. Smith and Co., Whitchurch. It is unsurprising that when this little gem won the RIBA Ibstock Downland Prize in 2006 it was described as 'a showcase for the bricklayer's craft'.[10]

The remodelling of Langton House exemplifies a type of project that has been the core work for ADAM Architecture: the restoration of existing houses with the design of substantial additions. Other examples

8   For a diagram showing the correctness of this detail, see John Ashurst and Francis G. Dimes (eds), *Conservation of Building and Decorative Stone*, vol. 2, Amsterdam 1990, fig. 4.82.

9   'Every type of bond can be found in the building, including English, Flemish, Header, English Garden Wall and Monk Bonds. In this way, the summer house suggests a giant apprentice piece, traditionally produced to demonstrate the skill of the bricklayer in his handling of materials, techniques and finishes.' Saumarez Smith's description of the project.

10   *Brick Bulletin*, Autumn 2006, p. 4.

*Opposite:* Historic house, Hampshire. The left hand bay and pedimented façade are the original miniature Palladian villa, the central and right hand bays are new.

*Clockwise from left:* The original miniature Palladian villa. The decorated flint and brick façade was discovered below old stucco and restored. The outline of the original front doorcase was still visible and was reproduced. The lower buildings on the left were added in the 19th century.

First floor plan

Ground floor plan. The original stair was lost and has been restored.

As first seen by the architect. The low buildings on the front were demolished to reveal the hidden villa behind.

Dining hall. This double-height room is where the new and old join. The arched window and door are original and were external.

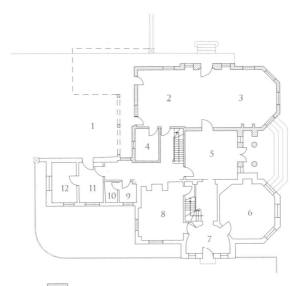

WORK BY ADAM ARCHITECTURE

EXISTING BUILDING

1  SERVICE COURT
2  KITCHEN
3  FAMILY ROOM
4  LARDER
5  DINING HALL
6  DRAWING ROOM
7  VESTIBULE
8  OFFICE
9  CLOAKROOM
10  WC
11  LAUNDRY
12  BOOT ROOM

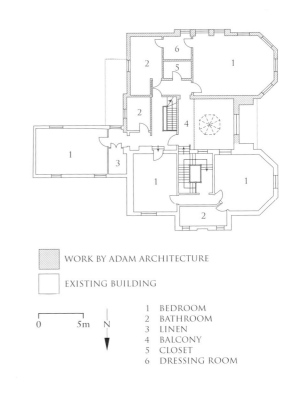

WORK BY ADAM ARCHITECTURE

EXISTING BUILDING

0        5m        N

1  BEDROOM
2  BATHROOM
3  LINEN
4  BALCONY
5  CLOSET
6  DRESSING ROOM

**Below:** *Extension to a manor House, Hampshire. The addition of large rooms to a medieval manor house in a contrasting style.*

**Opposite, clockwise from top left:** *Decorative details. The hart's tongue fern terracotta capitals and the obelisks were designed by the architect.*

*Drawing*

*Ground floor plan*

include a remodelled Historic House in Hampshire, an extension to a Manor House in Hampshire, a remodelled House in Ivor, Buckinghamshire, and extensions to a Farmhouse in Oxfordshire by Robert Adam; a Victorian Farmhouse extension in Hampshire, a Gothic Cottage renovation in Hampshire and a Medieval House restoration in Hampshire by Nigel Anderson; and a Cottage Ornée restoration in Yorkshire by Hugh Petter. There has also been some notable remodelling of institutional buildings including Petter's work at the British School at Rome (see Chapter 8) and Anderson's at Douai Abbey in Berkshire (see Chapter 6).

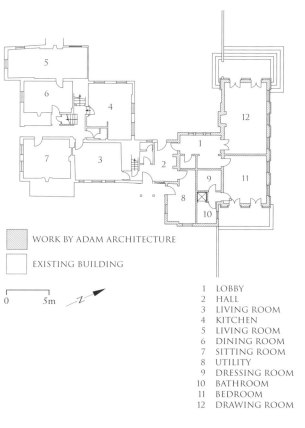

■ WORK BY ADAM ARCHITECTURE

□ EXISTING BUILDING

0    5m

1  LOBBY
2  HALL
3  LIVING ROOM
4  KITCHEN
5  LIVING ROOM
6  DINING ROOM
7  SITTING ROOM
8  UTILITY
9  DRESSING ROOM
10 BATHROOM
11 BEDROOM
12 DRAWING ROOM

**Left:** *Remodelled house, Ivor, Buckinghamshire*

**Above:** *View of entrance*

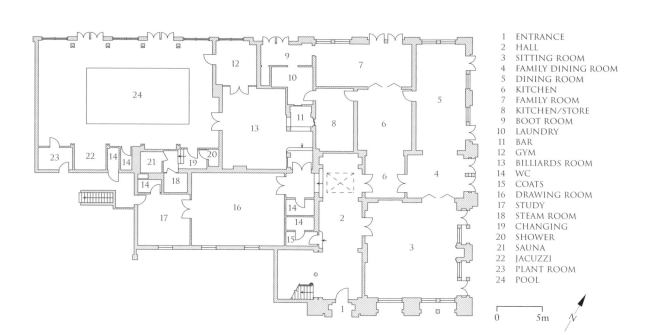

*Right:* Remodelled house, Ivor, Buckinghamshire. Ground floor plan.

*Below:* The tower and the garage are new, the rest of the building on this façade is re-faced. The irregular spacing of the bays on the main house, with a smaller central bay and equal side bays, is a rationalisation of the irregular original structure.

1   ENTRANCE
2   HALL
3   SITTING ROOM
4   FAMILY DINING ROOM
5   DINING ROOM
6   KITCHEN
7   FAMILY ROOM
8   KITCHEN/STORE
9   BOOT ROOM
10  LAUNDRY
11  BAR
12  GYM
13  BILLIARDS ROOM
14  WC
15  COATS
16  DRAWING ROOM
17  STUDY
18  STEAM ROOM
19  CHANGING
20  SHOWER
21  SAUNA
22  JACUZZI
23  PLANT ROOM
24  POOL

0        5m

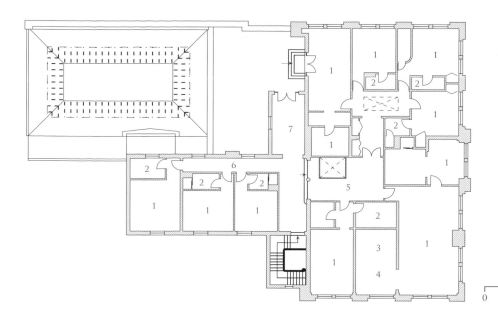

1 BEDROOM
2 BATHROOM
3 DRESSING
4 SITTING AREA
5 GALLERY
6 LANDING
7 SUN LOUNGE. TO ROOF TERRACE

0    5m    N

**Clockwise from left:** *Remodelled house, Ivor, Buckinghamshire. First floor plan.*

*Detail of tower. The high-level windows light the stair.*

*Entrance façade in its original state*

*Front door*

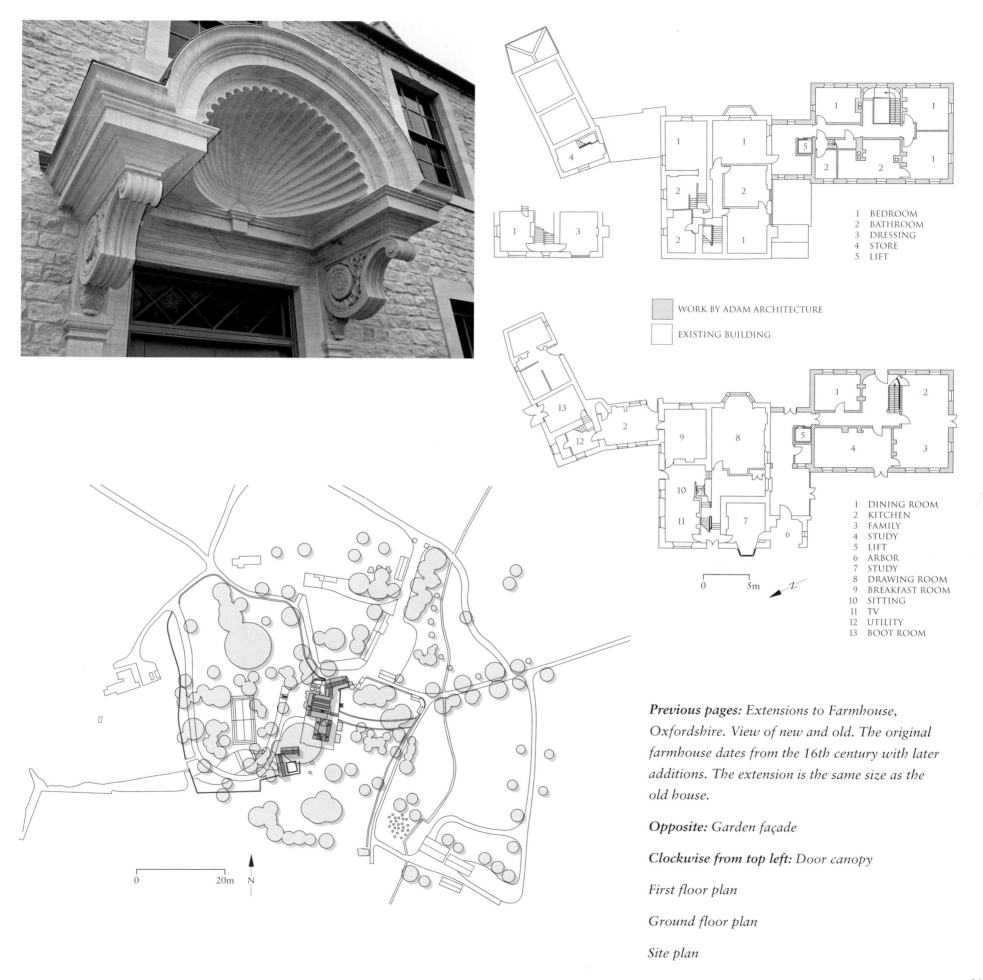

1 BEDROOM
2 BATHROOM
3 DRESSING
4 STORE
5 LIFT

▨ WORK BY ADAM ARCHITECTURE

☐ EXISTING BUILDING

1 DINING ROOM
2 KITCHEN
3 FAMILY
4 STUDY
5 LIFT
6 ARBOR
7 STUDY
8 DRAWING ROOM
9 BREAKFAST ROOM
10 SITTING
11 TV
12 UTILITY
13 BOOT ROOM

0        5m        N

0        20m        N

**Previous pages:** Extensions to Farmhouse, Oxfordshire. View of new and old. The original farmhouse dates from the 16th century with later additions. The extension is the same size as the old house.

**Opposite:** Garden façade

**Clockwise from top left:** Door canopy

First floor plan

Ground floor plan

Site plan

**Above:** *Victorian Farmhouse extension, Hampshire designed by Nigel Anderson. The new drawing room wing was conceived as a hunting box in the Artisan Mannerist style to which the original Victorian house was subsequently attached.*

**Opposite, clockwise from top left:** *Gothic Cottage renovation, Hampshire. Nigel Anderson enlivened an unprepossessing farm workers cottage with additions and architectural detailing in the Cottage Ornée idiom.*

*Medieval House restoration in Hampshire. Nigel Anderson's design stripped away Victorian cement render and plate glass sash windows to reveal the earlier jettied timber framing. Leaded casement windows were reinstated and the oriel bay reconstructed from fragments found within the house during the restoration works.*

*Cottage Ornée restoration in Yorkshire designed by Hugh Petter. The original house, designed in a vaguely Cottage Ornée style, was built in a woodland clearing some 30 years ago. Hugh Petter designed a significant extension and developed the architectural character of the original building.*

## NEW COLONIAL HOUSE, PARADISE ISLAND, BAHAMAS

The desire to continue architectural traditions is sometimes stronger in colonies and former colonies than in the mother country. Thus it is not surprising to find the classical work of ADAM Architecture as far afield as the Caribbean in the form of an elegant new house designed by Hugh Petter for an oceanfront site in the Bahamas. This Colonial house is located on the northern beach of Paradise Island.

Hugh Petter's client had chosen a beach-side location next to the Ocean Club and its golf links. The site is elevated about 30 feet above sea level, partly to minimise the impact of the storm surge during a hurricane, but also to allow one to look directly from the terrace out to the ocean. In 1995, the client founded the property investment group, Capital and Income Trust and worked closely with the architect Ken Shuttleworth, then of Foster and Partners. When it came to commissioning a design for his own house, the client knew he wanted a traditional architect and so Foster and Partners happily recommended ADAM Architecture.

In briefing the architect, the client described the pale yellow Regency villa near Lyme Regis in which he had once lived, and also talked about historic Bahamian architecture, which he had long enjoyed while visiting Nassau.[11] The grandeur of the local architecture illustrates the impact on Nassau of the many Loyalist refugees who moved there following the American revolutionary war. They brought with them the Georgian architectural traditions of Virginia and the Carolinas though now realised in the limewashed local coral stone rather than in brick.

This Colonial house, designed very much within this colonial masonry tradition, is built of concrete block and stucco, with a shingle roof. All of the wood trim both inside and out, from the verandah railings to the interior cornices, is made of mahogany, often painted, in order to withstand the effects of the ocean. In layout, the arrangement is similar to Nassau's government buildings, with a central porticoed block containing the main residential spaces flanked by a pair of lower two-storey dependencies. On one side, these contain a garage and office below and a nanny flat above, and, on the other, a games room and gymnasium below and two guest bedrooms above. The free-standing dependencies frame a formal lawn at the front of the house, which is surrounded on three sides by a bougainvillea-covered pergola and on the fourth is overlooked by the three-bay portico. The pediment of this portico, which rises to the full height of the main house, is echoed in the gables of the dependencies.

On the ocean side, two single-storey wings extend from the *corps de logis* to enclose a terrace with a swimming pool. The pool terrace, opening up dramatically to the ocean, offers a completely contrasting kind of outdoor experience from the lawn at the front of the house, where one feels embraced by the intimate scale, sense of enclosure and the presence of greenery. The landscape scheme was designed by Kim Wilkie.

To maximise ocean views a two-storey verandah extends the complete width of the house. It has a very different character from the portico on the landward side because it lacks a pediment, has a much wider spacing of bays, and, to compensate, has coupled columns. The classical order used throughout on both levels is a simplified Doric, almost indistinguishable from Tuscan, except for the pattern of ventilation holes in the soffit of the uppermost cornice that echo the sequence of mutules of a complete Doric order. This is only one example of the expert way in which Hugh Petter handles the classical canon, constantly paring it

---

11  See David Verey, 'The Georgian buildings of Nassau', *Country Life*, 28 October 1971, vol. 150, pp. 1134–1140.

*Previous pages:* New Colonial house, Paradise Island, Bahamas, designed by Hugh Petter. The landward façade provides shelter from the sea breeze. The house sits on the dune crest and the first glimpse that a visitor gets of the sea is on entering through the front door.

*Above:* The seaward elevation

down to make it absolutely appropriate for all aspects of the building, including its scale, materials, location, and building techniques. Although worn lightly, this learning should not come as a surprise as Petter was the senior tutor for the Foundation Course at the Prince of Wales's Institute of Architecture for six years. He has won Rome Scholarships not just once but twice and was responsible for the design of the recently completed extensions to the British School in Rome.[12]

12  On Petter's work at the British School see Elizabeth Meredith Dowling, *New Classicism: The Rebirth of Traditional Architecture*, New York 2004.

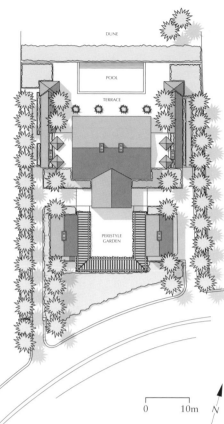

**Left:** *New Colonial house, Paradise Island, Bahamas. View of the ocean from the porch on the first floor.*

**Right:** *Site plan*

Above the entrance door the visitor is greeted by a carved tympanum by Dick Reid, probably one of the last examples of the work of this extraordinarily talented Yorkshire sculptor, who retired in 2004. From one of the landings of the staircase, a barrel-vaulted passage leads to the upper level of the front portico, a charming eccentricity of plan of the sort that one usually only finds in historic buildings. The interiors are designed by Monique Gibson, who worked closely with the client. The kitchen and breakfast room run the full depth of the house, with French doors opening onto the terrace at the end. Along the walls, white-painted cabinets rise from floor to ceiling, organised into bays by tall fluted pilasters. As with all the joinery in the house, the cabinets were built from scratch by local craftsmen. It was desirable to make many of the building elements out of raw materials on site, not just to have complete control over the details but also because of the high duties charged for the importation of construction materials to the Bahamas. Thus the exterior columns are all solid concrete. The result is a comforting solidity which one rarely finds in contemporary architecture, so that this feels like a house in which one would be safe riding out a hurricane. The other consequence of everything being made locally, just as the early colonists would have done, is that the building has a rare sense of rootedness. Though this Colonial House appears a highly formal building, with a symmetrical composition in plan and classical elevations, further exploration reveals that it also has that special quality of belonging that one finds in historic Colonial architectures.

The same celebration of *genius loci* that characterises Petter's Colonial House can also be discerned in his new modern classical villa for the predominantly early 19th-century environment of Cheltenham.

**Clockwise from top left:** *New Colonial house, Paradise Island, Bahamas. The double-height entrance hall.*

*First floor plan*

*Ground floor plan*

*The dining room looking through to the drawing room*

*Library*

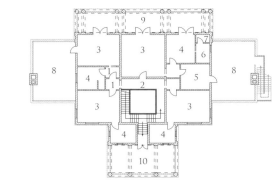

| | |
|---|---|
| 1 | LOBBY |
| 2 | LANDING |
| 3 | BEDROOM |
| 4 | BATHROOM |
| 5 | DRESSING ROOM |
| 6 | SHOWER |
| 7 | WC |
| 8 | BALCONY |
| 9 | VERANDAH |
| 10 | PORTICO |

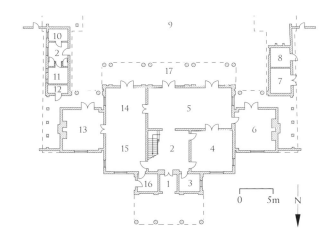

| | |
|---|---|
| 1 | LOBBY |
| 2 | HALL |
| 3 | WC/CLOAKROOM |
| 4 | DINING ROOM |
| 5 | DRAWING ROOM |
| 6 | LIBRARY |
| 7 | STORE |
| 8 | PLANT |
| 9 | POOL |
| 10 | SHOWER |
| 11 | WC |
| 12 | WINE CELLAR |
| 13 | FAMILY/TV ROOM |
| 14 | DINING AREA |
| 15 | KITCHEN |
| 16 | UTILITY ROOM |
| 17 | VERANDAH |

0    5m    N

# MODERN CLASSICAL VILLA, CHELTENHAM

This villa is an extremely restrained essay in regency taste entirely appropriate for the Spa town of Cheltenham. It is distinguished by a rigorous internal and external geometry with sequential square, octagonal and circular spaces. These are all held together by an entrance hallway with a remarkable monumental presence created by the skilful use of a cantilevered stone stair in an apsidal end that faces the entrance door and a stone floor. The interiors are ideally suited for the unpretentious lifestyle of the owner. The careful geometry and nicely selected detail have a calm and elegant character while being comfortable and functional. The rendered exterior is dominated by a three-bay Bath stone Doric portico. On one side, a particular delight is a pavilion, designed as a garden temple, which contains a guest cottage, utilities and garages. On the garden side a central octagonal bay dominates the façade as it opens out with large windows. A full-width terrace steps down first to a swimming pool, placed symmetrically as a formal pond, and then to a modest urban garden. This villa is an important achievement for Petter, demonstrating the adaptability of sophisticated formal design for modern everyday living and, in recognition of this it won the Giles Worsley Award for a New Building in a Georgian Context at the Georgian Group Awards in 2007.

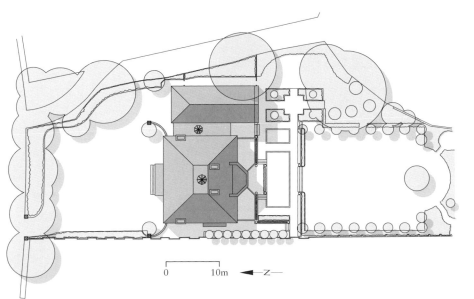

**Opposite:** *Modern Classical villa, Cheltenham designed by Hugh Petter. Detail of the entrance portico with the Ionic order of Eleusis.*

**Above:** *Entrance façade. The entrance portico uses the Ionic order to help the new house sit comfortably with its Regency neighbours. The low walls either side of the main façade define the entrance court beyond which are the garages.*

**Left:** *Site plan*

0        10m    ◄—N—

*Above:* Modern Classical villa, Cheltenham. The rear façade. A raised terrace with a swimming pool leads out to the main lawn.

*Opposite, clockwise from top left:* The main staircase is semicircular with cantilevered stone steps and landing, a simple metal balustrade and hardwood handrail

*Detail of the library linking through to the drawing room. A glass-roofed niche along the side of the drawing room improves the natural light level of that room while avoiding any overlooking issues with the neighbouring property.*

*First floor plan (top); ground floor plan (bottom). The main rooms are based on a module of 16 feet with a ceiling height of 12 feet.*

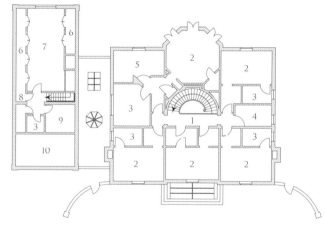

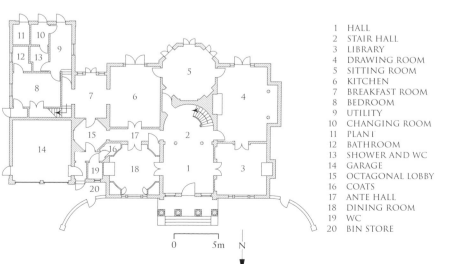

1   LANDING
2   BEDROOM
3   BATHROOM
4   LAUNDRY
5   DRESSING
6   STORAGE
7   PLAY ROOM
8   PLANT
9   OFFICE
10  VOID

1   HALL
2   STAIR HALL
3   LIBRARY
4   DRAWING ROOM
5   SITTING ROOM
6   KITCHEN
7   BREAKFAST ROOM
8   BEDROOM
9   UTILITY
10  CHANGING ROOM
11  PLANT
12  BATHROOM
13  SHOWER AND WC
14  GARAGE
15  OCTAGONAL LOBBY
16  COATS
17  ANTE HALL
18  DINING ROOM
19  WC
20  BIN STORE

0        5m        N

**Opposite:** *New Manor House, Hampshire, entrance façade. The new house replaces an original burnt down in the 1940s and is approximately the same size.*

**Clockwise from above:** *Garden façade*

*Stair hall*

*Front door canopy*

**Opposite:** *New villa, Kent, entrance façade. Designed in the manner of a Tudor hunting box, the building is a re-facing of a late-19th-century farmhouse.*

**Left:** *Garden façade*

**Above:** *Detail of entrance façade*

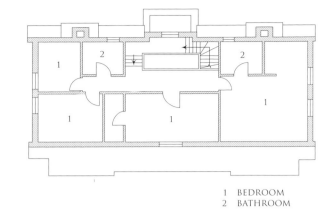

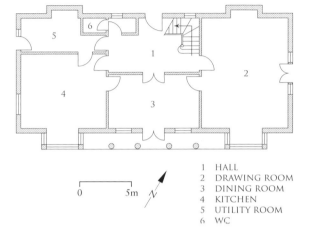

1  BEDROOM
2  BATHROOM

1  HALL
2  DRAWING ROOM
3  DINING ROOM
4  KITCHEN
5  UTILITY ROOM
6  WC

0        5m        N

**Opposite:** *New house, Hampshire, garden façade*

**Clockwise from top left:** *Entrance façade. The entrance is set behind buildings and has no outlook.*

*First floor plan*

*Ground floor plan*

*Detail of front door canopy*

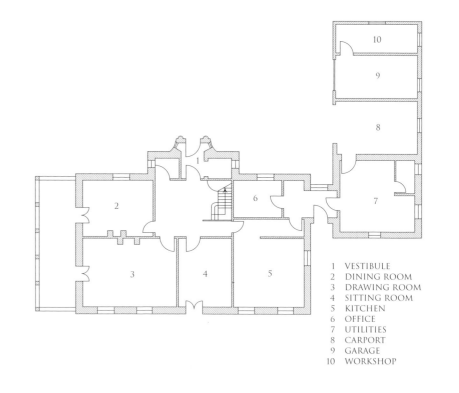

1 VESTIBULE
2 DINING ROOM
3 DRAWING ROOM
4 SITTING ROOM
5 KITCHEN
6 OFFICE
7 UTILITIES
8 CARPORT
9 GARAGE
10 WORKSHOP

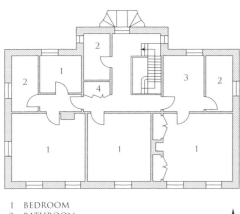

1 BEDROOM
2 BATHROOM
3 DRESSING ROOM
4 AIRING CUPBOARD

0       5m

*Opposite, clockwise from top:* New house, near Inverness, Scotland. Entrance façade.

First floor plan

Ground floor plan

Garden façade

*Above and left:* New house, Richmond, near London. Designed to fit into a row of historic 18th- and 19th-century houses.

*Above:* New house, near Stockbridge, Hampshire.
A house in the Arts and Crafts manner. Garden
façade.

*Right:* Entrance façade

*Opposite, clockwise from left:* Front door detail

*Bay window, dormers and chimneys*

*Entrance hall*

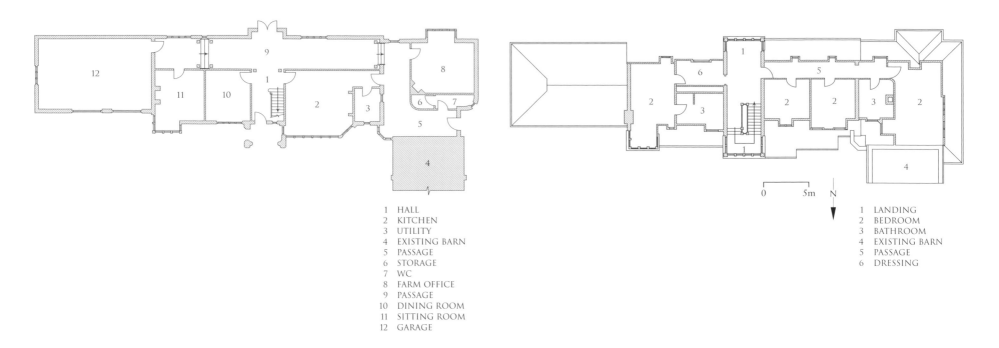

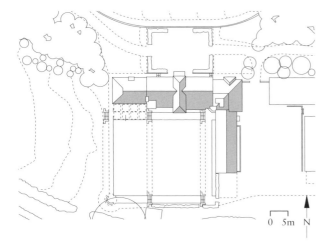

1 HALL
2 KITCHEN
3 UTILITY
4 EXISTING BARN
5 PASSAGE
6 STORAGE
7 WC
8 FARM OFFICE
9 PASSAGE
10 DINING ROOM
11 SITTING ROOM
12 GARAGE

1 LANDING
2 BEDROOM
3 BATHROOM
4 EXISTING BARN
5 PASSAGE
6 DRESSING

0    5m   N

***Clockwise from top left:*** *New house, near Stockbridge, Hampshire. Ground floor plan.*

*First floor plan*

*Stair*

*Site plan*

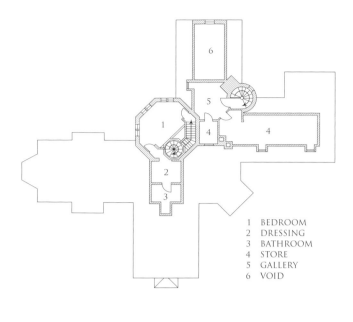

1 BEDROOM
2 DRESSING
3 BATHROOM
4 STORE
5 GALLERY
6 VOID

1 LANDING
2 BEDROOM
3 BATHROOM
4 DRESSING
5 WARDROBE

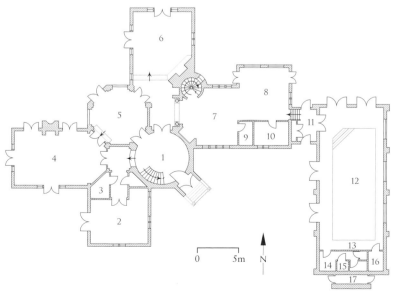

1 HALL
2 STUDY
3 WC
4 SITTING ROOM
5 DINING ROOM
6 FAMILY ROOM
7 KITCHEN
8 BREAKFAST ROOM
9 LARDER
10 UTILITY
11 LOBBY
12 POOL
13 CUPBOARD
14 CHANGING
15 SHOWER/STEAM
16 PLANT
17 BIN STORE

0    5m    N

***Clockwise from top left:*** *Arts and Crafts house, Derbyshire. Second floor plan.*

*A new house designed by Nigel Anderson on a hillside site. The façades follow the form and detailing of the local vernacular and suggest a building that has evolved over time around a central stone lookout tower. The layout is an early exploration of the 'butterfly' plan with radiating wings taking advantage of the spectacular views in all directions as well as providing sheltered garden areas within the highly exposed site.*

*Ground floor plan*

*First floor plan*

*Opposite:* New House, Wiltshire. The entrance front. A further exploration of the 'butterfly plan' by Nigel Anderson to take advantage of the far-reaching views from this site over the Wiltshire Downs. Here the façades are more formal and symmetrical with echoes of the country villas of John Nash. Key elements on the façades are of dressed Bath stone with the remainder having a rendered finish.

*Clockwise from left:* Nigel Anderson's Baroque design for a new house on the Wentworth estate in Surrey

A redundant and run-down workshop building converted by Nigel Anderson into a private house. The additions and alterations follow the idiom of the solid Victorian engineering character of the surviving original fabric.

Industrial workshop conversion in North Hampshire designed by Nigel Anderson

*Right:* Birstwith Hall, near Harrogate. The heart of this home is a late-17th-century double pile farmhouse. Over time the property was extended significantly on several occasions, each time without proper consideration to the overall plan. Hugh Petter demolished the staff quarters and rationalised the plan to create a comfortable, practical country home suitable for a family. The architectural character of the house was made more consistent by inserting new windows, removing unsightly details and extensive repairs to the historic fabric.

*Below:* Small country house at Betteshanger, Kent designed by Hugh Petter. Unbuilt.

*Opposite, clockwise from top:* Arts and Crafts farmstead designed by Hugh Petter. A new model farm in the Surrey Style for a young family with a rare-breed animal business. The main house is designed so that it appears to have grown in an incremental way. The centre looks like a medieval hall house with bargate stone walls on the ground floor and oak frame with a large central chimney. At either end are cross-wings designed to look as though they have been added later.

Georgian villa restoration, London. Hugh Petter designed a new chimneypiece in the drawing room of a listed mid-18th-century villa, previously derelict. The freehold is owned by the National Trust.

Georgian farmhouse renovation, Rochford, Essex. Restoration and extension to a listed small country house by Hugh Petter. New windows and a link to a brew house were added to the rear of the house.

# CHAPTER 5
# COUNTRY HOUSES

*'They had a country house. A house in the country is not the same as a country house. This was a country house.'*

Gertrude Stein, Blood on the Dining-Room Floor, 1933

From 1875 to 1975, the country house, a unique British contribution to world culture, was in apparently terminal decline. During this period, it has been estimated that as many as 1116 country houses fell victim to the slump in the agricultural economy, the human devastation of two world wars, extortionate rates of taxation and other, more mundane, depredations.[1] Perhaps partly as a result of the 1974 exhibition at the Victoria and Albert Museum, 'The Destruction of the Country House'[2], though more probably because of the dramatic reduction in taxes by the new Conservative government, the 1980s saw the tide turn in favour of the country house. There was a resurgence of interest in using these buildings for their original purposes, as family homes and the focus of an agricultural estate. A number of houses that had been occupied by institutions, most commonly boarding schools, were reclaimed and restored either by their original families or by new owners.[3] One difficulty facing those attempting to restore such houses was that often the contents had been sold when they were adapted for institutional use; finding sufficient furniture of appropriate scale and character could therefore be a challenge. When Lord Portsmouth was restoring Farleigh House, following the departure of the preparatory school which had occupied it since the Second World War, he commissioned a suite of heraldic furniture from Robert Adam rather than attempt to find a suitable set of antique dining chairs and other pieces.[4]

## SOLAR HOUSE AT WAKEHAM, SUSSEX

In 1975, The Hon. Brenda Carter, a trained radiologist, presented her invention of a portable 'Solar Wall' on the BBC's popular science programme, *Tomorrow's World*.[5] Consisting of a series of folding solar reflectors, the device was intended to enable anyone, even in a gloomy northern climate such as Britain's, to focus enough sunlight on themselves in order to develop a tan. The device never became popular, not least

---

1   John Martin Robinson, *The Latest Country Houses*, London 1984. Robinson, in choosing this title for his book, emphasised his optimism for the future of the country house, as opposed to the apparent pessimism of Clive Aslet, whose own book on the phenomenon was titled *The Last Country Houses*, New Haven 1982. See now also Giles Worsley, *England's Lost Houses*, London 2002.

2   Roy Strong, Marcus Binney and John Harris, *The Destruction of the Country House, 1875–1975*, London 1974.

3   Giles Worsley, 'Against the Tide', *Country Life*, January 1989, pp 90–91.

4   For more on the furniture for Lord Portsmouth see chapter nine below.

5   On The Hon. Brenda Carter's appearance on this programme in 1975 see Jackie Hunter, 'Tomorrow's World Today', *The Independent*, 6 May 1998, p. 5.

because within five years concerns began to emerge about the link between excessive exposure to the sun and malignant melanomas.[6] In architecture, however, there is nothing new about the desire to harness solar energy for light and heat: the *naos* of the Parthenon featured a shallow reflecting pool in front of Pheidias's figure of Athena Parthenos to ensure that there would be sufficient light to illuminate the gold and ivory statue. More recently, highly mechanised solar control systems have been employed in avant garde buildings, such as in Jean Nouvel's Institut du Monde Arabe, completed in 1987. Here the entire curtain wall of the building's façade is filled with thousands of photo-sensitive motorised apertures, just as one finds in the lens of a camera, so that the amount of light entering the building (and therefore its consequent solar gain) would be kept low on sunny days and maximised on overcast ones. The individual mechanisms, though simple in concept, were more complicated in realisation and immediately began to break down once the building was complete, so that this elegant idea – a Modernist moucharaby – has since become a maintenance nightmare.

Shortly before her death in 1993, Brenda Carter asked Robert Adam to collaborate with the solar heating expert Ray Maw on the design of a house that would be based around a system of passive environmental controls. The location, a hill with marvellous views over the Sussex downs, was the site of the former family home, which had burnt down in 1968.[7] Despite resistance from the local planning authority to some of the 'green' aspects of the proposal, Adam continued the project with the support of her son, Harold, and the house was completed in 2001. The result, architecturally, was Adam's most innovative design yet. It was based on two simple scientific ideas: Charles's law – that a gas at a constant pressure expands in relation to the rise in its temperature – and the principle of a greenhouse. In the latter, solar radiation passes through the glass panes of the greenhouse's structure to heat the ground and plants inside; they transfer heat to the air around them, which rises to the top of the greenhouse and is replaced by cool air that is in turn warmed. Since the warmer air is not allowed to escape into the atmosphere the greenhouse heats up. This system can be assisted through the use of a glazing material, which permits the shorter wavelength solar radiation to pass through, but does not allow the longer infrared radiation out – for this reason Adam and Maw used low-emissivity glass for the windows in the solar house. The crucial issue in applying these ideas to the design of a house is to achieve the maximum amount of control during varying weather conditions and at different seasons. Therefore the entrance front to the north has very little glazing, because here the potential for solar gain is minimal and one instead wishes to reduce heat loss through windows. On the south façade, on the other hand, 60 percent of the surface is glazed to maximise the absorption of the sun's energy, particularly by the black slate floor of the central double-height hall. The portico on this side of the house is cleverly designed with a deep projecting cornice to shade the windows when the sun is high in the sky – for instance at noon on a summer's day, when no additional heat is likely to be needed – but when it is low on the horizon, say on a winter afternoon, the slender columns scarcely interrupt the sun's rays allowing for the greatest possible solar gain. There is also a series of ducts and vents that allow cool air to be drawn into the house in the summer at the same time as hot air is being released through the central lantern; during cooler times of the year, the stack effect chimneys help draw warm air from the hall into the subsidiary spaces of the library, kitchen and bedrooms.

Adam's presentation drawing for the house provides a clue to the source of inspiration for his elegant portico with its slender cylindrical columns and pediment that breaks back dramatically in the centre. In the foreground of the drawing, next to an example of one of the steel column capitals, is a vignette of a

6   J Lee and D Strickland, 'Malignant melanoma: social status and outdoor work', *British Journal of Cancer*, vol. 41 (1980), no. 5, pp. 757–63.

7   Adam's inclusion of a phoenix in his presentation drawing is in reference to this fire.

Roman wall painting, just like those found at Pompeii. It features the kind of fictive architecture to which Vitruvius particularly objected because its highly attenuated forms could not actually be realised in stone. For us, accustomed as we are to seeing thin steel supports on Modernist buildings and industrial structures, they do not appear too insubstantial; rather their use as classical columns seems to restore the full decorative potential to a material which for the past 70 years has been stripped of its ornament through some spurious application of moral criteria to architecture. Adam's adaptation of the classical canon to steel is quite similar to the way in which Asher Benjamin, the early 19th-century American pattern book author, altered the proportions and details of the orders so that they would suit wood, the primary material available to him and his compatriots.

Over the entrance to the house a single word in Latin is most appropriately inscribed: LUCEAT, 'Let it shine'. This refers to the central theme of the house, the sun, and, at the same time, by reference to the Introit of the requiem mass, commemorates The Hon. Brenda Carter: 'Requiem æternam dona eis, Domine, et lux perpetua luceat eis' (Grant them eternal rest, O Lord, and let eternal light shine upon them).

*Opposite: Solar House at Wakeham, West Sussex. North elevation with minimum glazing for heat retention.*

*Above: South elevation with large areas of triple glazing for passive solar gain*

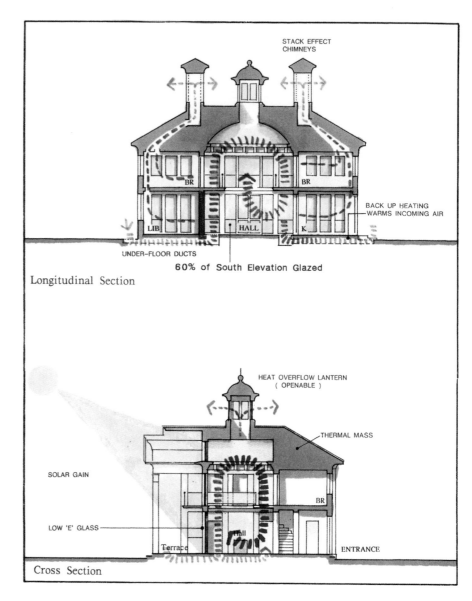

Longitudinal Section

STACK EFFECT CHIMNEYS

BR
BR

LIB
HALL
K

BACK UP HEATING WARMS INCOMING AIR

UNDER-FLOOR DUCTS

60% of South Elevation Glazed

Cross Section

HEAT OVERFLOW LANTERN ( OPENABLE )

THERMAL MASS

SOLAR GAIN

BR

LOW 'E' GLASS

Terrace

Hall

ENTRANCE

ARCHITECTS RAY MAW AND ROBERT ADAM · MCMXCIII

FOR THE HON. BRENDA CARTER AND HAROLD CARTER

SOLAR HOUSE AT WAKEHAM, WEST SUSSEX

***Clockwise from above:*** *Solar House at Wakeham, West Sussex. Pen and ink drawing showing the south elevation and two unbuilt wings all in brick. The walls were changed to stucco on construction. Standing on the right is Robert Adam with his client, Harold Carter. On the left is Ray Maw, who provided the technical advice on the use of passive solar energy and behind him is the Honourable Brenda Carter, Harold Carter's mother, who initiated the project and was a pioneer in the use of solar energy but died before construction began. A bird flies out of a fire in front of the house – an allusion to the phoenix as the new house was built on the site of the burnt-out family home – and is watched by a small dog – a 'canino' in Italian as a reference to Luigi Canina, the Italian architect who published a book on narrow classical orders. On the ground in the foreground are: a fragment of a wall painting from Pompei, showing the slender columns typically illustrated; an obelisk with a dung beetle pushing a dung ball inscribed, showing the use of Egyptian details and their worship of the sun; and three crowns, the symbols of Sweden as a reference to their innovative classical design from 1920s.*

*Diagrammatic sections showing the principles of the passive solar heating*

*Detail showing the portico that provides summer shading, the cupola that vents the central hall if it overheats, and the wind towers that vent the heated air naturally after it has passed through the building*

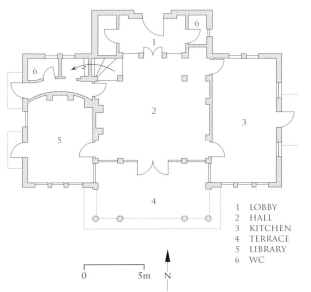

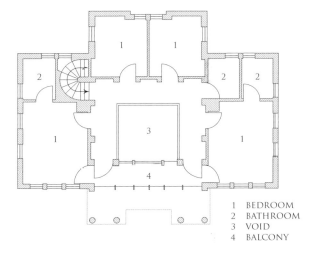

*Clockwise from left:* Solar House at Wakeham, West Sussex. Interior of open atrium living room with dark stone floors for heat retention and a gallery for access to first-floor bedrooms.

*First floor plan*

*Ground floor plan*

1 BEDROOM
2 BATHROOM
3 VOID
4 BALCONY

1 LOBBY
2 HALL
3 KITCHEN
4 TERRACE
5 LIBRARY
6 WC

0      5m    N

# THE REVIVAL OF THE COUNTRY HOUSE AND PPG7

At the end of the 1990s, a tremendous new impetus was given to the building of country houses by a short clause that had been slipped unobtrusively into a set of official planning guidance notes. These were issued by John Selwyn Gummer, the Secretary of State for the Environment, shortly before the Conservative government was defeated in the general election of May 1997. The relevant paragraph, 3.21, reads as follows:

*An isolated new house in the countryside may also be exceptionally justified if it is clearly of the highest quality, is truly outstanding in terms of its architecture and landscape design, and would significantly enhance its immediate setting and wider surroundings. Proposals for such development would need to demonstrate that proper account had been taken of the defining characteristics of the local area, including local or regional building traditions and materials. This means that each generation would have the opportunity to add to the tradition of the Country House which has done so much to enhance the English countryside.*

There were two points made by Gummer in this clause that are especially noteworthy. The first was that the justification for the country house was framed entirely in aesthetic terms, that is, that it should be 'truly outstanding in terms of its architecture and landscape design'. There was no discussion of what kind or how much of an economic impact it should have; no suggestion of a minimum size for either the house or the surrounding estate; no question of whether the estate should be a functioning agricultural concern or merely a small landscaped park; or if employment and affordable housing was to be provided for estate workers, etc. So that while economic arguments have often been used to support 'Gummer's Law' as it became known,[8] there was nothing in its phrasing that implied such a concern. Rather, it seems that its prime intent was, as stated, to allow individuals 'the opportunity to add to the tradition of the Country House which has done so much to enhance the English countryside'.

The second point, which seems hardly to have been commented upon,[9] is that Gummer implies (although he personally denies it) a virtual requirement that the house should be traditional in its style. He reminded local planners of the applicant's 'need to demonstrate that proper account had been taken of the defining characteristics of the local area, including local or regional building traditions and materials.' It is extremely difficult to imagine how a rigorous neo-Modernist house could reflect the character, building traditions and materials of any historic place.

Almost immediately, the Weekend Property section of *The Times* invited three architectural firms to propose different designs to illustrate the kind of houses that might result.[10] Border Oak of Hereford designed a neo-medieval idyll built of green oak beams and wattle-and-daub panels, while Baker-Brown McKay, who had won RIBA's 'House of the Future' competition in 1993, sunk its techno-fantasy into a ditch, with 'virtual reality' areas inside and an organic garden on its roof. Robert Adam, whose designs, both in plan and

---

8   See, for instance, the report partly funded by ADAM Architecture: Peter Prag and Roger Gibbard, *Private Investment in the Countryside: An assessment of the role of new houses and estates in sustaining the rural economy and environment*, Reading 2003.

9   See, though, Keith Miller, 'Plots on the landscape', *The Daily Telegraph*, 27 October 2001, p. 5: 'These breathily imprecise qualities are only slightly refined by the next couple of sentences, which mention 'local or regional building traditions and materials' and 'the tradition of the Country House'. So, if you were thinking of hiring some trendy modernist firm from the Smoke to knock you out a futuristic number in extruded titanium, forget it.'

10  Christine Webb, 'Three fantasies of a manor reborn', *The Times*, 8 March 1997, Weekend Property section.

*A Greek Revival country house with a central dome designed to illustrate an idealised classical country house*

elevation, were the most prominently featured in the article, produced a compact, easily legible square plan, loosely derived from the Villa Rotonda tradition of Mereworth and Chiswick. The style of the façade, however, was Greek Revival rather than Palladian, with a tetrastyle portico of baseless Doric columns rising the full height of the house and a prominent triglyph frieze running around on all four sides. On top, a large belvedere, in the form of an Ionic tholos, housed the lantern by which the double-storey octagonal hall below was lit. Christine Webb's accompanying text made it clear that 'of our three fantasies … [Adam's] is the most likely to coincide with the wishes of Cotswold planners, who usually expect designs to fit in with the local character of an area'.[11] This invaluable piece of initial publicity helped ensure that ADAM Architecture would receive a number of commissions for country houses, including even some under PPG7, over the next few years.

In the five years following the publication of these guidelines nearly 50 applications were made based on the provisions of paragraph 3.21, though more than half of these were for sites where there were existing houses or farm buildings, or where there had previously been a house. By 2002, planning permission had been granted for 14 new country houses and been refused for 12, though two of the latter applications, including one designed by Adam, were subsequently won on appeal. The controversy surrounding applications based on the PPG7 paragraph was such that in March 2003 it was even adopted as a storyline in the long-running and popular radio programme, *The Archers*.[12]

11   ibid.

12   Chris Arnot, 'A Dastardly Plot in Ambridge', *The Daily Telegraph*, 8 March 2003, p. 11.

By then it had already been rumoured that Mr Blair's government intended to eliminate the clause – the 'toffs' charter' as it had sometimes been caricatured by Labour supporters.[13] Indeed Andrew Bennett, MP for Denton and Reddish, had tabled an amendment to an early day motion with the support of five Old Labour cronies, which attacked it in terms of naked class warfare: 'this House … further believes that if the countryside is to be preserved by not building ordinary houses, it is even more important that it should not be polluted with big houses for the arrogant, vulgar and rich'.[14] As early as April 2001, Beverley Hughes, the government planning spokeswoman, had informed Parliament that the clause would be removed.[15] But in May 2004, the Housing and Planning Minister Keith Hill was lobbied by both Lord Foster, Britain's most famous high-tech architect, and the RIBA President George Ferguson to ensure that Gummer's clause would be retained.

This lobbying effort was so successful that three months later, a new Planning Policy Statement (PPS7) was issued to replace John Gummer's PPG7, in which it was stated (Paragraph 11):

> *Very occasionally the exceptional quality and innovative nature of the design of a proposed, isolated new house may provide this special justification for granting planning permission. Such a design should be truly outstanding and ground-breaking, for example, in its use of materials, methods of construction or its contribution to protecting and enhancing the environment, so helping to raise standards of design more generally in rural areas. The value of such a building will be found in its reflection of the highest standards in contemporary architecture, the significant enhancement of its immediate setting and its sensitivity to the defining characteristics of the local area.*[16]

Hill announced that, 'Changing the face of new country house architecture from a pastiche of historical styles to innovative cutting-edge design is essential if the best of British architecture is to be encouraged'.[17] And, as if to confirm his role in the decision, Lord Foster himself issued a statement: 'It is wonderful news that the government has recognised the role that good design can play in shaping the way we build in the countryside. This is a very progressive initiative'. The press immediately smelled a rat and denounced the government for 'shamelessly showering favours upon a Modernist architectural clique' led by Foster.[18] Whether there will be much call for such houses remains to be seen as cutting edge Modernist designs certainly had not proved popular before and even now two of the Modernist Houses from the old PPG7 are up for sale without being built, one is set to be changed to a traditional house and one has been changed – by Robert Adam.

One infamously 'progressive' design, for which planning permission had been obtained under PPG7, was a half-buried starfish-shaped house in Cheshire by the firm Ushida Findlay. After three years this had still failed to find a patron despite the original high-profile design competition run by the RIBA and a thousand

---

13  This phrase was quoted by Elizabeth Walton, 'How To Build A New Stately Home', *The Field*, March 2002, pp. 68–71. See also Ferdinand Mount, 'In Prescott Country, Only the Gypsies Win', *The Sunday Times*, 8 August 2004.

14  See Hansard, *Official Report*, 29 Jun 2004, vol. 423, c. 57WH.

15  See Hansard, *Official Report*, 23 April 2001; vol. 367, c. 82W: 'The Government believe that there is a need for more affordable housing in rural areas, and do not see the current planning exception for isolated large dwellings which may be built in unsustainable locations as consistent with that priority, or with its objectives for the countryside more generally. We therefore intend to consult on amendments to PPG7 to remove the exceptions policy which allows such large dwellings to be built.'

16  Office of the Deputy Prime Minster, *Planning Policy Statement 7: Sustainable Development in Rural Areas*, Norwich 2004.

17  Cahal Milmo, 'End of the Classical Mansions', *The Independent*, 4 August 2004, p. 7. The issue of style was raised in a written question to Hill from Alan Howarth MP, with Adam's involvement; the response deliberately avoided dispelling the notion that avant garde design was being encouraged.

18  Ross Clark, 'Little houses are special, too', *The Sunday Telegraph*, 8 August 2004, p. 20.

*New country house, Hampshire. A cubic design with large areas of window.*
*The tower houses the farm office.*

121

*Clockwise from left:* New country house, Hampshire, entrance façade

Garage building, with staff accommodation above

Detail above garden entrance

expensively printed brochures. Its realisation was dealt another blow when the architects, previously best known for their work in Japan, went into voluntary liquidation in 2004. In 2007 the developers finally gave up on trying to sell their futuristic daydream and approached ADAM Architecture to provide a more viable design for the site. As of autumn 2006, only four proposals had been granted planning permission under the new PPS7, one being a huge 40,000-square-foot house designed by the architects Feilden Clegg Bradley for a site near Grimsby.[19]

So what was achieved in the seven and a half years between PPG7, which clearly favoured traditional country houses, and PPS7, which appears to mandate neo-Modernism? Of the two dozen designs for new country houses that were granted planning permission during this period, relatively few have so far been completed.[20] Were they, as predicted by Jonathan Glancy in an article brimming with class resentment and ideologically tilted towards neo-Modernism, 'a virulent rash of second-rate houses for late flowering country squires'?[21] The first to be finished was Wootton Hall, Staffordshire, designed by Digby Harris, of Francis Johnson and Partners, for the brewery heir John Greenall. Constructed on the site of a mid-18th-century house that had been demolished in 1935, it was in an extremely restrained Regency idiom reminiscent of Wyatt or Soane. Similar restraint characterised Quinlan Terry's Great Canfield, a red brick and stone house in the Georgian vernacular of Essex for the businessman Philip Seer. Not all new country houses of this period were so understated. For Lord Rothermere, the young chairman of Associated Newspapers, Terry designed a modestly sized house of Chilmark and Portland stone, onto the entrance front of which was grafted an elaborate portico of giant composite columns complete with a sculptured pediment bursting with the Rothermere arms.

Robert Adam's only PPG7 house to be completed, a new country house in Hampshire, was itself not without controversy. The clients wanted to build a house as an appropriate focus for the 1700-acre estate they already farmed. Though still in their mid-30s, they had begun thinking ahead to their own children growing up and they envisaged passing on the house and estate to them. Fifty acres surrounding the house were set aside to be managed as parkland, though the current sensitivity to the preservation of natural habitats meant that the landscape design, by Barton Wilmore Environmental, was more a series of subtle interventions rather than a single sweeping statement as it might have been in the 18th century. This also meant that the siting of the house in relation to the existing landscape features had to be handled with particular delicacy.

In response to the requirements of function and site, Adam broke the 15,000-square-foot programme of the house down into four parts: a block of staterooms, a family wing, an estate office pavilion and a separate range of garages and outbuildings. This subdivision allowed him to create an unusual asymmetrical arrangement with the various parts wheeling around the domed estate office pavilion, which anchors the composition at the centre. Thus the house fits picturesquely into its landscape and the amount of sunlight

19   The first to be granted permission was a design for a house on the former site of Coston Hall in Leicestershire, designed by Paul Bancroft and FPCR, see James Rose, 'Surprise Winner in Country House Stakes', *Building Design*, 2 June 2006, p. 6. Another project that might fall into this category is a minimalist house designed by Andrei Bowbelski for a site in Buckinghamshire, though it seems still to be shrouded in secrecy; see Pat Bramley, 'Blocks on the Penn landscape', *Bucks Free Press*, 24 October 2005. Craig Hamilton's house for the Lowther estate, blending Michelangelesque detail with Palladian form was granted permission on appeal; as of the time of writing it is apparently the only traditional or classical house to have succeeded since the introduction of PPS7, see Marguerite Lazell, 'PPS7 suffers classic case of identity crisis', *Building Design*, 8 September 2006, p. 6.

20   For accounts of these houses see the catalogue by Neil Guy for the exhibition 'The New English Country House' held at the RIBA in September 2003.

21   Jonathan Glancey, 'Brideheads? Baloney', *The Independent*, 28 February 1997, p. 6.

*New country house, Hampshire, main garden façade*

125

reaching the gardens is carefully maximised. Despite this overall asymmetry, each individual component exhibits the formal balance one might expect to find in a grand country house. The outcome, recalling the work of Schinkel both in idiom and layout, is an extraordinarily lucid composition, which differs markedly from the Palladian tradition in which a house, strung out along a single orthogonal axis, is constrained by an overarching and artificial bilateral symmetry. According to this latter model, typical of the grander Georgian country house, a single, repetitive façade subsumes all the different activities of the household behind false correspondences, so that identical pavilions in flanking wings might house a sculpture gallery on one side and suites of service rooms on the other. While such concerns could be dismissed as the fallacious application of a Modernistic morality to architecture, there are consequences for the everyday ease of use of the house. In a more organic plan, as one might find in a Nash villa or an Arts and Crafts house, the *parti*, or the basic concept underlying the plan, is arranged to ensure the best views out to the natural landscape and the most harmonious fit within it. Numerous examples of this kind of picturesque planning are found in Adam's work, most notably at the riverside country house in Dorset, which is based on the kind of sophisticated butterfly plan favoured by Lutyens and other Edwardian architects.[22]

This house was initially refused planning permission. Adam responded by producing an extremely thorough statement, which documented every aspect of the scheme and explained the reasoning behind each design decision, particularly through reference to local precedent and to the history of the site. This kind of report has become a standard production for the firm for all projects that are likely to be controversial and the directors find them invaluable presentation tools.[23]

Keith Durrant, the planning inspector, noted in his report that the house was 'truly outstanding in terms of its architecture and landscape design and would significantly enhance its immediate setting and wider surroundings ... It has evolved as a design under the direction of a skilled architect with a reputation for an innovative approach to the classical traditions, reinterpreted for the 21st century.'[24] What was indeed most striking about this house was the handling of the classical idiom. Not since the great prodigy houses of Elizabethan England had the proportions of window to wall in a traditional house been so dramatically tipped in favour of glass. Adam opened up magnificent views to the countryside from the staterooms, setting the expansive windows in an elegant grid of attenuated piers. To enhance the flat, planar quality of the masonry, the details of the orders are carefully stripped away; the tall pilasters marching around the four-square block containing the rooms of parade are thus a pared-down version of the simplest of all Corinthian columns, those of the Horologion of Andronikos in Athens, the so-called 'Temple of the Winds'. In the family wing, by contrast, brick is substituted for the crisp stone of the main block, and the windows, now smaller, take on squarish proportions. The sense of stepping down in the building hierarchy is confirmed by the pilasters, still full height, but now denuded of all details to leave mere strips of brick, though their pairings continue to echo the rhythms of the *corps de logis*. The language evoked now shifts from Schinkel at the Schauspielhaus or Thomson at Moray Place to Behrens or even Rossi. Finally, as one crosses over the yard to the garage wing, the idiom descends to a simple brick vernacular, complete with dormer windows. At every point in the composition, the elision of classical elements, perhaps the trickiest part of abstracting and modernising the language, is rigorously thought through. As one

22  On the precedents for the butterfly plan used by Adam, see David Watkin's 'Robert Adam: A Critical Review' in the exhibition catalogue *Classical Design in the Late Twentieth Century: Recent Work of Robert Adam*, London 1990, p. 12.

23  These brochures have proved particularly useful in projects where a historic building is being reordered or extended, such as the remodeled Historic House in Hampshire.

24  Charles Clover, 'Couple's £3 million home beats ban on rural building', *The Daily Telegraph*, 30 January 2001, p. 11.

*New country house, Hampshire, pediment over front door*

moves around the house, mouldings disappear and then later re-emerge exactly on cue, following the internal logic of the orders. Even their materials change to communicate precisely their relative importance within the hierarchy of parts; thus the single-storey Doric order of the curving entrance portico to the family wing has a bold architrave and cornice of stone, but a reticent frieze of brick.

Paul Hanvey played a crucial role at this house in managing the project from the planning stage onwards, paying particular attention to 'the stonework detailing and its interface with the structure, being a combination of load-bearing masonry and precast concrete columns and beams'.[25] The interiors, also by ADAM Architecture, were a separate stage of the contract, and here again Hanvey's involvement was vital, 'to ensure that the junction of window frames and room cornices was built to the finest possible tolerance within a 6–10 millimetre deviation.'[26]

25   Paul Hanvey, undated project description.

26   ibid.

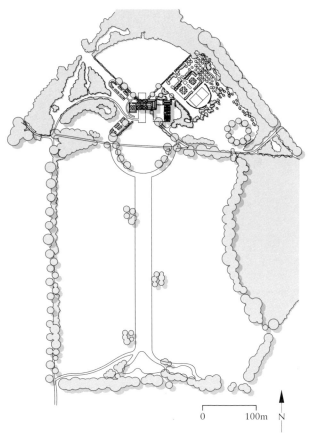

**Clockwise from top left:** *New country house, Hampshire, central window mullion and crest on tower*

*Stair*

*Site plan*

**Opposite, clockwise from left:** *Entrance hall*

*First floor plan*

*Ground floor plan*

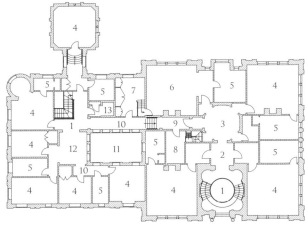

| | |
|---|---|
| 1 STAIR HALL | 8 LINEN |
| 2 LANDING HALL | 9 HALL |
| 3 OCTAGON LANDING | 10 CORRIDOR |
| 4 BEDROOM | 11 COURTYARD |
| 5 BATHROOM | 12 NURSERY HALL |
| 6 MASTER BEDROOM | 13 LIFT |
| 7 DRESSING ROOM | |

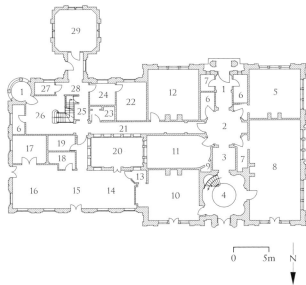

| | |
|---|---|
| 1 VESTIBULE | 16 FAMILY ROOM |
| 2 OCTAGON HALL | 17 NURSERY |
| 3 INNER HALL | 18 PANTRY |
| 4 STAIR HALL | 19 STORE |
| 5 LIBRARY | 20 COURTYARD |
| 6 CLOAKROOM | 21 CORRIDOR |
| 7 LOG STORE | 22 FISHING/GAMES ROOM |
| 8 DRAWING ROOM | 23 LIFT |
| 9 CUPBOARD | 24 UTILITY ROOM |
| 10 DINING ROOM | 25 BOOT ROOM |
| 11 BILLIARD ROOM | 26 HALL |
| 12 SITTING ROOM | 27 BATHROOM |
| 13 CHINA | 28 OFFICE HALL |
| 14 KITCHEN | 29 OFFICE |
| 15 BREAKFAST | |

## NEW QUEEN ANNE HOUSE, DORSET

By comparison with the new country house in Hampshire, where permission was won only on appeal, another country house commission handled by ADAM Architecture went swimmingly.[27] Nigel Anderson was asked to design a house for a site in Dorset for the sculptor George Bingham. He had bought a 149-acre farm in 2002 knowing that the previous owner's application for building on its redundant concrete yard had just been denied. By comparison to other country house projects, Bingham's budget was rather constrained – a million pounds – so the palette of materials chosen was solid and unpretentious: lime render over load-bearing masonry for the walls, brick chimneys, natural slate roofs, and small-paned timber sash windows. The local council unhesitatingly granted permission with deliberations at the meeting lasting a mere ten minutes. Afterwards, the chairman was quoted as saying that it 'was a very beautiful house and it deserved to be built.' The two-storey central block was perfectly framed by smaller flanking pavilions under steeply pitched roofs, and the overall simplicity of the composition was enlivened by a judicious sprinkling of oval 'oeil de boeuf' windows.

Other new country houses by directors of the firm that have recently been completed include Nigel Anderson's new Palladian house in East Sussex, and a new Palladian villa in Berkshire by George Saumarez Smith, in the tradition of the English Palladians and John Carr of York.

---

27   Jonny Beardsall, 'An estate of grace', *Sunday Telegraph*, 6 March 2005, p. 3.

**Opposite:** *Queen Anne style house, Dorset, designed by Nigel Anderson. The estate office side wing with the dog kennel below its masters entrance echoing the oeil de boeuf windows on this façade.*

**Above:** *The entrance façade of the elegant essay in the Queen Anne style described as 'a very beautiful house that deserved to be built'*

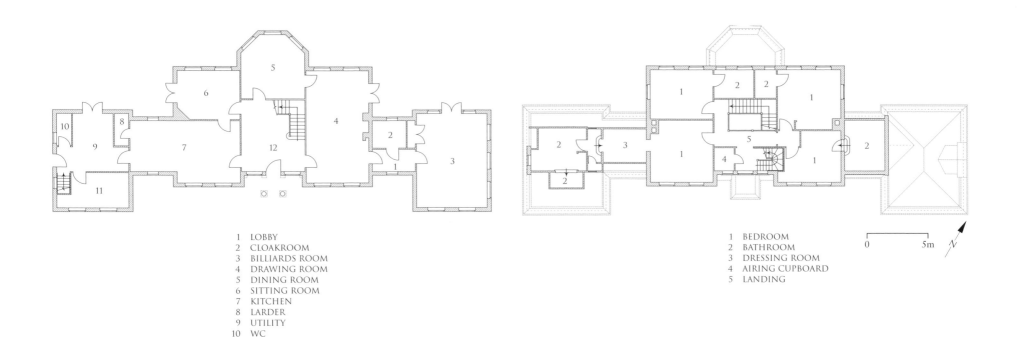

| | |
|---|---|
| 1 | LOBBY |
| 2 | CLOAKROOM |
| 3 | BILLIARDS ROOM |
| 4 | DRAWING ROOM |
| 5 | DINING ROOM |
| 6 | SITTING ROOM |
| 7 | KITCHEN |
| 8 | LARDER |
| 9 | UTILITY |
| 10 | WC |
| 11 | OFFICE |
| 12 | HALL |

| | |
|---|---|
| 1 | BEDROOM |
| 2 | BATHROOM |
| 3 | DRESSING ROOM |
| 4 | AIRING CUPBOARD |
| 5 | LANDING |

0        5m

*Clockwise from top left:* Queen Anne style house, Dorset. Ground floor plan.

*First floor plan*

*Garden façade with restored farm buildings in the background*

# NEW PALLADIAN HOUSE, EAST SUSSEX

The new Palladian house in East Sussex is perhaps the most rigorously symmetrical exploration of the Butterfly Plan produced by the practice so far. A rectangular two-storey central block has a giant order Doric entrance portico. This is flanked on both sides by attached single-storey pavilions projecting diagonally from the front and rear. These pavilions in turn embrace two-storey-high circular drum 'towers' with conical roofs that are detached from the main body of the house. Within and at both main floor levels, arcaded hallways and landings run the whole length of the central axis of the interior. These are terminated at both ends by the drum towers and punctuated at their mid-point by tiered and vaulted galleries rising through three floors and top-lit by a circular roof light or oculus.

*New Palladian house, East Sussex. The garden façade of Nigel Anderson's most rigorously symmetrical*
*'butterfly plan' design. It overlooks the lake within the valley below and has a central sun loggia within the*
*Ionic Giant Order portico. The circular end pavilions each contain dramatic vaulted double height spaces.*

*Above:* New Palladian house, East Sussex. The front
façade with Doric giant order entrance portico.

*Right:* Ground floor plan

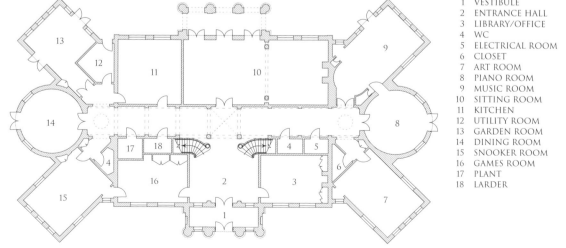

1  VESTIBULE
2  ENTRANCE HALL
3  LIBRARY/OFFICE
4  WC
5  ELECTRICAL ROOM
6  CLOSET
7  ART ROOM
8  PIANO ROOM
9  MUSIC ROOM
10  SITTING ROOM
11  KITCHEN
12  UTILITY ROOM
13  GARDEN ROOM
14  DINING ROOM
15  SNOOKER ROOM
16  GAMES ROOM
17  PLANT
18  LARDER

1 BEDROOM
2 BATHROOM

0    5m    N

*Clockwise from top left:* New Palladian house, East Sussex. The garden façade.

*Detail of the front entrance portico*

*The central gallery area rising through all floors of the house to the rooftop oculus*

*First floor plan*

# NEW PALLADIAN VILLA, HAMPSHIRE

George Saumarez Smith designed the new Palladian villa in Hampshire at the centre of a 70-acre farming estate in an Area of Outstanding Natural Beauty facing the North Downs to the west of Newbury. The house replaced a farmhouse that had been substantially altered and engulfed with modern additions. The new house forms part of wider improvements to the estate including the construction of new farm buildings and extensive landscaping works.

The design is in the Palladian tradition, and draws particularly on Palladio's villa-farms as appropriate to a building at the centre of an agricultural estate. The plan is based on one of Palladio's unbuilt projects, the Villa Ragona at Le Ghizzole, published in the *Quattro Libri dell'Architettura*. This villa was used as a plan-type for several 18th-century English houses including Stourhead in Wiltshire. In contrast to other English Palladian houses, however, this new Palladian villa has been designed entirely in Venetian feet, the unit of measurement used by Palladio. This gives the house a more generous scale as well as a more direct connection with the work of Palladio and his contemporaries.

The house also draws on the English villa tradition exemplified by architects such as Robert Taylor and John Carr of York. In particular, the introduction of canted bays on the east and west elevations gives the house a distinct English character. At the centre of the house, a cantilevered stone staircase is overlooked by vaulted landings reminiscent of the work of Sir John Soane.

It was a specific intention that the house should serve as a model of a low-technology sustainable house. The construction is solid and robust, using locally traditional materials including handmade red bricks, Portland stone and Welsh slate. The heating and hot water for the house is supplied by a geothermal heating system. The plan form also has the flexibility to be adapted over time. This is a perfect demonstration of how the Palladian tradition can serve as a model for sustainable building.

The house is meticulously crafted and Saumarez Smith worked closely with local builders, RJ Smith and Co. The project involved successful collaborations with the interior decorator William Graham, the landscape designer Guy Thornton and the sculptor Simon Smith, who modelled and cast two delightful little monkeys that sit inside the balustrade of the main staircase. These subtle and surprising little figures are a good example of the features that, in the hands of an imaginative architect, can give a house the permanent and unique signature of its owners and architect.

Hugh Petter is hoping to follow the success of these houses with the construction of one of the most dramatic country house designs to come out of ADAM Architecture: a new English Baroque house in Berkshire.

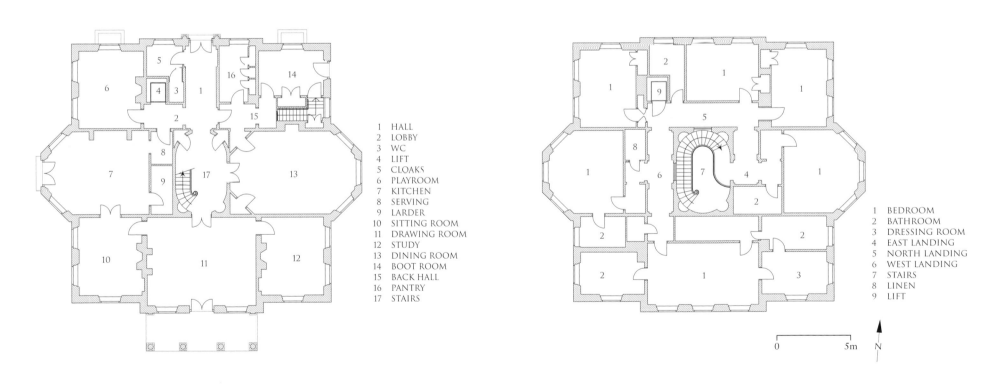

1 HALL
2 LOBBY
3 WC
4 LIFT
5 CLOAKS
6 PLAYROOM
7 KITCHEN
8 SERVING
9 LARDER
10 SITTING ROOM
11 DRAWING ROOM
12 STUDY
13 DINING ROOM
14 BOOT ROOM
15 BACK HALL
16 PANTRY
17 STAIRS

1 BEDROOM
2 BATHROOM
3 DRESSING ROOM
4 EAST LANDING
5 NORTH LANDING
6 WEST LANDING
7 STAIRS
8 LINEN
9 LIFT

0        5m    N

**Opposite:** *New Palladian villa, Hampshire, designed by George Saumarez Smith. The main garden front facing south, with the projecting portico of Ionic columns.*

**Left:** *Ground floor plan*

**Right:** *First floor plan*

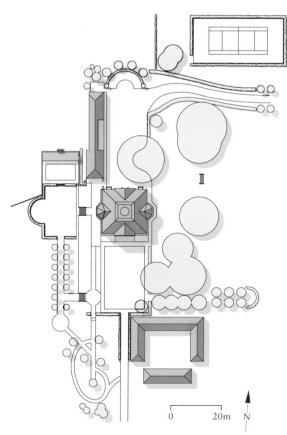

**Clockwise from left:** *New Palladian villa, Hampshire. The west front of the house, with the angled bay of the kitchen in the centre.*

*The front door with engaged Ionic columns and door surround, all in Portland stone*

*One of the two monkeys on the staircase, modelled by the sculptor Simon Smith and cast in bronze, together with the typical balustrade pattern*

*Site plan*

0     20m    N

# NEW ENGLISH BAROQUE COUNTRY HOUSE, BERKSHIRE

This new English Baroque Country house in the grand manner proposed for a site south of the Royal town of Windsor would replace an undistinguished house that is a waste of a remarkable setting. The design is firmly in the tradition of English Baroque architecture. Castle Howard, Yorkshire, built from 1702 by Sir John Vanbrugh with Hawksmoor's assistance, is a key source.

The imposing west entrance front of the English Baroque house is flanked by long, single-storey wings in the Ionic order, containing garages and a swimming pool. The entrance front has a portico of four free-standing Corinthian columns supporting a pediment filled with a decorative bas-relief which, like the other carved work at the English Baroque house, will be by the two finest sculptors and carvers in Britain, Dick Reid and Alexander Stoddart.

The east garden front, which commands a view down the parkland to the lake and woodland beyond, remarkably also has a portico of free-standing Corinthian columns. Although the house was planned to have a domed cupola, the east front has instead been enhanced with the addition of a terrace, double staircase, and seven-bay orangery that bears some resemblance to the Grand Trianon at Versailles. Despite the many historical precedents for aspects of the design, the house is at the same time thoroughly of the 21st century, with interior spaces such as club room, bar, gymnasium and cinema.

Petter has also designed a series of smaller buildings that form a kind of commentary on the language and character of the big house. These include the lake lodge, a little residential Doric temple, an octagonal timber structure and the workshop and garden store. He has also designed a dower house, a clever building in the Doric order with an L-shaped plan recalling pavilions near Paris such as the Pavillon Français at Versailles.

Since PPS7 was introduced in August 2004 the situation has looked much bleaker for the classical country house, however progressive its plan or details. Two high-profile projects by Robert Adam have been denied planning permission explicitly for stylistic reasons. The first was a new Manor House, designed as an ambitious U-shaped house for a site near Compton, Berkshire, in an Area of Outstanding Natural Beauty. The centre of the main tripartite façade was to have been dominated by a freestanding Corinthian portico of traditional Palladian form, while the two wings running back from this *corps de logis* were to be in the Tudor revival and Italian baroque styles respectively. The component parts of the design were not self-consciously progressive in terms of the handling of their details, but the fundamental premise was quite original: that the house had notionally developed over time, and that this imagined evolution was made evident through the proposed combination of styles. Even though the application had been lodged in June 2004, before the introduction of the PPS7, the refusal of permission was couched very clearly in the terms of the new Statement: the recommendation baldly stated that 'the design proposed is not contemporary in approach but rather an historical pastiche which does not accord with the advice contained within para[graph] 11 of PPS7.'[28]

The second project to suffer as a result of the stylistic prescriptions of PPS7 was a four-storey house designed for a disused chalk pit quarry site in the North Wessex Downs, again an Area of Outstanding Natural Beauty. All of Adam's knowledge and experience from building the solar house in Sussex went into the design of the sophisticated passive solar heating and energy efficiency systems running throughout the structure. The façade

---

28   West Berkshire Council, Downlands Area Planning Sub-Committee, Report, 15 December 2004, http://www.westberks.gov.uk/media/doc/d/r/0401570_1.doc.

*New English Baroque country house, Berkshire, designed by Hugh Petter. Perspective of the garden front and its landscape.*

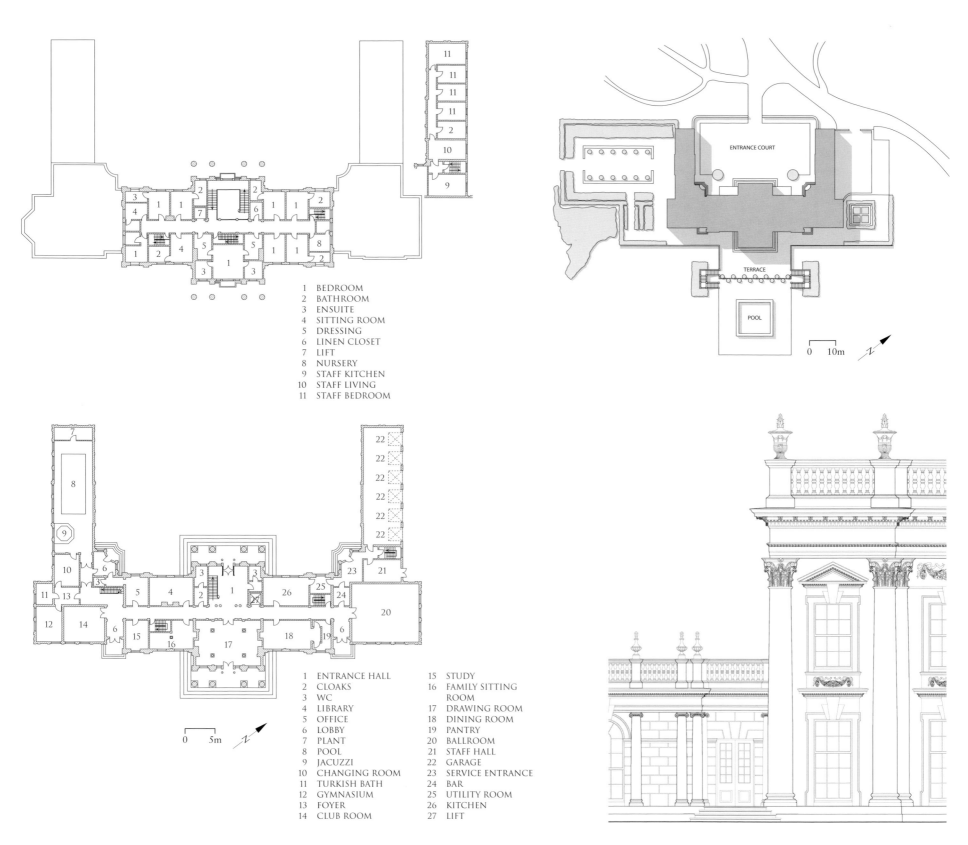

1 BEDROOM
2 BATHROOM
3 ENSUITE
4 SITTING ROOM
5 DRESSING
6 LINEN CLOSET
7 LIFT
8 NURSERY
9 STAFF KITCHEN
10 STAFF LIVING
11 STAFF BEDROOM

| | |
|---|---|
| 1 ENTRANCE HALL | 15 STUDY |
| 2 CLOAKS | 16 FAMILY SITTING |
| 3 WC | ROOM |
| 4 LIBRARY | 17 DRAWING ROOM |
| 5 OFFICE | 18 DINING ROOM |
| 6 LOBBY | 19 PANTRY |
| 7 PLANT | 20 BALLROOM |
| 8 POOL | 21 STAFF HALL |
| 9 JACUZZI | 22 GARAGE |
| 10 CHANGING ROOM | 23 SERVICE ENTRANCE |
| 11 TURKISH BATH | 24 BAR |
| 12 GYMNASIUM | 25 UTILITY ROOM |
| 13 FOYER | 26 KITCHEN |
| 14 CLUB ROOM | 27 LIFT |

**Clockwise from top left:** *New English Baroque country house, Berkshire, designed by Hugh Petter.*
*First floor plan.*

*Site plan*

*Bay study of the main façade*

*Ground floor plan*

*A new manor house, Berkshire with different parts designed in different classical styles, unbuilt*

was entirely glazed with two projecting semicircular bays framing the continuous horizontal balconies of the taller central block. This proposal was Adam's clearest departure yet from the traditional plan typology of the English house, having much more in common with the stacked porches or 'piazzas' of historic American houses, such as those in Charleston, South Carolina. Though it was approved by Basingstoke and Deane Borough Council, it was 'called in' by the Secretary of State following objections from neighbouring landowners and went to a public enquiry, which lasted an unprecedented eight days. The objectors were represented by two barristers, including a Queen's Counsel, and also engaged expert witnesses, including a London-based neo-Modernist architect, Russell Brown, who later admitted his extreme ideological bias: 'There is a style war going on here.'[29] The resulting refusal of permission, though hardly surprising considering the funds expended opposing the application at the public enquiry, was important in its implications: amongst other issues, the secretary of state noted that the project was not of an 'innovative nature to meet the requirements of paragraph 11 of PPS 7'.[30] Since the design was patently innovative, and in fact had departed so far from the country house typology so as to be hardly recognisable as one, the only gloss that can be put on this phrase is that the proposal was not judged sufficiently Modernist.

29  Will Hurst, 'Adam's house fails to impress', *Building Design*, May 19, 2006, p.7.

30  Press release, 2 Harcourt Buildings, http://www.2hblaw.co.uk/lc_cms/page_view.asp?ID=897.

More recently there is evidence that the tide is turning. Two projects that demonstrate with conviction and panache that a traditional new country house can exactly satisfy the PPS7 requirements to be 'innovative', 'truly outstanding and ground breaking' have been running neck and neck for a permission to build. One is by Robert Adam and the other by Hugh Petter. At the time of writing, Robert Adam's design for a new country house in Cheshire has just won a landmark planning consent. Hugh Petter is, at the time of writing, managing the planning system to secure an approval on his ground-breaking country house design in Surrey.

Both designs use the latest developments in sustainable building and demonstrate that reducing carbon consumption is not a high-tech affair based on complicated mechanical engineering but is best achieved with traditional design and construction. Indeed, in 2007 the firm worked with leading environmental engineers, Atelier Ten, on a research project that showed, once and for all, that insulated solid-wall construction has better energy saving credentials than even the most technically advanced glass walled construction. Although environmental engineers all know this, when the results of the research were published they were not popular among architects and most engineers kept their heads down.[31] The engineers earn large fees providing 'greenwash' calculations for Modernist architects who have to pretend to be sustainable while designing the same glass and steel buildings they have always designed.

---

31 Atelier Ten, *A Study of the Energy Performance of Two Buildings with Lightweight and Heavyweight Facades*, 2008, published by ADAM Architecture.

Robert Adam continued to work with Atelier Ten on the new country house in Cheshire while on the country house in Surrey Hugh Petter adopted the clever tactic of working with the British Research Establishment, which still carries the status of its origins as a government research organisation although it is now an independent consultancy. The outcomes were similar.

Thick walls allow for extensive insulation and the use of local materials and traditional construction, the fundamental principles of all traditional design, reduce heat loss and the use of energy to transport building products. Tall windows, a classical standard, set into these solid walls are larger on the south side and smaller on the north side and so control the amount of energy gained from sunlight and allow light to penetrate deep into the rooms behind. The use of energy from natural sources, such as rapeseed oil or 'biomass' (harvested fast-growing timber crops), or from heat exchangers, capitalising on differences in soil temperatures and air temperatures, have no impact on the exterior of the building. Even the latest devices can be comfortably contained in a traditional design: solar heating and photovoltaic panels can be set up in roof wells created by the pitched roofs and windmills that can be used to generate electricity are no larger than the wind-driven pumps that are an established feature in the countryside. The combination of the latest research with traditional design, which evolved in a time of high-cost energy, is being pioneered by the firm and is truly innovative, pointing the way to the future.

## PIONEERING COUNTRY HOUSE, SURREY

Petter's country house in Surrey will replace a bungalow from the 1960s that sits uncomfortably in gardens created for a much grander 19th-century pile. The owner has had his eye on this plot since 1990 and when it came up for sale in 2005 he felt that it would be right for an imposing Classical house. Normally the local council would only contemplate a replacement that was 10 percent bigger than the existing structure, but Hugh Petter found that the planners recognised that this site, with commanding views, needed a house in proportion. Working closely with the landscape architect Mark Darwent of Colvin and Moggridge Landscape Architects, the new house has been carefully designed to fuse with the surviving fragments of the original garden layout and to integrate into its sensitive parkland setting.

On the north side, Petter has designed a freestanding portico of giant Corinthian columns. The west and east elevations will have a centrepiece of interlocking Tuscan columns (two tiers of small orders ingeniously incorporated within a double-height one), inspired by the Renaissance architect Bramante's Ninfeo at

*Opposite: New house on a disused quarry site in Hampshire, south façade. An innovative development of classical design for achieving maximum passive solar gain.*

*Above: Country House, Surrey, designed by Hugh Petter. Landscape section showing the south façade of the new house and how it fuses with the gardens that survive from the earlier building on the site. Drawing by Mark Darwent of Colvin and Moggridge Landscape Architects.*

Existing Pavilion
to be dismantled and re-erected

Extent of Basement

Service Courtyard and Service entrance
(Retaining walls to Service Courtyard not shown for clarity)

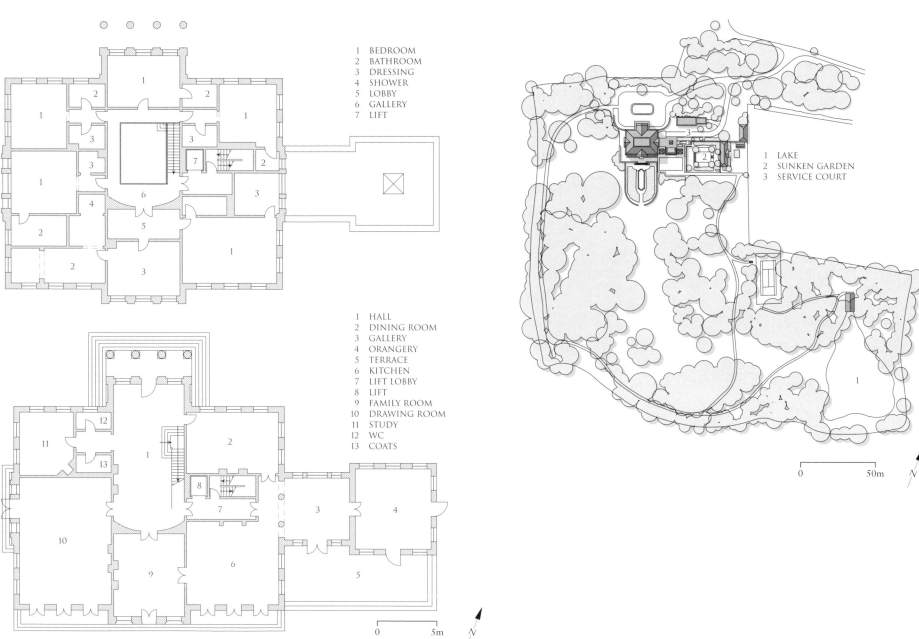

1 BEDROOM
2 BATHROOM
3 DRESSING
4 SHOWER
5 LOBBY
6 GALLERY
7 LIFT

1 HALL
2 DINING ROOM
3 GALLERY
4 ORANGERY
5 TERRACE
6 KITCHEN
7 LIFT LOBBY
8 LIFT
9 FAMILY ROOM
10 DRAWING ROOM
11 STUDY
12 WC
13 COATS

1 LAKE
2 SUNKEN GARDEN
3 SERVICE COURT

0        5m

0        50m

Genazanno, near Rome. The result, without any direct precedent, is therefore an innovative piece of classicism, carried out in a way that is literate in the classical language. This is a piece of high architecture, which will dominate a fine mature landscape. The planning system, as is so often the case, has proved to be difficult. Petter and his client's advisors are confident that this important building will soon receive the necessary permission.

## SUSTAINABLE COUNTRY HOUSE, CHESHIRE

Much as Ushida Findlay's design for a starfish-shaped house, as described above, was seen by Modernist architects in 2001 as the defining proof that country houses did not have to be traditional, so its replacement by a traditional design is a highly significant event.

The new owner of the site wanted a home for his family rather than a speculative venture such as the enterprise that had led to the failure of the Ushida Findlay design. A real brief always gives a better sense of reality and character to a design. Robert Adam worked closely with the owner and his family to develop the proposal. At the same time, he introduced Atelier Ten to work alongside him in developing a sustainable design. He also worked closely with the landscape architect Chris Burnett. At regular intervals in the development of the design Adam was careful to take the team to discuss the proposals with the local council so that they could understand the originality of the emerging proposals – so avoiding the simplistic Modernist idea that to be original a building has to be outrageously unusual.

The house is a relatively austere rectangular block in local stone, with an attached single-storey recreational wing projecting into the garden alongside a garage courtyard. On the north side, the central entrance bay projects forward and, at each end, the walls break forward to frame the façade. The treatment of the classical orders on the elevations is quite unique.

The details of the order itself are wholly individual. The capitals are a highly literal development of the story of the origins of Corinthian capital by the Roman author Marcus Vitruvius Pollio – normally just known as 'Vitruvius'. Vitruvius describes the Corinthian capital as originating in a representation of a basket of grave goods for a young maiden, capped with a roof tile and with an acanthus plant growing up around it. The beauty of this accidental arrangement, according to Vitruvius, led the Corinthian sculptor Calimachus to invent the Corinthian capital. Adam has taken up this story and represented it quite literally in the Cheshire house order. Adam's capital has a four acanthus stems at each corner of a simple basket-weave decoration and the abacus that tops the capital is simplified to a simple square tile. The base of the column is also changed from the series of concave and convex rings that typify the Corinthian order to

*Opposite, clockwise from top: Country house, Surrey. This country house, designed by Hugh Petter and the Building Research Establishment, will be zero carbon. It is designed to sit on the site of a 19th-century house that was demolished previously. The original service entrance on the east side at the lower level becomes the family entrance for the new house and leads also to a swimming pool in an orangery which looks out onto a sunken garden that survives from the earlier building.*

*Site plan*

*Ground floor plan*

*First floor plan*

another ancient type – a base made of acanthus leaves sprouting from where the column rises – except in this case, unlike the capital, the motif is dramatically simplified to a ring of fluted petals.

The use of this order, particularly on the front, is also unique. The full column and capital are only fully shown once on each side of the entrance. Each side of the entrance the capital merges with the wall and becomes a repeated Greek key pattern. On the ends of the façade the capitals only appear, clasping the sides of the projections, with the column suggested only by a slight taper in the walls themselves.

The south side of the house has large full-height French windows on the ground floor with large windows above. This façade is distinguished by a rectangular forward break in the elevation with the full new Cheshire house order expressed.

Even the windows themselves are unique. Developed with Atelier Ten, the triple-glazed windows eschew the conventional English vertical sliding sash to create a more energy-efficient three-pane type based on continental European side-hung window, with a central wooden column and insulated internal shutters. On the recreation wing, the normal use of fully glazed windows for an indoor swimming pool would have resulted in an unacceptable loss of energy. Adam has developed a version of the most elemental three-part window, with an arched centre, developed in Venice. This local Italian window type was elaborated with full classical orders by the architects Sebastiano Serlio and Andrea Palladio to create a distinctive and much-used version named either after these architects or after the city itself: the Venetian window. At the house in Cheshire the Venetian windows to the pool are reduced to their origin as simple cut openings filled with large panes of triple glazing.

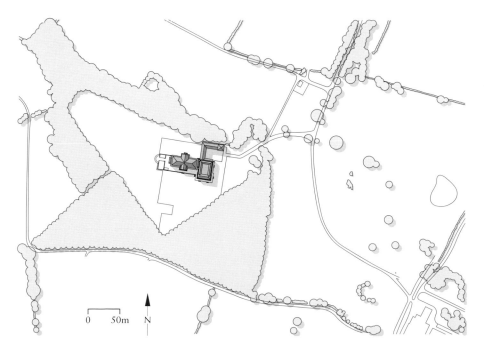

**Left:** *Country house, Cheshire. A house designed for energy efficiency and an inventive use of classical detail. North façade.*

**Top:** *South façade, with pool building on the east end*

**Above:** *Site plan*

0   50m   N

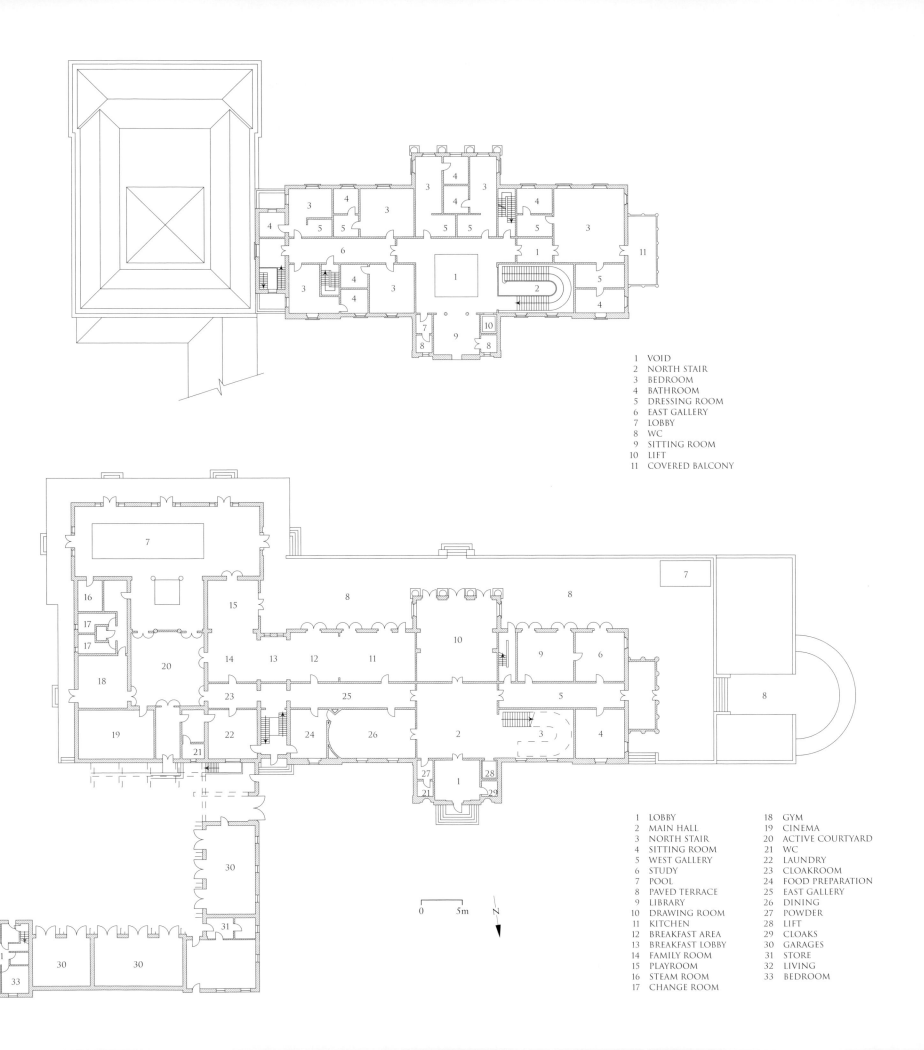

1 VOID
2 NORTH STAIR
3 BEDROOM
4 BATHROOM
5 DRESSING ROOM
6 EAST GALLERY
7 LOBBY
8 WC
9 SITTING ROOM
10 LIFT
11 COVERED BALCONY

| | | | |
|---|---|---|---|
| 1 | LOBBY | 18 | GYM |
| 2 | MAIN HALL | 19 | CINEMA |
| 3 | NORTH STAIR | 20 | ACTIVE COURTYARD |
| 4 | SITTING ROOM | 21 | WC |
| 5 | WEST GALLERY | 22 | LAUNDRY |
| 6 | STUDY | 23 | CLOAKROOM |
| 7 | POOL | 24 | FOOD PREPARATION |
| 8 | PAVED TERRACE | 25 | EAST GALLERY |
| 9 | LIBRARY | 26 | DINING |
| 10 | DRAWING ROOM | 27 | POWDER |
| 11 | KITCHEN | 28 | LIFT |
| 12 | BREAKFAST AREA | 29 | CLOAKS |
| 13 | BREAKFAST LOBBY | 30 | GARAGES |
| 14 | FAMILY ROOM | 31 | STORE |
| 15 | PLAYROOM | 32 | LIVING |
| 16 | STEAM ROOM | 33 | BEDROOM |
| 17 | CHANGE ROOM | | |

0   5m

N

With the sustainable house in Cheshire, the pioneering country house in Surrey to follow and similar projects coming forward at the time of writing, ADAM Architecture is setting a new direction in the development of the English country house. It is perhaps an irony that this direction has in part been stimulated by a poorly worded UK government policy that seemed to favour Modernism. But the need to address energy use in new building is a real modern issue and, if this can be combined with the traditions that sustain the cultural individuality of the English countryside and remain universally popular, it will be a great step forward.

**Opposite:** *Country house, Cheshire, first floor plan (top); ground floor plan (bottom)*

**Above:** *Drawing of north elevation and details*

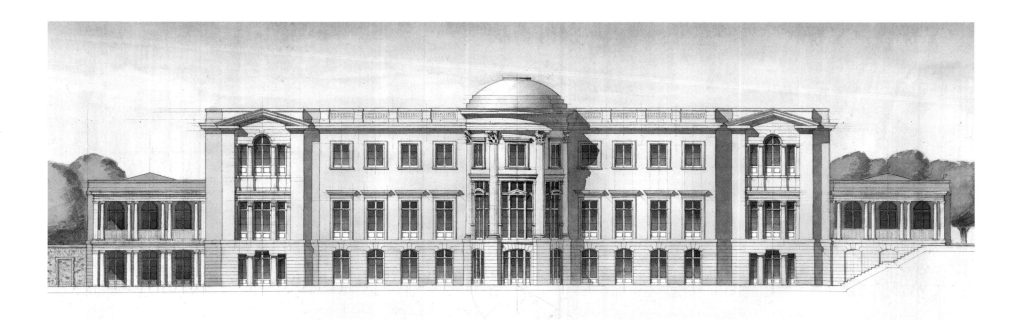

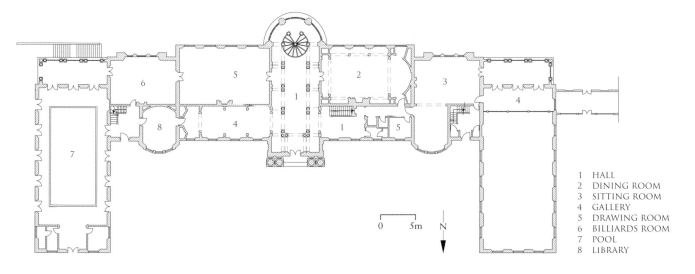

| | |
|---|---|
| 1 | HALL |
| 2 | DINING ROOM |
| 3 | SITTING ROOM |
| 4 | GALLERY |
| 5 | DRAWING ROOM |
| 6 | BILLIARDS ROOM |
| 7 | POOL |
| 8 | LIBRARY |

0    5m    N

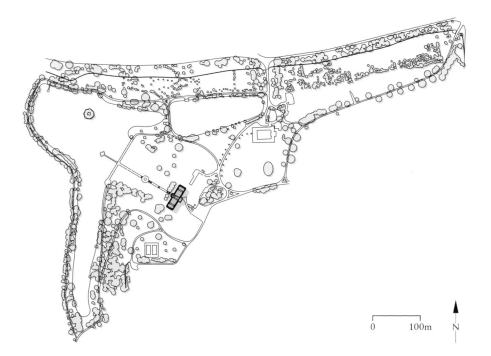

0    100m    N

**Opposite top:** *New house, Great Tew, Oxfordshire. A new house built around surviving fragments of a previous house. All work in this view except right hand wing (with blind windows) would be new. Unbuilt.*

**Opposite bottom:** *Palladian villa, Windsor. Unbuilt.*

**Top:** *New house in Surrey, on the site of a house burnt down in the 1950s. This façade faces a large man-made lake. Construction to commence soon.*

**Centre:** *Ground floor plan*

**Left:** *Site plan*

**Below:** *Regency house in North Hampshire, entrance façade. Nigel Anderson's design for this replacement house has a low-key Regency flavour to reflect its rural setting. The asymmetrical entrance façade is punctuated by a three-storey projecting tower and entrance porch with a lead Trafalgar canopy.*

**Opposite, clockwise from top:** *Main garden façade. This long symmetrical front contains the main living rooms and principal bedrooms that take advantage of the expansive countryside views beyond.*

*First floor plan*

*Ground floor plan*

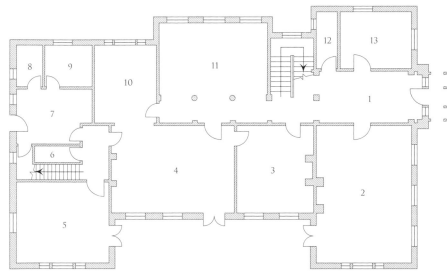

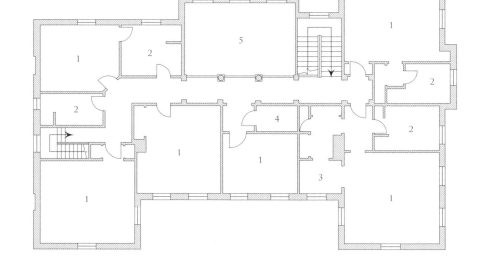

| 1 | ENTRANCE HALL | 8 | SHOWER ROOM |
|---|---|---|---|
| 2 | DRAWING ROOM | 9 | LAUNDRY |
| 3 | MORNING ROOM | 10 | BREAKFAST ROOM |
| 4 | KITCHEN | 11 | DINING HALL |
| 5 | PLAY ROOM | 12 | WC |
| 6 | STORE | 13 | STUDY |
| 7 | BOOT ROOM | | |

| 1 | BEDROOM |
|---|---|
| 2 | BATHROOM |
| 3 | DRESSING ROOM |
| 4 | LINEN |
| 5 | VOID OVER DINING HALL |

0    5m    N

*Above:* New Queen Anne house, the Chilterns, designed by Hugh Petter. The new house is approached via an existing chestnut avenue terminated by the arch of the service wing. The new house, to the side of this avenue, dominates the parkland setting in which it sits. Unbuilt.

*Right:* Site plan by landscape architects Colvin and Moggridge. Unbuilt.

*Opposite, clockwise from top:* Georgian country house, Hertfordshire. South and west façades restored and remodelled by Hugh Petter.

*Garden pavilion*

*New stable block*

*East façade restored and remodelled*

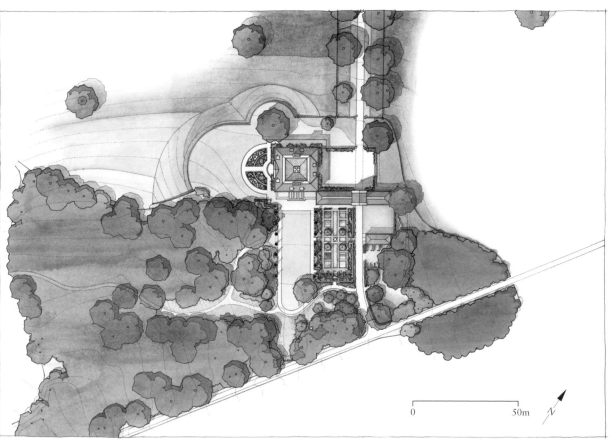

0          50m

## CHAPTER 6

# SPECULATIVE HOUSING

*'Lord, Thou hast given me a cell*
*Wherein to dwell,*
*A little house, whose humble roof*
*Is weather-proof:*
*Under the spars of which I lie*
*Both soft, and dry;'*

Robert Herrick (1591–1674), *A Thanksgiving to God for his House*

Today it requires a leap of the imagination to associate speculative housing with a mastery of the classical tradition, but it was not always thus. Residential development was conducted along broadly classical lines in Britain from early in the 17th century through to the middle of the 20th century. The first such scheme was Covent Garden, laid out by Inigo Jones in the 1630s for the Earl of Bedford following continental models such as the Place Royale (now the Place des Vosges) in Paris.[1] Throughout the Georgian period, a more or less simplified classicism was the norm for urban speculative development. Mostly it was astylar, without columns or pilasters articulating façades, but the unified front of a terrace of houses would generally indicate through its horizontal divisions an implicit classical order, from a rusticated base to a crowning parapet. Occasionally, these orders would become boldly explicit, turning a row of simple town houses into a single monumental façade, such as in the work of John Wood the Elder in Bath,[2] the 18th-century Robert Adam in Edinburgh and John Nash in London. The last of these, Nash, complemented his grandiose metropolitan terraces facing Regent's park with two quaintly rustic Park Villages to provide an architectural fantasy of *rus in urbe*. In this prototype of suburbia, Nash skilfully drew on traditional idioms, such as the Italian villa, the Gothick castle and the cottage ornée, to create the effects of variety and individuality that were lacking in his monotonous façades fronting the park. As we shall see, these styles remain effective today in alleviating our *ennui* with the faux Modernism of public buildings and the consumerist neo-vernacular of the private sector.

By the second half of the 20th century speculative housing had come to be completely ignored by both the professional and the educational wings of the architectural establishment. The reasons for this are not hard to discern. Firstly, while European Modernism had initially concerned itself with cheaply produced housing for the industrial masses, it had never gained a hold in the popular imagination as an appropriate style for the individual suburban home. This still retained the pseudo-vernacular look that had become popular 50 years earlier in the 1920s. Secondly, the design of spec-built private housing seems to have been considered *infra dignitatem* – too low on the hierarchy of building types to concern architects, at least from the point of view of architecture schools and the various professional bodies. While social housing projects of vast

---

1   Arthur Channing Downs, Jr., 'Inigo Jones's Covent Garden: The First Seventy-Five Years', *The Journal of the Society of Architectural Historians*, vol. 26 (1967), no. 1, pp. 8–33.

2   It perhaps should be noted that the present Robert Adam playfully attacked the work of Wood the Younger in the *Sacred Cows* column of the Prince of Wales's architectural magazine, *Perspectives on Architecture* in November 1994.

*A sketch illustrating a group of gothic revival houses for a site in Winchester in an area characterised by late-19th-century gothic revival housing. Unbuilt.*

scale and inhumanity were seen as suitable laboratories for the new architecture, which was being forged by the luminaries of the profession such as the Smithsons and Erno Goldfinger, the individual private house was not thought worthy of attention. The basic problem of spec building from the point of view of the self-consciously avant garde designer was that a developer needing to sell his product on the open market had a very specific idea of what they knew would sell; the result was that all types were reduced to their lowest common denominator in order to maximise the potential market. In social housing, of course, the ultimate inhabitants of a building had no choice – before the advent of 'community architecture' and other participatory approaches to design, they were not involved in the decision-making process in any shape or form, and had little option other than to accept the housing that they were offered.

Adam is unique among today's traditional practitioners in having been concerned with speculative housing from the beginning of his career. When he was making a name for himself in architectural journalism in the mid 1970s, he tackled a subject that was anathema to the avant garde acolytes working in that field: pattern books for suburban houses.[3] Adam pointed out that, historically, architects of the calibre of Sir John Soane had happily published pattern books for simple houses, yet now the profession had 'turned away from such common fare' and noted that any architect doing so would be struck off. He then profiled some firms selling sets of construction drawings to the general public, including one that expected 4000 houses to be

3   Robert Adam, 'Pattern Books', *Building Design*, 24 September 1976, pp. 16–17.

built from their designs that year. He then quoted the comments of the RIBA President, Eric Lyons, on the designs being sold: 'The cynical exploitation of people's fantasies is deplorable … the idea that a house should be an expression of individuality is absurd.'[4] For Adam this concern with the provision of regular homes for the man and woman in the street would become a recurring theme in his public utterances, but it is also more quietly reflected in the kind of bread-and-butter work he and his firm has undertaken during the last 25 years.

In 1995 Adam established the Popular Housing Forum with funding from the Jerwood Foundation. This was intended to bring together a group of developers, architects, property journalists, planners and estate agents to review the way in which houses were then being designed. The timing was fortuitous because the government had just begun to re-examine Britain's future housing needs and, in November of the following year, John Selwyn Gummer, Secretary of State for the Environment, presented a green paper to Parliament entitled *Household Growth: Where Shall We Live?* It predicted that by the year 2016, 4.4 million new homes would have to be built in Britain, one million more than were then being planned.

This increase was not needed to accommodate population growth – this was not in fact occurring – but because of a dramatic change in demographics. Increasingly Britons were living alone, either from choice when young, or, when older, through necessity following the breakdown of a marriage or the death of a spouse. The rise of the single-person household was expected to account for 80 percent of this increased need in housing. Gummer earned immediate plaudits for emphasising the need to focus attention on brownfield locations, setting an 'aspirational' goal of building 60 percent of the new houses needed on previously developed sites. He could, however, be as aspirational as he liked because he and his party were, predictably enough, out of office within months. Following the publication of this green paper, popular housing immediately became a topic of vigorous media attention. Most commentary was focused on the location of new developments, asking whether they should occur mostly in existing cities or sprawl across the countryside, but also issues of housing type – for instance whether we should be building apartments, terraced houses or suburban detached villas – were also discussed. With the intense public scrutiny of the subject, it was not difficult for Adam to secure funding from a number of bodies including the now-defunct Department for the Environment, Transport and the Regions for a study of popular attitudes to the design of homes. It was conducted by Dr Sally Malam and Helen Angle of the market research agency, BMRB International (formerly known as the British Market Research Bureau), with surveys, interviews and focus groups being held in different parts of Britain.

The resulting report, cleverly entitled *Kerb Appeal*, was couched in the language of Blairite market research and confirmed, with the support of innumerable statistics, what anyone who has ever glanced in an estate agent's window in a British High Street could have told you. It noted that the general public preferred homes that they viewed as 'traditional' and 'individual' and which exhibited what they thought of as 'character'. Eighty percent of those surveyed stated a preference for new homes that 'fit in with existing housing' and, when shown houses in different styles, only four percent preferred those in a Modernist idiom. This focus on aesthetics, rather than the core issue of urban design, made *Kerb Appeal* of 'limited value' according to one academic,[5] and it was generally derided in the broadsheet newspapers. In the *Sunday Times* for instance, Hugh Pearman, referring to the kind of neighbourhood preferred by the study's

4  ibid. p. 17.

5  ibid., p. 122.

*Five new houses built in a farmyard in the centre of the village of Bradley in Hampshire. The larger single house is a converted barn. The four new houses are built in what was the open yard.*

participants, coined the term 'Carland', a play on Sir John Betjeman's derogation of the suburban communities of the Metropolitan Railway commuter belt as Metroland. He concluded his review, in deep pessimism, with the words: 'in Carland, nobody can hear you scream.'[6]

The truth was that nothing much had changed in the two decades since Adam's first article on pattern book designs: the profession was still turning its back on popular housing and the public still craved the pablum they had always been given by developers. In July 1997, 21 years after Adam had quoted the inane comments of a past RIBA President, Eric Lyons, the newly elected president, David Rock addressed the question of housing with this exhortation: 'Let's throw away our Borsetshire Design Guides, our dog-eared pattern books ... "It's time for a change"'.[7]

6   Hugh Pearman, 'Home is Sweeter When Detached', *Sunday Times*, 20 September 1998. The phrase is, of course, itself a play on the wording of the advertising poster for Ridley Scott's 1979 film, *Alien*.

7   Quoted in Christine Webb, 'Home design captures the spirit of the age', *The Times*, 6 September 1997.

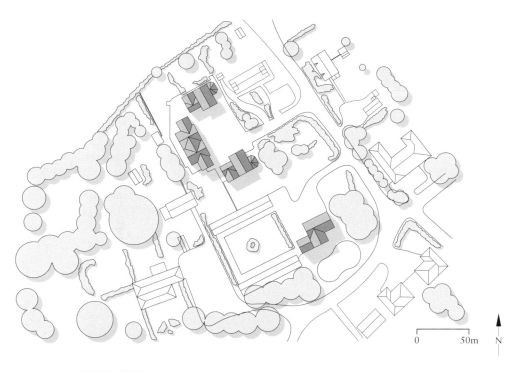

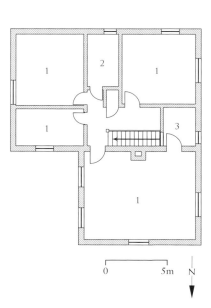

*Opposite:* Houses in farmyard, Hampshire. The single house is a modest classical design.

**Clockwise from left:** *Site plan*

*First floor plan*

*Ground floor plan*

The porch on the single house is supported on brackets shaped as griffons. The griffons are designed to be cut from flat timber sections by a carpenter.

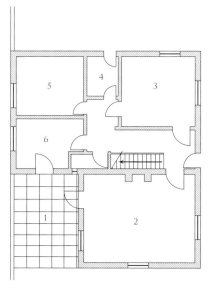

1  PAVED AREA
2  SITTING ROOM
3  DINING ROOM
4  UTILITY ROOM
5  KITCHEN/BREAKFAST ROOM
6  STUDY

1  BEDROOM
2  BATHROOM
3  ENSUITE

Adam's own work in this field shows considerable originality, and little dependence on pattern books, except perhaps of the historic kind. After joining the firm of Evans, Roberts and Partners in 1977,[8] one of his earliest projects was a proposal for six houses on Garnier Road, Winchester, paired to form three handsome villas in a mid-Victorian red-brick idiom. Like many projects for speculative housing undertaken over the next three decades, it remained unbuilt. It is inherent in the nature of this kind of speculative work that a surprising percentage never gets beyond the drawing board – often because the developer is refused planning permission, fails to secure funding or is unsuccessful in even purchasing the land. A few years later a similar Victorian idiom was employed in a successful scheme for five houses on a derelict farmyard in Bradley, Hampshire. Four of the houses, all in a simple gothic brick vernacular, frame a courtyard, reflecting the form of the original enclosed yard, while the fifth, still in brick but with a more 17th-century classical flavour, stood apart. The way in which decorative effects could be economically achieved is evident in the details of the gothic houses: steeply pitched roofs, trefoil-pierced barge boards and polychromatic brickwork such as glazed soldier courses marching across the façades to form sill and lintel courses for the windows. Over the last 15 years much of the same vernacular detail has crept into the work of the volume housebuilders, but it is generally applied in a heavy-handed way compared with Adam's light touch. The main house is less decorated, with only a simple brick cornice and timber architraves framing the front door and main windows, but it derives a strong sense of presence from the symmetry of its façade and the proportions of its openings.

In the same year, 1981, Adam began what was to become a fruitful relationship with a local builder, Bendall Developments, with a row of brick houses near the centre of Winchester on Hyde Church Path. He had been at school with the Bendall brothers, and one of them, John, was an immediate contemporary. These compact two- and three-storey terraced houses, enlivened by oriel windows and bracketed cornices, face a charming leafy footpath; their associated parking and access for vehicles hidden in a courtyard behind. Adam achieved here what all developers dream about – making the most of an awkwardly shaped site that was previously considered unusable. He did it in a way that seemed entirely natural and organic, thus satisfying the planners and enhancing the neighbourhood at the same time.

A few years later, Bendall Developments approached Adam for a design for a site that was much more straightforward, but at the same time much more sensitive. New Alresford was founded by the Cluniac Abbot of Glastonbury and Bishop of Winchester Henri of Blois towards the end of the 12th century. During the 14th century it prospered as the location of a major sheep market, though, as result of a devastating fire in 1689, most of its surviving fabric dates from the 18th century. Adam was given the opportunity to design three new houses on its main thoroughfare, Broad Street. He adapted the standard Georgian town house plan to incorporate a ground floor garage in each of these compact four-bedroom houses, placing the main rooms at the back, with the drawing room on the first floor and a kitchen/dining room below. The façade proportions are based on a series of related square openings, thus making the garage doors, slightly hidden in shadow, echo the nearby Georgian shop fronts. Though there was no space for a transom or fanlight over the front doors, they are given prominence on this wide street by being framed with a full classical order, composed with tapering Tuscan pilasters, reminiscent of those used by Inigo Jones at St Paul's, Covent Garden. These three houses, occupying plots scarcely 18 feet wide, are a perfect example of how a hallowed prototype, in this case the Georgian terraced house, can be updated to accommodate modern needs such as a garage and ensuite bathrooms without sacrificing any of the elegance of proportion and detail of the originals.

8   Evans, Roberts and Partners was later known as Winchester Design, and then, more recently, as Robert Adam Architects and now ADAM Architecture.

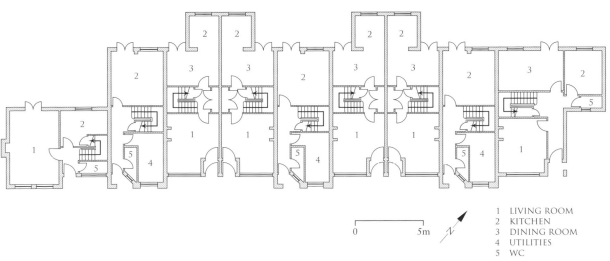

*Above:* Hyde Church Path. A row of narrow houses facing onto a medieval churchyard in Winchester. A variety of heights, oriel windows on the taller houses and simple brick details create interest on otherwise simple houses.

*Left:* Ground floor plan

0        5m    N

1  LIVING ROOM
2  KITCHEN
3  DINING ROOM
4  UTILITIES
5  WC

The sensitive way in which he dealt with the site on Broad Street in Alresford earned Adam the opportunity to tackle a much more delicate location with essentially the same programme three years later. Wimborne Minster was built by the Normans in the middle of the 12th century on the site of an Abbey founded by St Cuthberga in 705 AD. Edward II made the church a Royal Peculiar in 1318, and while it suffered greatly during the depredations of Henry VIII, his daughter Elizabeth I restored at least some of the Minster's confiscated wealth. It was on a site immediately adjacent to this most historic church that a local builder wanted to construct two new two-bedroom cottages. Adam, working closely with Nigel Anderson, produced a scheme of extreme subtlety and understatement with clay tile roofs, pale render walls, and timber jetties, cornices and architraves. The relationship of the individual houses to the site is quite similar to Hyde Church Path in that the front doors open onto a paved precinct across the road from the minister, while vehicular access for the cottages is at the back. The houses therefore have two fronts; the rear façade of each is symmetrical, using small kitchen windows to create a sprightly dance in triple time, a sarabande with an accented middle beat. At the front of the houses the tune is quite different with wide drawing room

*Opposite:* Three houses in a market street in Alresford, Hampshire. The garage doors are recessed to lessen their impact on the street and their square proportions are echoed elsewhere in the design. Originally intended as row of identical stucco houses, the different orientations and variety of materials were imposed by the local council.

*Above:* Two houses adjacent to the Minster in Wimbourne, Dorset

windows alternating with narrow doors, all under a unifying Doric frieze. This lolloping rhythm, like that at Alresford, echoes a more commercial layout, though this time perhaps medieval rather than Georgian shop fronts.

Cricket has been played at Weybridge Green, Surrey, since 1814, when the publican of the Stag and Hounds was given permission to level the gravel pits to create a pitch. In the mid 1990s, following an investigation of the monopoly held by breweries on both the wholesale and retail sale of beer, the government required many public houses to be sold.[9] Thus the site of the public house facing the Green at Weybridge became available for development. Bewley Homes commissioned Adam to design a row of four houses that would harmonise with the surrounding homes, but also provide an interesting backdrop to the open space of the Green. Unlike the previous terraces he had designed for the centres of towns, here Adam wanted something much more varied, reflecting the edge condition of the site and mediating between the variegated suburban fabric and the park. Though they are in fact of similar sizes, the impression one gets from the façades is that they are of very different scales, ranging in appearance from a cottage to a grand five-bay regency town house. The use of dormers, parapets and a three-storey centrepiece enhances this sense of variety and suggests a gradual development over time. Coherence and unity are, on the other hand, provided by the narrow palette of materials: render, slate, brick chimneys and white-painted timber window frames. As with the other terraces, the parking is at the rear, though this time it is approached through a central opening in the row. The success of the scheme can be judged from the fact that it was premiated in the National Home Builder Design Awards 1998, the Elmbridge Borough Council Design/Conservation Awards 1998, and the RIBA Southern Region National Housebuilder Design Awards 1998.

Following these accolades, Bewley Homes unsurprisingly asked Adam's firm to work on several other speculative projects. One was a new classical mansion with a double-height Doric portico for a three-and-a-half-acre site on the Wentworth Estate designed by Nigel Anderson. Another, less specific, project resulted in Adam drawing a series of villa types for the developer. These were exploratory studies, not intended for any specific site, but designed to show how slight alterations in style could give the same basic stuccoed shell a great deal of variety. Here we find Regency villas in the Grecian, Italianate and Gothick modes, all faintly recalling the work of Nash in the Park Villages, or of Schinkel at the Court Gardener's Villa at Schloss Charlottenhof. There is, of course, an impeccable precedent for such an exercise: Sir John Soane had taken a similar approach to stylistic variations on a theme when in 1825 he presented different versions of his church designs in a drawing by J.M. Gandy.[10] The enduring market appeal of Adam's projects for Bewley Homes can be judged from the fact that when the houses in the courtyard, which his firm designed in 1996 for Winkfield Place, Windsor, come on the market today, they can command prices upwards of one and a quarter million pounds.

The main reason a developer bothers to engage the services of a nationally known architect is because of the added value that they can provide in one form or another. In the case of a trendy apartment block in an unfashionable part of London, the name recognition of a Foster or a Rogers might be just the cachet needed to sell. In the case of Adam, however, it is the clear public preference for traditional design combined with his reputation and commercial understanding of the market that makes his work attractive. A perfect example of the kind of added value provided to a developer is the terrace of four houses designed by Adam

---

9   On this phenomenon see John Douglas Pratten, 'The changing nature of the British pub', *British Food Journal*, vol. 105 (2003), pp. 252–62.

10   On this drawing, entitled 'A groupe [sic] of churches, to illustrate different styles of architecture', see Gerald Carr, 'Soane's Specimen Church Designs of 1818: A Reconsideration', *Architectural History*, vol. 16 (1973), pp. 37–53, 89–94.

*A row of four houses facing the village green in Weybridge, Surrey. Each house is different, creating a picturesque profile to the green.*

*Above:* New country house on Wentworth Estate, Surrey, entrance façade. Nigel Anderson's design is a simply detailed symmetrical composition that relies on the scale and detail of its central Doric portico for visual impact and appeal as a speculative house on the open market.

*Right:* Ground floor plan (left); first floor plan (right)

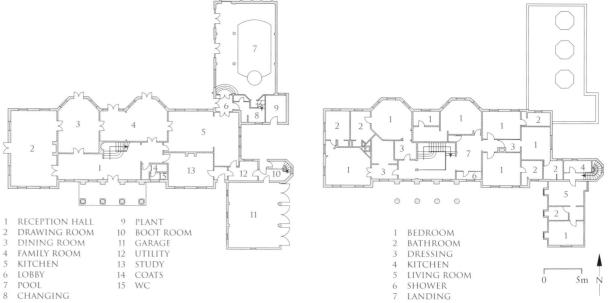

| 1 | RECEPTION HALL | 9 | PLANT |
|---|---|---|---|
| 2 | DRAWING ROOM | 10 | BOOT ROOM |
| 3 | DINING ROOM | 11 | GARAGE |
| 4 | FAMILY ROOM | 12 | UTILITY |
| 5 | KITCHEN | 13 | STUDY |
| 6 | LOBBY | 14 | COATS |
| 7 | POOL | 15 | WC |
| 8 | CHANGING | | |

| 1 | BEDROOM |
|---|---|
| 2 | BATHROOM |
| 3 | DRESSING |
| 4 | KITCHEN |
| 5 | LIVING ROOM |
| 6 | SHOWER |
| 7 | LANDING |

0    5m  N

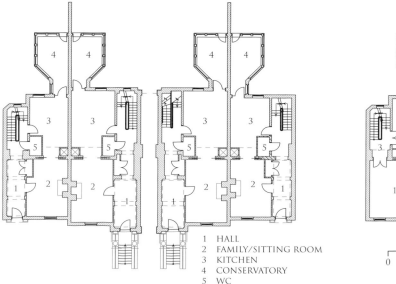

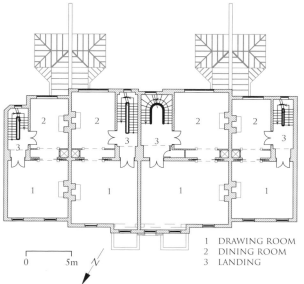

*Above: A terrace of four houses in St John's Wood, London. The outermost houses are reduced in scale and impact by the use of brick and very simple details.*

*Left: Ground floor plan (left); first floor plan (right)*

1 HALL
2 FAMILY/SITTING ROOM
3 KITCHEN
4 CONSERVATORY
5 WC

0    5m    N

1 DRAWING ROOM
2 DINING ROOM
3 LANDING

**Top left:** *A terrace of four houses in St John's Wood, London. The houses are a unified design with the access arch to the rear as the central feature, flanked by two porticos.*

**Top right:** *Doric portico from one of the central pair of houses*

**Right and opposite:** *Coed Darcy, Swansea, Wales. The first phase of a new town near Swansea with 4000 houses, a shop and home working facilities. The steep site creates interest naturally. The buildings in different areas are designed to create a series of distinct places each with its own character.*

in 2000 for Galliard Homes at Marlborough Place, St John's Wood in London, replacing a worn-out collection of 19th-century buildings. Here the idiom is easily recognisable, a stripped late-Regency exercise in brick and stucco, echoing the work of the Cubitt family in Bloomsbury, Belgravia and Pimlico.[11] The designs are tailored to the market with built-in garages and just the kind of bedrooms, dressing rooms and other facilities demanded at this high-value end of the market. The houses were designed as a complete composition with a central pair of large houses, stepping down to two smaller houses conceived as wings of the centre block. Careful gradation of the classical orders adds emphasis to the centre. The wings become skilful compositions of minimal classical detailing while maintaining their status by association with the complete assembly. At first the project was rejected by the planners but when it was taken to a government appeal the inspector allowed the project to go ahead, stating that 'I am of the view that … the buildings would at the very least be the equal of those of the nearby listed in terms of architectural interest'. The houses were sold well before the builder completed construction.

In spite of his increasing reputation Adam continues to work with speculative housing developers. He enjoys the raw commercial edge and the closeness to the real market. Above all, he believes that it is vital that this kind of housing, which dominates the built environment in the UK, should be improved. The poor quality of popular housing is a much greater threat to traditional design than perennially unpopular Modernism.

---

11    On the probable designer of all these developments, the laziest but most talented of the Cubitt brothers, see the present author's
      'Cubitt, Lewis (1799–1883)' in the *Oxford Dictionary of National Biography*, Oxford 2004.

*Above:* Coed Darcy, Swansea, Wales. A terrace of large houses facing a narrow green.

*Right:* A group of small houses and apartments grouped around a private courtyard

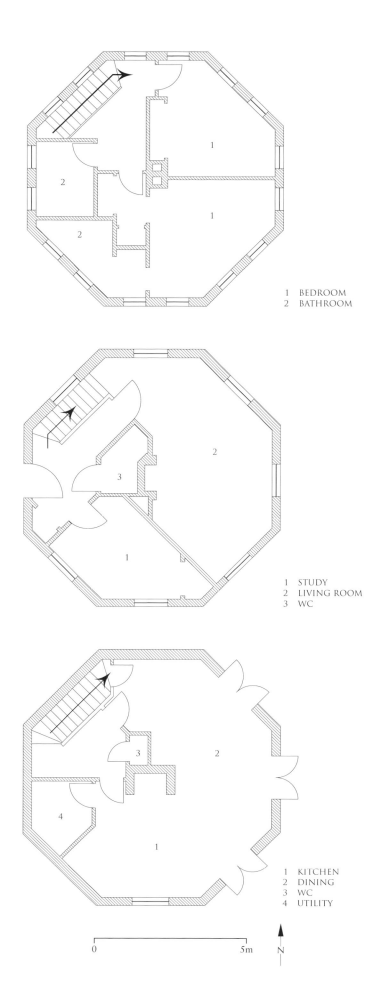

*Above:* Kitcombe Folly. This octagonal 'folly' building forms part of a further speculative housing scheme designed for Bewley Homes by Nigel Anderson on the site of redundant quarantine kennels in East Hampshire. The plan form explores how compact an octagonal footprint can be while still remaining viable as a family home. The rubble stone base and chimney suggest a building constructed from the ground on which it is located.

*Right, from top:* Second floor plan, first floor plan, ground floor plan

1 BEDROOM
2 BATHROOM

1 STUDY
2 LIVING ROOM
3 WC

1 KITCHEN
2 DINING
3 WC
4 UTILITY

0          5m          N

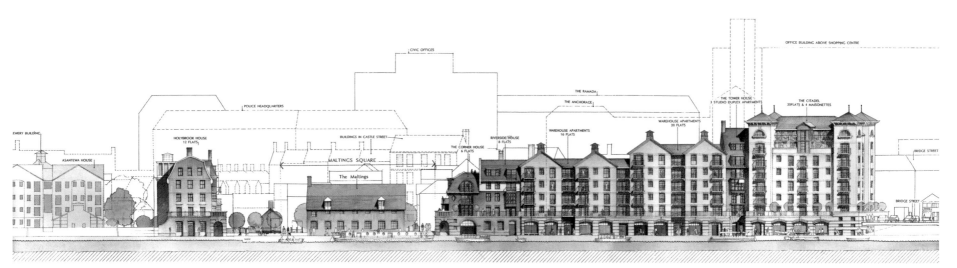

***Clockwise from top left:*** *Bear Wharf canalside development, Reading, riverside view. Nigel Anderson's scheme for Bewley Homes containing 89 apartments alongside the River Kennet in the heart of Reading emulates the 19th-century character and scale of the brewery and warehouse buildings once on this site.*

*View over the River Kennet from the upper levels of the development*

*Watercolour view of the overall scheme illustrates the varying scale of the new buildings from their lowest adjacent to the listed and retained 'Maltings' building up to the highest eight-storey 'Citadel' section facing Reading's Oracle shopping complex.*

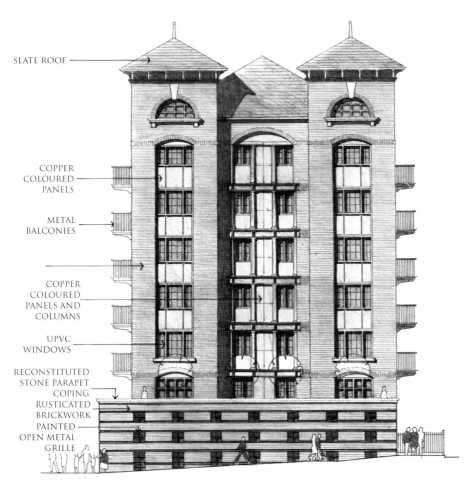

SLATE ROOF

COPPER
COLOURED
PANELS

METAL
BALCONIES

COPPER
COLOURED
PANELS AND
COLUMNS

UPVC
WINDOWS

RECONSTITUTED
STONE PARAPET
COPING
RUSTICATED
BRICKWORK
PAINTED
OPEN METAL
GRILLE

THE CITADEL

**BAY STUDY  1:100 SCALE**

*Clockwise from left:* Bear Wharf, Reading. Preliminary design study for the 'Citadel' building.

*Site plan*

*Typical floor plan*

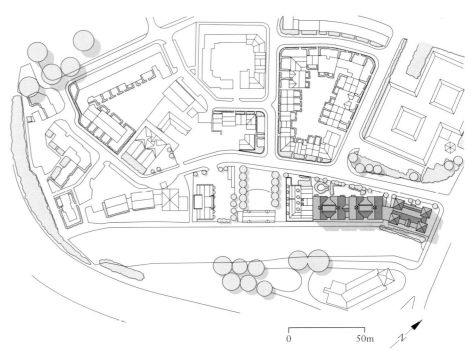

0    50m

1  BEDROOM
2  LOUNGE
3  BATHROOM
4  ENSUITE
5  KITCHEN
6  BALCONY
7  SHOWER ROOM
8  LIFT

0    5m    N

**Above:** Conversion work and residential development at Douai Abbey in Berkshire. In the largest of the practice's collaborations with Bewley Homes, Nigel Anderson designed 33 apartments within the redundant Grade II listed 19th- and early 20th-century school complex and a further 44 new apartments and houses on the site of later and more utilitarian school buildings.

**Opposite top:** The new apartments and houses are set out in a series of courtyards and quadrangles having the collegiate character and scale of the original Douai Abbey complex as well as other traditional educational building groups

**Right, and opposite bottom:** The individual new buildings follow the stylistic cues of the earlier school building complex

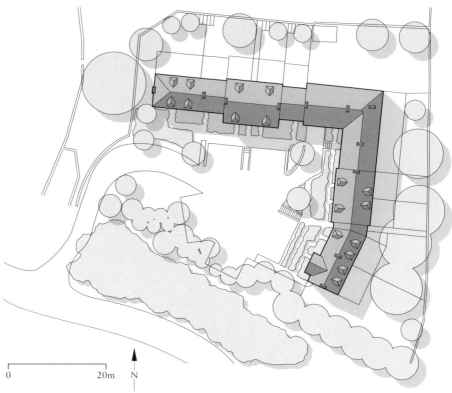

*Clockwise from above:* Blue Ball Hill Winchester. A court of 14 new houses on a sloping site adjoining a listed building in Winchester, designed by Hugh Petter. The restricted palette of brick and tile reflects the predominant character of the city, with subtle variation in character and detail to reflect the relative size and importance of each house.

*Blue Ball Hill site plan*

*Avenel, Kilmacolm, Scotland. Six new houses in an established landscape setting, designed in the Scottish Arts and Crafts tradition by Hugh Petter.*

**Opposite:** *Plot 4 (top) and plot 1 (bottom), Avenel, Kilmacolm, Scotland. Two of six new houses in the Scottish Arts and Crafts tradition with roughcast walls, simple stone details and steep sloping slate roofs.*

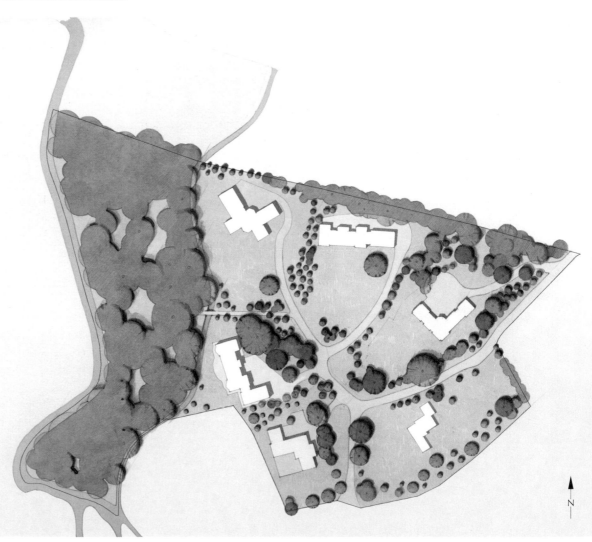

0        20m      N

**Top, left and right:** *New housing development, Radlett, north of London. The individual houses face onto the side street.*

**Right:** *Site plan*

**Opposite:** *A dense development of 21 apartments on a prominent corner site on the Watling Street, a Roman road leading out of London. The apartments were built over car parking but have domestic frontages onto the road.*

0          20m    N

CHAPTER 7

# URBAN DESIGN AND MASTERPLANNING

*'The pseudoscience of planning seems almost neurotic in its determination to imitate empiric failure and ignore empiric success.'*

attributed to Jane Jacobs

Since 1980 there has been a burgeoning revival of traditional urbanism in both Europe and America. The initial stimulus came from the theorists Leon Krier and Christopher Alexander and was perhaps first taken up by the American practitioners Elizabeth Plater-Zyberk and Andres Duany. The movement has since gained such momentum on both sides of the Atlantic that today it is embraced by government agencies and star architects alike. Beginning in the late 1970s, Krier argued that traditional communities were being destroyed by the twin evils of the functional zoning imposed by Modernist planners and the sprawling suburban development engulfing our countryside. He observed that the urban *quartier* or neighbourhood was the basic building block of the polycentric city, and therefore the restoration of community had to begin with this fundamental unit of the built environment.

With simple, almost cartoon-like drawings Krier illustrated how the old, established places that we love, like market towns and village-like urban neighbourhoods, depend for their special character on a mix of functions, an organic plan, and a coherent palette of styles and materials. He showed how these ideas could be implemented through unrealised projects such as a school for the new town of Saint-Quentin-en-Yvelines (1978). The growing acceptance of this revival of traditional urbanism, or New Urbanism as it has become known in America, is attributable to several factors. Amongst architects it has perhaps found favour because, unlike the classical revival in architecture, urban design is seen as above and beyond the issue of style, though authentically Modernist buildings are clearly antithetical to traditional urbanism. The very concept of style is anathema to many architects who had been told by Hegelian historians that the question of style had been transcended with the advent of Modernism. A second reason for the acceptance of the New Urbanism is the forceful argument put forward by environmentalists that the recent trend in global warming is a result of man-made greenhouse gas emissions. Proponents of this increasingly fashionable cause have demonised the dependence on the motor car, which is virtually mandated by suburban morphologies, advocating instead modes of mass transit which require a very much denser and interconnected development than has been common in recent years. Thirdly, there has been a shift in popular perception of what constitutes the ideal living environment: away from the post-war suburban fantasy complete with privet hedges or picket fences, to a more community-orientated ideal, which embraces a range of 'lifestyle' options from a luxury metropolitan penthouse to a rustic cottage in a close-knit village.

Among all the disciplines of design, town planning is particularly challenging because of the complexity of its realisation and the time that must pass before one can fairly judge the results. It is an art of the long term: communities take time to become rooted, commercial ventures can often take a few years to become established, public buildings are almost always the last to be built and trees, the crucial softening elements of landscape, grow very slowly. It is only developers who operate on a large scale and with a great deal of foresight who build the public components, such as schools, libraries, churches and village halls, at the same time as the residential portion of a scheme. One noteworthy example of such an approach is that of the Disney Corporation at the town of Celebration near Orlando, Florida, where a full range of public and commercial buildings, including a cinema and a post office, was constructed at the same time as the first residents arrived. The success of urban design is also dependent on the quality of the architecture and unfortunately the control of the masterplanner is often limited to writing building codes. Sometimes they can play a part in reviewing architectural designs, but fee structures rarely allow for this, and this role is either delegated to a so-called 'town architect' or design board, or, worse still, left up to the local planning authority to approve drawings. Even the best urban design, if realised with indifferent architecture or badly executed buildings, can sink beneath a sea of poor details.

## THICKET MEAD, SOMERSET: A RURAL DEVELOPMENT

In 1988 Robert Adam was asked by the Duchy of Cornwall to masterplan an H-shaped site of 14 acres at Thicket Mead on the edge of Midsomer Norton, a former mining village about 9 miles from Bath.[1] Adam worked on this project with Nigel Anderson. The initial scheme boldly suggested shifting the course of the A362 road so that a public building, which he proposed placing in the centre of the site to link two neighbourhoods, would be directly visible from the main road. His plan called for the creation of three formal public spaces, one circular and two semicircular. These would be framed by buildings that were arranged in different ways to form crescents. The central public building, intended to be a church, consisted of a tall rectangular nave aligned with the approach road and flanked by two lower curving wings coming forward on either side to shape the space in front. This unusual Baroque composition was clearly much on Adam's mind in the late 1980s because he used the similar curved forms in his contemporaneous competition entry for a new building Worcester College, Oxford, and for a site in Thamesmead for Ideal Homes. The second crescent was defined by the gable ends of eight identical freestanding houses, while the third was created from a terrace of nine cottages that helped enclose a circular green with an obelisk at its centre. The formality of this scheme, with its pure geometrical shapes and repetitive house types, perhaps reflects the proximity of Midsomer Norton to Bath, famous for its 18th-century Circus and Crescents by both John Wood the Elder and the Younger. It is also reminiscent of 19th-century model villages such as Port Sunlight. The formalism of the design was not the only unusual aspect that set it apart from conventional developments of the period: Adam had taken great care in the location of parking, giving the two residential crescents a rudimentary system of back alleys and wherever possible placing garages behind houses. The circulation through the site was continuous, with none of the familiar cul-de-sacs terminated by 'hammerheads' or turning circles. The idiom of the houses was a pared-down vernacular with high pitched roofs, quite different from the fussy details and low spreading roofs of suburbia, one of which was already represented on the site in an inconveniently pre-existing bungalow.

By the time the project for Thicket Mead was unveiled three years later in 1991 it had evolved into something quite different. The large axially placed public building still anchored the scheme, but now the two subsidiary spaces had become completely irregular and, to achieve the relatively high density of ten

---

1   Marcus Binney, 'Prince plans new rural idyll', *The Times*, 16 December 1991.

**Opposite top:** *Thicket Mead masterplan. A small urban extension of 137 houses in the Somerset town of Midsommer Norton. The masterplan was executed by the architects Tetlow King.*

**Opposite bottom, left and above:** *Thicket Mead views. The buildings are all in locally typical materials: Doulting stone, Blue Lias stone, stucco and slate and clay pantile for the roofs.*

**Top:** *Site plan*

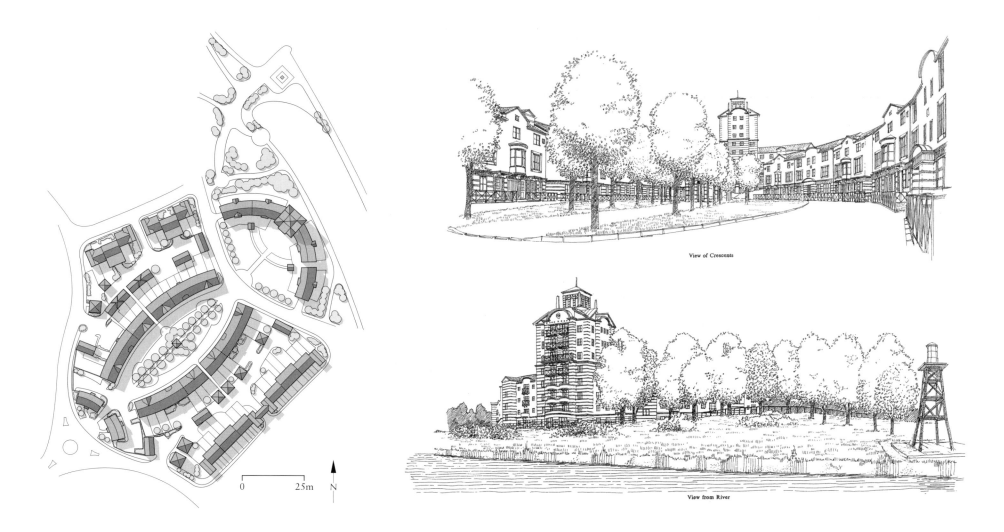

View of Crescents

View from River

*Clockwise from above: Thamesmead near London, competition-winning design, plan. The development of 60 houses and 184 apartments was centred around a space described by a double ellipse plan focused on a tall apartment block overlooking the River Thames. Unbuilt.*

*Thamesmead near London, views*

*Competition submission for Worcester College Oxford. A half-elliptical plan that gave a logical form to various restrictions on the site. Unbuilt.*

houses per acre, there were now very few detached houses, most of them having been replaced by terraces of cottages behind which were tucked parking courts. Just as at the Duchy's contemporary scheme of Poundbury, the overall character was now of a place that had grown up gradually over time. It was, however, rather greener and more rural than the Duchy's Dorchester project with the village greens echoing the rustic idyll of John Nash's Blaise Hamlet rather than the paved *piazzette* of Italian hill towns. Adam's youthful studies of the textural richness of the urbanism of Rome's Campus Martius had been successfully translated into a British context.

Thicket Mead perfectly illustrates the painful slowness with which even the smallest urban design schemes proceed. In 1997, nearly a decade after Adam was commissioned, and even though outline planning permission had already been granted by Bath and North East Somerset council, nothing had been built. Despite the unusual quality of the scheme, there was an element in the community that objected vociferously,[2] and a public meeting was held by the Duchy in an attempt to assuage local fears about the project.[3] Construction finally began over a dozen years after the initial designs were drafted, and though the ambition of the scheme was slightly curbed – there is no major church and the main road had to stay where it was – the result is certainly worth the wait. The difficult balance between coherence and variety is carefully achieved through restraint in the choice of materials and by keeping roof pitches and window proportions similar. At Poundbury, on the other hand, the first phase of construction, involving just 70 houses, suffered from a too-rich palette of materials, including slate, tile, brick, stone, flint and render. The result, as even the masterplanner would admit, was rather over-egged. At Thicket Mead it seems just right. The project won prizes and commendations for both design and construction in Bath and North East Somerset Council's Building Control, Building & Design Quality Awards in 2003 and 2004. It is all the more remarkable that this was built by Persimmon Homes, one of Britain's largest housebuilders, and illustrates eloquently that this quality can be achieved with fiercely commercial developers in the normal housing market.

## FIELD FARM, SHEPTON MALLET: AN URBAN EXTENSION

Two years after he began work on the designs for Thicket Mead, the Duchy of Cornwall commissioned Adam to provide another masterplan, this time for a much larger site about 9 miles away, at Field Farm in Shepton Mallet, again working with Nigel Anderson. Here the Duchy was in partnership with a local farmer, David Vagg, and together they wished to develop 37 acres with a hamlet of 360 houses.[4] Shepton Mallet is a rural town just to the south of the Mendip Hills with fewer than 9000 inhabitants and so the proposal, unveiled in 1993, represented a substantial addition to the existing community. Planning permission was obtained relatively smoothly in 1995, and the first phase of construction, 100 homes on 10 acres, began the following year with Bloor Homes as the builder and Melvyn King of Tetlow King responsible for the detailed design following the masterplan.[5] Adam and King worked closely together to

2    Renny Jones, 'DON'T RUIN OUR COUNTRYSIDE; Rally call to fight Duchy 'overdevelopment', *Bristol Evening Post*, August 5, 1997, p. 2.

3    Renny Jones, 'Duchy gives town a say on new housing', *Bristol Evening Post*, 12 July 1997, p. 5.

4    Hugh Pearman, 'Small is beautiful but is big better?', *Sunday Times*, 14 March 1993.

5    Christine Webb, 'Village-style development gets royal seal of approval', *The Times*, 13 December 1995.

achieve the best result for the first phase. The stone used for dressings came from the quarry only a few miles away at Doulting, which had provided stone for the construction of Wells Cathedral in the Middle Ages. A 20-foot-tall obelisk, made of stone donated by the quarry, was erected on the site in 1999. The plan follows similar principles to the earlier Duchy project: higher density than conventional development; an unusual variety in house type; the public spaces closely framed by buildings; the use of local materials and construction idioms; and motor cars subordinated in parking courts or garages set back behind frontages. Field Farm differs from Thicket Mead in that its much larger size allows for real connectivity throughout the site, both for vehicles and pedestrians, and even accommodates a mix of tenures and uses, with live-work units included in the last stages of the development.

As it progressed the scope of the project was extended to the south, enlarging the scheme to 550 homes, and by March 2006 it was almost three-quarters complete. ADAM Architecture was retained by the Duchy to oversee the implementation of the plan and to ensure that its design code was being followed correctly. In the final phase it was determined that some of the more prominent sites should be assigned to a number of younger traditional architects: thus George Saumarez Smith was selected to design a curving terrace of five three-storey houses to face a public space. The Late-Georgian austerity of his design is complemented by an appropriate restraint in the handling of materials: plain ashlar on the front and lime render with stone quoins to the rear. This is an experience Saumarez Smith is now taking to the South West Quadrant phase of Poundbury with his friend and colleague Ben Pentreath. With compact terraces such as this, the final density of the homes at Thicket Mead rose to be in line with current government guidelines. The *Planning Policy Statement 3 (PPS3): Housing*, published in November 2006, emphasises the commitment to a minimum density of 30 houses per hectare, or over 12 per acre.[6] It also urges local planning authorities to develop design policies that are aimed at 'Creating places, streets and spaces which ... have their own distinctive identity and maintain and improve local character', a phrase that could almost have been written with Field Farm in mind.[7]

In February 2007, the Commission for Architecture and the Built Environment (CABE) featured this southern extension of Field Farm (known as Dukes Rise, Tadley Acres) as one of the exemplary case studies in its *Housing Audit Assessing the Design Quality of New Housing in the East Midlands, West Midlands and the South West*. In praising Adam's work drawing up standards and guidelines for the overall layout, house design, landscaping, roads and car parking, the authors of the audit quoted his development brief, which had accompanied the masterplan: 'Building design and materials, by the consideration of the effect of building groups, can use standard house types and natural local materials to give added character and quality within normal construction prices.'[8] Here was the bottom line for landowners and developers: if traditional urbanism and architecture could add value without adding cost, then it was clearly a winning formula. Admittedly, in Britain, since the price of housing is primarily affected by the restricted supply, such considerations might seem to be of less concern than in America, where in many regions even a slight marketing advantage can become invaluable if a housing boom evaporates overnight.

6   '30 dwellings per hectare (dph) net should be used as a national indicative minimum to guide policy development and decision-making', *Planning Policy Statement 3 (PPS3): Housing*, Norwich 2006, p. 17. This level had been first outlined in the earlier *Planning Policy Guidance 3: Housing (PPG3)*, Norwich 2000.

7   ibid., p. 7.

8   Commission for Architecture and the Built Environment (CABE), *Housing Audit: Assessing the design quality of new housing in the East Midlands, West Midlands and the South West*, London 2007, p. 29.

*Field Farm masterplan. A major urban extension to the Somerset town of Shepton Mallet. The plan has 360 houses and apartments, a shop and employment uses. It was built over a period of 15 years. The first phases were in the north and development continued southwards with the masterplan itself being extended for the final phases. Most of the masterplan was executed by the architects Tetlow King but some phases were undertaken by other architects and the final phases had different young architects designing individual buildings.*

**Above and opposite top:** *Field Farm, Shepton Mallet. The buildings are all in locally typical materials: Doulting stone, Blue Lias stone, stucco and slate and clay pantile for the roofs. The buildings are grouped around a varied series of streets, greens and squares.*

**Opposite below:** *A terrace of five houses at Field Farm designed by George Saumarez Smith*

# POUNDBURY, DORSET: HOUSING WITHIN THE MASTERPLAN

For nearly two decades Poundbury has served as a high-profile example of traditional urbanism being applied to extend a town not through piecemeal growth at the edges but by adding entire new neighbourhoods. As an inspiration for a revival of traditional town design, however, it has one major drawback: it could provide visual paradigms and typological prototypes; but its process of development is so unconventional – with vast consultancy fees upfront and slow initial progress with a small-scale local builder to ensure the highest level of quality control – that it does not offer a model for development that could be readily understood by the volume house builders. Field Farm, on the other hand, provides a ready template for major town additions by showing that through a close cooperation between landowners, masterplanner and volume house builder, a traditional design of the highest quality can be achieved in a reasonable timeframe and result in good profits.

The relationship with the Duchy of Cornwall has continued with new projects tackled by the other directors of the firm. In 1999 Nigel Anderson won a competition for 30 dwellings in the second phase of Poundbury. His scheme, working within the existing masterplan, combining free-standing houses, terraces and flats, has a traditional urban character, drawing on nearby historic towns such as Bridport to create a sense of stylistic variety that seems natural and unforced. Since then Anderson has designed residential and commercial buildings in a further three phases of the development of the town.

**Opposite:** *Poundbury, Dorset. A more recent apartment building designed by Nigel Anderson. The scale and increased formality of the design reflect the position of the building close to what will become the centre of Poundbury.*

**Left:** *'Pink Castle' in the context of some of the other houses Anderson designed in his first involvement at Poundbury*

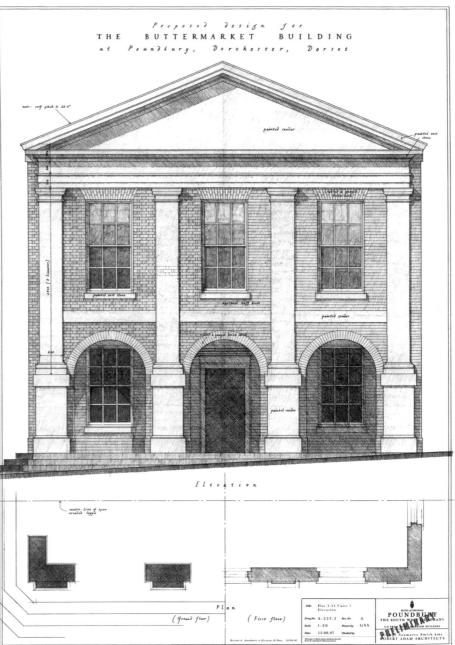

*Left:* An informal building group of flats and houses using local materials in one of his earlier projects at Poundbury

*Right:* Design for the Buttermarket Building at Poundbury, Dorset, by George Saumarez Smith

# ROCESTER, STAFFORDSHIRE: A TOWN CENTRE REDEVELOPMENT

In the mid 1990s Adam tackled two urban design projects that were quite different from the villages for the Duchy of Cornwall in that they consist of delicate interventions in existing communities rather than *de novo* construction on greenfield sites. The first was in Rocester, an East Staffordshire village with a distinguished history of continuous occupation stretching back to the Romans. In 1781 Richard Arkwright bought a corn mill next to the village on the River Dove and turned it into a water-powered mill for spinning cotton. This industry transformed Rocester into an important trading location and the mill remained the main employer until the middle years of the 20th century, when that role was taken over by the privately owned firm of J.C. Bamford (Excavators) Ltd. (JCB). In the 1960s Uttoxeter Rural District Council replaced the spinners' cottages in the village with modern maisonettes and flats.[9] These, three decades later, had become run down and were such a blight on the centre that a competition was held for its redesign. Robert Adam won the commission with a scheme that reintroduced a mix of shops and houses and provided a new focal point for the main public space at the intersection of the High Street, Mill Street and Ashbourne Road. Here, most imaginatively, he proposed building a brick market cross, just as one finds in numerous other historic towns and villages which, like Rocester, have been shaped by trade and commerce. The phased intervention, which has completely rehabilitated the character of the village, was realised through the collaboration of four partners: Miller Homes, the developers; the local borough and parish councils; and Sir Anthony Bamford, JCB's chairman and chief executive, who donated a parcel of land for the project.

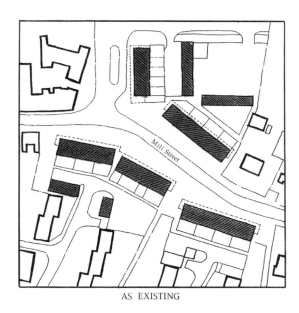

AS EXISTING

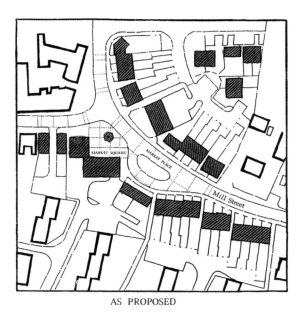

AS PROPOSED

*Left: Rocester, Staffordshire, competition-winning design. The remaking of the centre of the village with 35 houses, 15 flats and 3 shops, a police station and a new market cross. Original and new plan. The masterplan realigned the crossroads to give views of a new market cross from all approach roads.*

*Right: Rocester plan. The original building massing was restored and new urban spaces created.*

---

9 'JCB chief cuts ribbon for the "new" Rocester', *Derby Evening Telegraph*, 23 September 1999, p. 21.

**Opposite:** *Rocester, Staffordshire. A new market cross with a central column inscribed to record the Bamford family's support for the project.*

**Centre and left:** *Before and after views. Run-down 1960s concrete apartment blocks were demolished and new buildings designed to act as focal points at the street intersections.*

**Top:** *Small simple terraced houses in Rocester*

*Trowse, Norwich, Norfolk. Masterplan for major village expansion of 76 houses. The opportunity to expand the village was created by the construction of a new road bypassing the city of Norwich. The original radial road out of the city passed through the village but was cut off. The old public house serving travellers was made into a new focus for the area.*

## TROWSE, NORFOLK: A HISTORIC VILLAGE MASTERPLAN

Like Rocester, the village of Trowse, just outside Norwich in South Norfolk, grew up in close association with a local industrialist. In this case, though, it was the 19th-century mustard manufacturer, Jeremiah Colman, and Trowse was planned as a model village to provide housing for workers at the factory in much the same way as the Cadburys did at Bournville. Though the vast mansion that Jeremiah built nearby has long since been sold, the Colman family still own much of the land surrounding the village and take a keen paternalistic interest in its welfare.[10] Following plans for the construction of a new bypass to relieve Trowse of traffic in the early 1990s, they approached Adam to devise a masterplan for the north of the village now that the old thoroughfare, known simply as The Street, was relatively free of traffic. Adam's scheme for 76 new houses has just the balance of formal urbanism and informal architecture that one expects from a model village: squares of various sizes are created from rows of cottages in a Norfolk vernacular of red brick and render and a gentle crescent enclosing a green provides a sense of arrival from the main road. From this semicircular village green one is led into the

---

10   Ross Clark, 'Cutting the mustard: a model village for Mondeo Man', *The Daily Telegraph*, 6 October 2001.

**Top and bottom left:** *Trowse, Norwich, Norfolk. The buildings are all in locally typical materials: brick and stucco and clay and clay pantile roofs. Building forms are also typical of the area and selected features reflect details particular to this village.*

**Below:** *Site plan*

heart of the site through an angled street that is handsomely framed by a matched pair of Dutch gables.[11] Derek Brentnall, part of the team at ADAM Architecture, described it thus: 'Crescents look like arms opening to embrace you. Our approach was to keep the houses simple, but even simple crescents are welcoming.'[12]

## NEWQUAY, CORNWALL: A PATTERN BOOK FOR FUTURE DEVELOPMENT

In 2003 the firm added another and quite different project to its growing and diverse urban design portfolio. Hugh Petter was commissioned by The Prince's Foundation to write a pattern book for another Duchy development on the North Cornish Coast at Newquay. The conceptual masterplan for the development was prepared by Leon Krier and Colum Mulhearn and lays out the urban extension with some 3000 houses in the Chapel Valley on the southeast of the town. Petter's pattern book sought to codify the characteristics of the local architectural and urban form in such a way as to be useful to designers who, in time, would work upon the development. In 2004, The Prince's Foundation led what they call an 'Enquiry by Design (EBD)' public consultation in Newquay. This process, promoted by New Urbanism in the US under the term 'charrette', has proved to be a highly effective way of identifying needs of the local community and bringing them along with, what is almost always controversial, new development.

The intention at Newquay was not only to create a distinctive north coast Cornish town, but also to create a development that would act as an example for the increasing demand for environmental sustainability in new building. Sustainable measures include: a town design like Poundbury that will promote walking and cycling with most daily activities being available within a 10-minute walk of home; one job for every new household; in keeping with the local desire (discovered at the public consultation) 40 percent of the housing at affordable (below market) prices; where possible local materials; and an integrated public transport in action as soon as the first buildings are finished.

Later in 2006 Petter was commissioned again, this time by the Duchy directly, to write the building code for the Newquay scheme. Petter's codes are an important event in the development of traditional urban design and coding. It is a pioneering fusion of local character analysis, urban design and building design guidance all under an overarching sustainability strategy incorporating not only the usual details for achieving low-energy design but also energy, water, transport and food. These codes will undoubtedly be influential in the growing discipline of code writing and add a significant new area of expertise to the firm.

At the time of the public launch of the project in 2007, Tony Juniper, director of Friends of the Earth said:

> 'This inspirational proposal shows that sustainability really can be at the heart of a large development. Although there is growing awareness of the need for action, there is still a perceived shortage of solutions that people can relate to.

> 'The plans put forward by the Duchy could make an important difference, not only in providing local solutions in Cornwall, but in demonstrating what is possible right across the country. Friends of the Earth is pleased to offer its support in making this scheme a real beacon of hope.'

In 2007 The Prince's Foundation was appointed to act as the coordinating masterplanner and Petter was commissioned to be the phase masterplanner.

---

11  Adam also used Dutch gables to demarcate the entrance to a site in his mixed-use scheme for Watling Street, Radlett, Hertfordshire.

12  Jenny Knight, 'Builders take a bet on crescent-shaped future', *Financial Times*, 19 October 2002, p. 3.

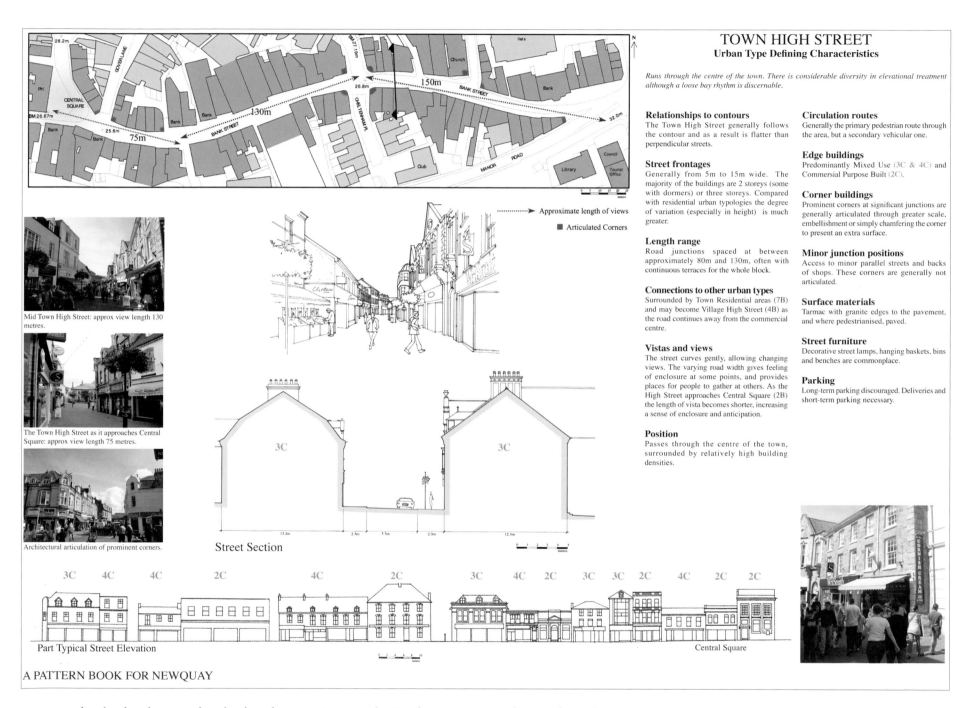

# TOWN HIGH STREET
## Urban Type Defining Characteristics

*Runs through the centre of the town. There is considerable diversity in elevational treatment although a loose bay rhythm is discernable.*

**Relationships to contours**
The Town High Street generally follows the contour and as a result is flatter than perpendicular streets.

**Street frontages**
Generally from 5m to 15m wide. The majority of the buildings are 2 storeys (some with dormers) or three storeys. Compared with residential urban typologies the degree of variation (especially in height) is much greater.

**Length range**
Road junctions spaced at between approximately 80m and 130m, often with continuous terraces for the whole block.

**Connections to other urban types**
Surrounded by Town Residential areas (7B) and may become Village High Street (4B) as the road continues away from the commercial centre.

**Vistas and views**
The street curves gently, allowing changing views. The varying road width gives feeling of enclosure at some points, and provides places for people to gather at others. As the High Street approaches Central Square (2B) the length of vista becomes shorter, increasing a sense of enclosure and anticipation.

**Position**
Passes through the centre of the town, surrounded by relatively high building densities.

**Circulation routes**
Generally the primary pedestrian route through the area, but a secondary vehicular one.

**Edge buildings**
Predominantly Mixed Use (3C & 4C) and Commersial Purpose Built (2C).

**Corner buildings**
Prominent corners at significant junctions are generally articulated through greater scale, embellishment or simply chamfering the corner to present an extra surface.

**Minor junction positions**
Access to minor parallel streets and backs of shops. These corners are generally not articulated.

**Surface materials**
Tarmac with granite edges to the pavement, and where pedestrianised, paved.

**Street furniture**
Decorative street lamps, hanging baskets, bins and benches are commonplace.

**Parking**
Long-term parking discouraged. Deliveries and short-term parking necessary.

> Approximate length of views
> ■ Articulated Corners

Mid Town High Street: approx view length 130 metres.

The Town High Street as it approaches Central Square: approx view length 75 metres.

Architectural articulation of prominent corners.

Street Section

Part Typical Street Elevation          Central Square

A PATTERN BOOK FOR NEWQUAY

*A pattern book of architectural and urban form in Newquay by Hugh Petter. A sample page from the urban form section of the pattern book looking at the particular character of the High Street in Newquay.*

## GREAT COVERT, HAMPSHIRE: A SUSTAINABLE TOWN EXTENSION

In 2006 Hugh Petter was commissioned to act as the masterplanner for another sustainable urban extension, this time for a mixed-use development with 1050 houses on a redundant commercial woodland area on the edge of Chandlers Ford in Hampshire, a dormitory town virtually contiguous with Winchester and Southampton. The new town, provisionally called after its location – Great Covert – will be self contained but also give new facilities to and act as a focus for a series of uninspired post-war housing estates nearby. The new town will have a central green with shops, new jobs, schools and recreational facilities all within a ten-minute walk of every new house.

## WESTERN HARBOUR AND GRANTON HARBOUR, EDINBURGH: URBAN DEVELOPMENTS ON THE FIRTH OF FORTH

At another level of density and of a totally different character and set of requirements, Robert Adam has been working for six years on a masterplanning project of breathtaking scale: Edinburgh's Western and Granton Harbours, encompassing nearly 180 acres of redundant docks and landfill. Adam was called to this project by the involvement of his client for 198–202 Piccadilly (see Chapter 3, Commercial Developments), Ed Bellhouse of Bellhouse Joseph, who had taken both a shareholding and a role in managing the rather chaotic development of the waterfront masterplans of Forth Ports, the owners of Edinburgh's docks at Leith. Asking Adam to take on these huge masterplans, then already designed and under management by another architect, was a massive leap of faith by Bellhouse and Forth Ports.

The original masterplans were prime examples of what Adam has more recently christened 'big box and boulevard' plans – simple grids of wide streets and blocks filled with large single-use buildings. Sales of plots

SITE BOUNDARY

**Opposite:** *Great Covert, a new dense, mixed-use urban extension to Chandlers Ford in Hampshire, designed by Hugh Petter. The scheme, designed to set high standards for sustainability, will deliver a high proportion of affordable housing and employment space while reflecting the particular character of towns in and around the Test Valley.*

**Left:** *Western Harbour, Leith, Edinburgh. Aerial view of development area. The area was created within the breakwater of the 19th-century harbour enclosure on the River Forth.*

**Below:** *Computer-generated view. Construction has begun at the south end of the new plan.*

and the construction of buildings in the plans had already begun. In a dramatic move, Bellhouse and Adam identified these plans as future disasters and froze their development while new plans were prepared.

Adam immediately formed a masterplanning team including the London firm of landscape architects, Landscape Design Associates, and highways engineers Alan Baxter Associates (and later Arup). This team would guide the development of the masterplan as Adam adopted a design workshop approach to the masterplanning process. These workshops could include the client, real estate advisors and even the City Council. The workshops made sure that everyone had a part to play and, most importantly, felt the design was theirs – Adam preferred to call himself the 'chair of the masterplanning team' rather than 'the masterplanner'. There were two outcomes of this process. First, in a practical and aesthetic sense, all the complexity of differing pressures and requirements could find their expression in the plan and avoid later conflict. Second, in an almost mystical sense, Adam describes the moment when all the members of the team knew instinctively that they had achieved the right plan and, from that moment, they were not designing something new but refining a living thing.

The team had to take the original masterplan and keep to the original 3500 residential units for each plan, the same commercial area and mix and the same quantity of open space. To break down the simplistic geometry, tighten up the wide streets and keep the building heights down, Adam analysed other historic ports on the River Forth and further afield in northern Europe. He was adamant that the examples should be as local as possible and in similar climatic conditions. This paid off when the new design was wind tested and it was established that wind speeds, in an area prone to high winds, decreased dramatically within the plan.

As the projects developed and learning from this experience, Adam drew up four guiding principles for the design process: repeat success, life is complicated, don't waste space and save energy locally. The two plans exhibit these principles very clearly. The form and character of attractive and successful local towns is repeated. The plans and building form have a natural complexity driven by apparently conflicting practical considerations, avoiding grand and overblown gestures – as Adam says 'every problem should be a design opportunity, provided you know in time'. The building heights have been kept down and the streets have been narrowed as much as possible, based on the principle that every square metre must be accounted for. To facilitate this process, digital three-dimensional models were tested to ensure that suitable daylight levels could be achieved at every point at street level. This was a much more sophisticated technique than the old standard street cross sections and is a model example of the benefits of new technology brought in to traditional design. Finally, the use of local stone, the improved climatic conditions and mix of uses ensure that the underlying principles of the design are sustainable.

Robert Adam was given very specific instructions about design codes on day one by Ed Bellhouse. He was told that the codes should allow traditional as well as modernist design, quite unlike the codes Adam had produced for his previous masterplans. Adam turned to his experience of working in Beirut, Lebanon where

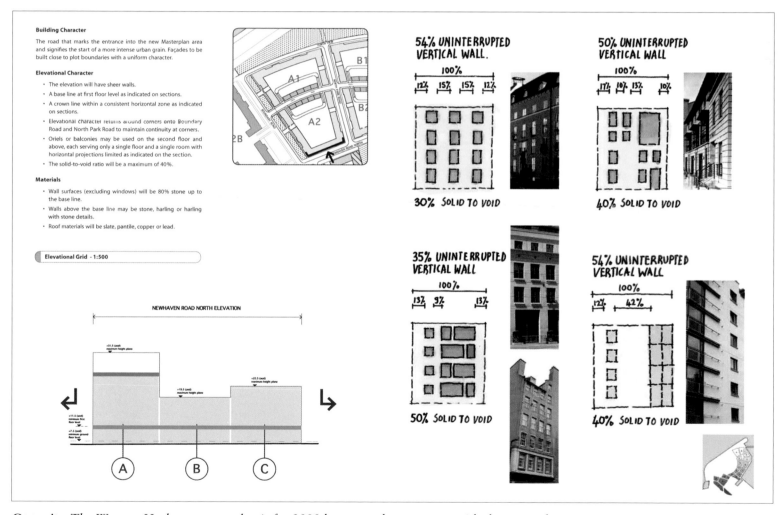

*Opposite: The Western Harbour masterplan is for 3000 houses and apartments with shops, employment uses and a school. The original masterplan was formed with large single-function blocks and four of these remain on the north shore. The new masterplan reflects the complex plans of historic ports on the River Forth.*

*Above: The masterplan is controlled by simple obligatory codes*

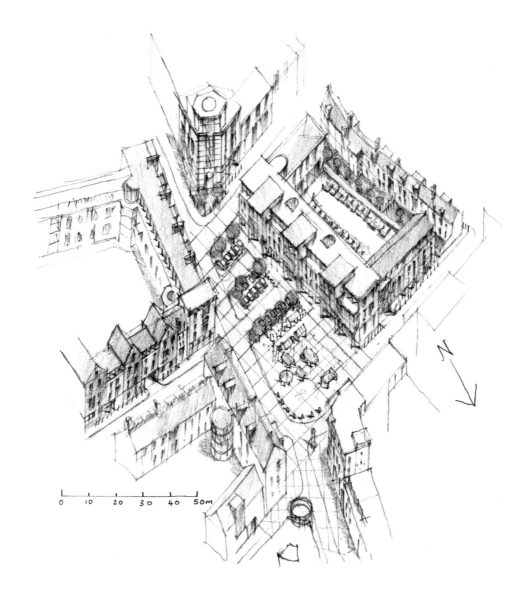

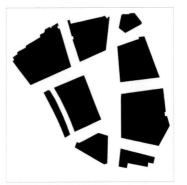
Proposed North Square

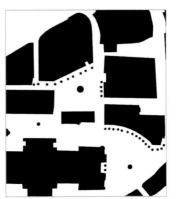
Paternoster Square, London

St. Andries Square, Antwerp

Wroclaw, Poland

the British masterplanner Angus Gavin had drawn up a series of codes that could be simply administered in any style with objective rules. This seemed to be an excellent model as it avoided a subjective design review process, with all the controversy this entails, and cut out the risk of him or some future administrator imposing their personal taste. Early work with these codes has proved their effectiveness. They form part of the land sale and allow the designer complete freedom within clearly defined limits. They are now being administered at almost arm's length by Adam's assistant in Edinburgh, Nigel Gilkison.

As these plans in Edinburgh are at an early stage and have been delayed by the recent economic slowdown (something Adam anticipated, saying that the schemes should be flexible enough to weather at least two recessions), it is hard to assess their success in built form. There have, however, been two tests of quite different kinds: an independent assessment of land value, ignoring any aesthetic improvements, gave a value increase of £10 million over the old scheme with identical accommodation and mix; in 2007 the Western Harbour plan won the prestigious Congress for the New Urbanism Charter Award.

View across Central Park.

*Opposite: Western Harbour, Leith, Edinburgh. North Square. All public spaces were tested against successful local or regionally typical comparative spaces. Views and details were developed as part of the plan.*

**Clockwise from left:** *View across Central Park*

*View along street towards harbour*

*Commercial square off Main Street*

Commercial Square off Main Street.

View along Street towards harbour.

209

The Charter Award takes ADAM Architecture's urban design and masterplanning full circle to the pioneering work of the New Urbanists. Adam and his fellow directors have followed an unusually diverse series of paths in their enquiring exploration of traditional urban design. This ranges from Adam's early work with the Duchy of Cornwall, to Nigel Anderson's work at Poundbury, through to Hugh Petter's innovative sustainable pattern book, to George Saumarez Smith's work at Field Farm and Poundbury, and finally to the unique planning and design control work for large-scale plans in Edinburgh. Put together, this work is a considerable contribution to the new field of traditional urbanism and a legacy for the future.

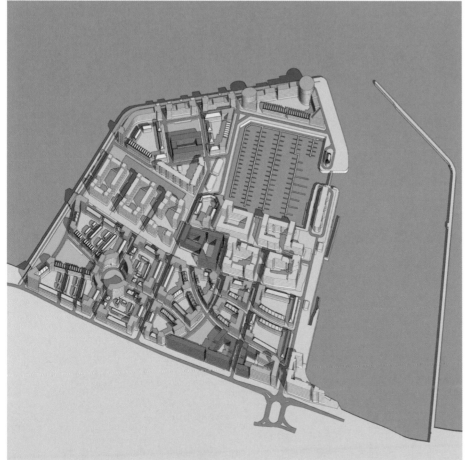

*Clockwise from top left:* Granton Harbour, Leith, Edinburgh. Aerial view of development area. The area has been created inside a redundant 19th-century coal harbour. It is currently occupied by industrial buildings and some further land fill is taking place.

The area to be re-planned was divided by the remnants of the original plan, the new areas were divided into 'quarters', each with a character related to its particular characteristics created by location, outlook and relationship with other areas

The masterplan is for 3000 houses and apartments with shops and employment uses. The original masterplan sits across the middle of the area and consists of large blocks and wide streets. The new masterplan has the form of an historic port and is the same size as Leith itself in the 18th century.

*View across Oxcraig Park towards Lighthouse*

*View from Harbour Square towards Marine Parade West*

*Forth View Gardens looking West.*

***Clockwise from top:*** *Three-dimensional view shows the different heights of the buildings, all created by daylight testing, orientation, views, proximity to other buildings, and the character of the area*

*Forth View gardens looking west*

*View along Garden Mews north looking south*

*View from Harbour Square towards Marine Parade West*

*View across Oxcraig Park towards lighthouse*

*View along Garden Mews North looking South*

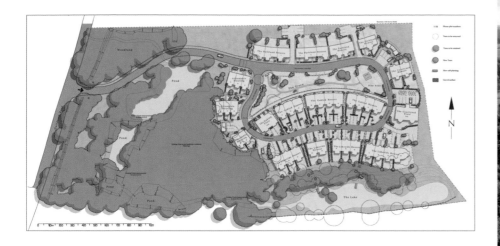

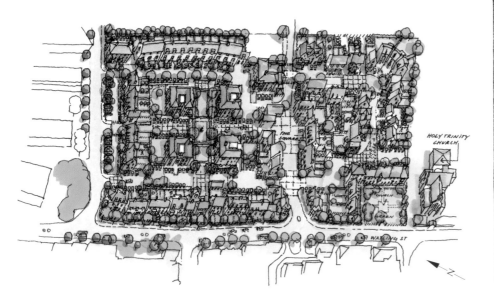

Aerial View of Church Green.

**Clockwise from top left:** *New sustainable housing plan, Surrey. The plan was oriented to provide maximum passive solar gain for each house while creating variety and a pleasant outlook for each dwelling.*

*Computer-generated aerial view*

*Frogmore, Hertfordshire. An aerial view of part of Nigel Anderson's scheme for Barwood Developments of 183 new houses and apartments that replace redundant industrial buildings adjoining the district of Park Street to the south of St Albans in Hertfordshire. This view illustrates a new village green intended to enhance the setting of the adjacent parish church and the southern approach to the village conservation area within which it is located.*

*Frogmore site plan*

*Above:* Tregunnel Hill, Newquay. A development of 200 new houses with employment space on land owned by the Duchy of Cornwall, designed by Hugh Petter.

*Below:* Masterplan for urban extension to Newquay by Hugh Petter, working in association with The Prince's Foundation for the Built Environment

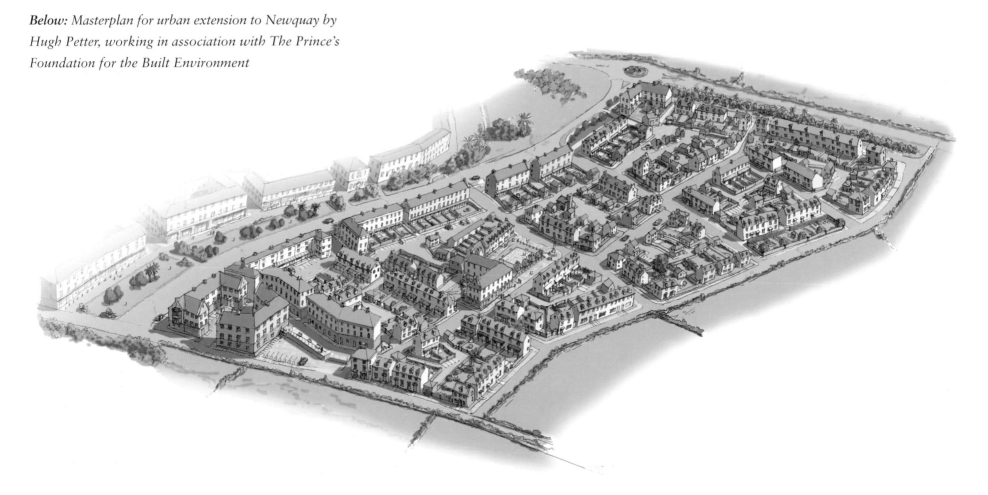

# CHAPTER 8

# PUBLIC BUILDINGS

*'What do we, as a nation, care about books? How much do you think we spend altogether on our libraries, public or private, as compared with what we spend on our horses?'*

John Ruskin, *Sesame and Lilies*, 1864[1]

In Britain today, architects working within the classical idiom are almost entirely restricted to residential projects.[2] While in America the number of classical public buildings is growing apace, most notably in the university sector, here in the United Kingdom those erected in the last two decades can easily be counted on two hands, with only a handful being responsible for all of them. Five years ago, Giles Worsley expressed the hope that, perhaps in time, 'architects working in the Classical tradition will be able to break out of their beleaguered bastion' of private residential architecture, 'particularly as the damning effect that association with the HRH The Prince of Wales has had fades.'[3] Since Worsley wrote these words, however, not a single new classical public building has broken ground in the UK, despite the continued lavish spending on capital projects of public money from lottery and other government sources. Though there currently seems to be almost no light on the horizon, it is worth considering the substantial contribution Robert Adam has made to this field.

## BORDON LIBRARY, HAMPSHIRE

Bordon is a small town in East Hampshire, mid-way between Portsmouth and London, which has played an important role as the location of a British army base and training ground since 1863. During the 1970s and 1980s the population grew markedly as a result of the development of a series of banal brick housing estates. The focus of this new community is not a traditional high street, but an ill-kempt 1970s shopping precinct, the Forest Centre. Adam was commissioned by Hampshire County Council to design a small freestanding public library on a site adjacent to this shopping centre in 1984. The commission was an example of the enlightened judgement of Colin Stansfield Smith, whose visionary patronage as head of the Hampshire County Architect's Department from 1972–1992, earned him the award of the RIBA gold medal in 1990 and a knighthood in 1993. Adam took as his typological model the ancient basilica, the archetypal civic building of the Roman Empire, which generally consisted of a tall, timber-roofed rectangular nave, surrounded by a lower aisle on all four sides. This building type

1   John Ruskin, *Sesame and Lilies: Two Lectures Delivered at Manchester in 1864*, New York 1867, p. 47.

2   The exhibition held by the Traditional Architects Group (TAG) at the Prince's Foundation in 2004 made this unhappy fact abundantly clear.

3   Giles Worsley, 'A touch of classicism', *The Daily Telegraph*, 2 November 2001, p. 26.

*Library at Bordon, Hampshire. Entrance showing brick decoration.*

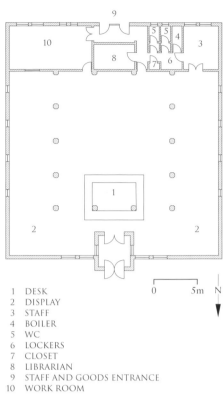

1  DESK
2  DISPLAY
3  STAFF
4  BOILER
5  WC
6  LOCKERS
7  CLOSET
8  LIBRARIAN
9  STAFF AND GOODS ENTRANCE
10  WORK ROOM

*Opposite, clockwise from top left: Library at Bordon, Hampshire. Designed in the manner of a Romanesque basilica.*

*Ground floor plan*

*Capitals at the springing of the entrance arch representing hart's tongue fern in terracotta*

*Bordon Library interior*

had also been chosen by Constantine's architects for the first purpose-built Christian churches in Rome at the beginning of the fourth century, though, for liturgical reasons, they adapted it to create a strong longitudinal axis.

Historically, the building type for a library has usually been a long shallow space raised up off the ground in order to preserve books from the dangers of damp and to maximise the amount of natural light in the reading room. For Bordon library, Adam chose a different model, the basilican form, because the clerestory lighting of its nave allowed him to design a square, deep building that was much more cost effective but still had ample natural light. The space of the nave is framed on all four sides by chamfered brick piers supporting low wide brick arches; above these, pairs of rectangular windows march rhythmically down the sides of the reading room and at either end a large thermal window terminates the central axis. This high central nave, forming the main reading room, is a strikingly noble space, especially so considering that this was built at a time when public architecture in Britain was generally mean in scale and proportions, partly as a result of the influence of Modernism, and partly because of the parsimony of local governments. Adam has also achieved a great effect with relatively economical means in the treatment of the exterior. He uses an imaginative mix of different coloured bricks to create a polychromatic façade, which is further enlivened with banding patterns and roundels. These are complemented by some consciously neo-antique features, such as the use of terracotta tiles laid in with the regular bricks to imitate the thin *bipedales* of ancient Rome, and, beneath the ground floor windows, panels of diagonally set bricks recalling *opus reticulatum*. Further interest is provided by bands of cast terracotta ornament made by David Birch in the form of the leaves of the harts-tongue fern. In their upright, half-furled form they resemble the lowest rank of leaves in a Corinthian capital, though the fern was chosen because it was much more appropriate to Hampshire than the acanthus. These ornamental bands run around the piers of the main entrance to mark an impost from which the arch springs.[4] Finally, the eaves are celebrated with protruding bricks set at an angle to form a kind of dentil cornice, particularly noticeable in the gable of the nave.

The library was well received in the press. Rowan Moore, the Cambridge-trained architect brother of the editor of *The Spectator* Charles Moore, was warm in his praise: 'Here he has achieved the classical building that is also recognisably modern'.[5] In his survey of up-and-coming stars of British architecture, Moore placed Adam in the company of Eric Parry and John McAslan, and identified his particular contribution as 'his catholic interpretation of the Classical, which includes Romanesque and Gothic ... he has gone to war on the prevalent orthodoxy that classical equals Georgian'.[6]

4   Adam used this terracotta ornament to great effect in three of his residential projects: his own house, Crooked Pightle; Kingsmead, Preston Candover; and the extension to Manor Farm, Weston Patrick.

5   Rowan Moore, 'Who's going to be Who?', *Blueprint*, October 1986, p. 46.

6   ibid.

The Messel family was one of the more prominent of the creative dynasties of 20th-century Britain, and while Lord Snowdon is undoubtedly their most famous scion, the most inventive was surely the set designer and portraitist Oliver Messel. His grandfather, the German banker Ludwig Messel, bought a partly ruined Tudor house and 600-acre estate in the Sussex Weald in 1890 and there proceeded to lay out a garden of rare South American and Far Eastern plants. Ludwig's son Leonard bequeathed the garden to the National Trust in 1953, though the house, which had been rebuilt in the 1920s and then devastated by fire in the 1940s, continued to be used by the family. In 1993, following the death of Ludwig's daughter Anne, Countess of Rosse, it was decided to open a suite of rooms in the house to the public. In anticipation of

*Above:* *Nymans Gardens Visitors' Centre, Sussex. The restaurant is designed as a marquee with a copper roof, with each alternate strip chemically coloured blue.*

*Opposite:* *View across the public areas with the original pavilion designed by Philip Jebb*

increased numbers of visitors, the National Trust commissioned Robert Adam to expand the existing tea-room and lavatories into a much more ambitious set of facilities, including a full restaurant, shop, offices and ticketing pavilion. Oliver Messel had long before contributed some small pavilions to the site, and Philip Jebb had built an octagonal trellis-work gazebo and a clapboard ticket booth in the 1980s. Jebb was a self-effacing but highly talented classical architect who had worked, perhaps too consciously, in the shadow of Raymond Erith during the post-war period.[7] He had a long association with the National Trust and been responsible for the visitor facilities at Chartwell, Winston Churchill's house in Kent, and Claremont in Surrey. If it were not for his age and infirmity – he died aged 68 in 1995 – he might well have been given the commission to expand on his earlier work at Nymans.

---

7   See the necrological notices by Alan Powers, 'Enjoying a Classical Taste', *The Guardian*, 30 May 1995, p. 12, and Louis Jebb, 'Obituary: Philip Jebb', *The Independent*, 13 April 1995, p. 16.

**Clockwise from above:** *Detail of canopy over restaurant entrance*

*Restaurant interior. The inside of the curved roof is hung with a matching fabric ceiling to maintain the impression of a marquee.*

*Nymans Gardens Visitors' Centre. Lavatories are in an existing re-clad brick building.*

*Nymans Gardens site plan*

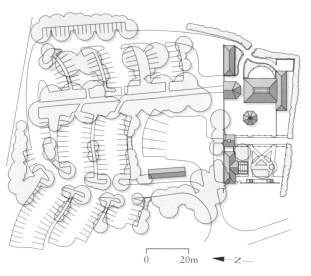

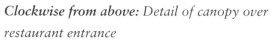

0    20m

An initial idea of uniting all the new visitor functions in a single large building was soon dismissed by Adam because the result would have been too bulky and intrusive for the sensitive site. Instead he proposed the charming conceit of breaking the programme down into a series of smaller pavilions. This decision enabled him to continue the idiom in which Jebb had already begun and allowed the existing buildings to be retained. Four out of the five new buildings are clad in painted weatherboarding with Doric pilasters at the corners and a variety of trellis-work cupolas on top. In these the simple rustic style of early American timber structures such as the dependencies at Colonial Williamsburg are combined with the urbane sophistication of French garden *pavillons* made out of *treillage*. Low fences are constructed of trellis panels, anchored by obelisks and framed by swags; these line the paths that guided visitors to and from the garden. The form of the reception pavilion also serves to help direct the flow of visitors. Its gabled façade, which faces the car park, is flat, but with four square piers boldly projecting to assert its importance among the other buildings. On entering, visitors unexpectedly find themselves inside an octagonal space with the four different possible exits – to the garden, offices, restaurant and shop – arrayed in front of them.

The restaurant, with its kitchens and service areas, requires a very much larger space than the other buildings, so Adam designed the dining room to seem like a temporary marquee that had been set up among the smaller wooden pavilions and gazebos. Its tall blue and green striped copper roof sits lightly on a colonnade of trellis-work pilasters behind which a row of patio doors can be opened up completely. Inside, the structural steel columns, painted with diagonal stripes like barber's poles in the same colours as the roof, support a striped tented ceiling. A sequence of *treillage* swags and pilasters frames the servery end and simultaneously conceals the series of vertical radiators that heat the interior during the winter. The whole playful fantasy cleverly evokes the spirit of Oliver Messel's whimsical stage sets and the fanciful holiday villas that he designed for his aristocratic patrons on the island of Mustique.

The contributions of Paul Hanvey, the technical director who managed the project, to the success of the scheme was significant; he was involved in all aspects of its realisation, from testing the patinating chemicals used to create the contrasting stripes on the copper to ensuring that a custom-designed light fitting complied with current regulations.

A pre-existing lavatory block adjacent to the car park was transformed into a Greek Revival temple by adding square Doric columns at either end to form porticos. Its sides are clad in grey painted weatherboarding which, articulated by pilasters and pierced by lunettes, makes it resemble a stable or dairy by Soane. Despite the programme being split between several different buildings rather than lumped together, these new facilities were achieved very economically, partly as a result of building the new structures out of cheap concrete block and only cladding them with timber. The whole project cost only £500,000, but the result was phenomenal from a commercial point of view; within a short time they were receiving nearly 150,000 visitors a year and the shop and restaurant were generating some of the highest revenues of all National Trust properties. The magical setting, with its garden party-like atmosphere, even attracts frequent enquiries from couples looking for a location to hold their wedding reception.

## THE SACKLER LIBRARY, OXFORD

The Ashmolean in Oxford is Britain's oldest museum. It first opened its doors on Broad Street in 1683, though much of the original collection had been on public display 50 years earlier in 'The Ark', a cabinet of curiosities established by John Tradescant at his home in Lambeth. In the 1830s, C.R. Cockerell designed a new building

*Sackler Library, Oxford. At the back the upper floors of a small segment of the main library are visible.*

to house both the museum and the Taylorian Institute of Modern Languages on the corner of St Giles and Beaumont Street. The result, a supremely accomplished essay in a rich, early-Victorian classicism, incorporated the results of Cockerell's own first-hand research into Ancient Greek architecture. Together with the German archaeologist Karl Haller von Hallerstein, Cockerell had excavated the temple of Apollo Bassitas at Bassai, which Pausanias had attributed to Iktinos, one of the architects of the Parthenon.[8] The unique Ionic order which they discovered there, with its flaring bases and arched capitals, was adopted by Cockerell for his new museum building in Oxford. By 1990, the university had begun to consider redeveloping the area to the north and west of the Ashmolean, an underutilised space within the urban block behind the museum. It was constrained to the west and south by rows of Georgian terraced houses in Beaumont Street and St John Street, but to the north the site opened up into an alleyway called Pusey Place. The programme was ultimately rather ambitious: in addition to bringing together a number of collections of books on related topics including the Ashmolean's own library and that of the History of Art department, it was also to include the Griffith Institute of Egyptology and the Near East, an extension of the Institute of Archaeology and a new gallery of 20th-century art for the museum, the Sands gallery and the first new Ashmolean gallery for 40 years.

---

8   On this temple, see now F. A. Cooper, *The Temple of Apollo Bassitas*, Vols 1, 3 and 4, Princeton, NJ, 1992-96.

The university had just appointed a new Deputy Director of the Campaign for Oxford who, by chance, had been trained as an art historian: Gerard Vaughan had recently completed a D.Phil. thesis on the antiquarian collector Charles Townley (1737–1805) and his circle and was therefore particularly interested in the Ashmolean project, proposing as it did a huge improvement in the facilities for art historical and archaeological research. In order to approach potential benefactors he wanted to have some compelling images of what the new library might look like once complete and so, without undertaking a formal competition process, Robert Adam was asked to produce some sketches and a feasibility study.[9] One of the philanthropists approached, Dr Mortimer Sackler, so liked what he saw that he agreed to fund the library part of the project, but insisted that Adam's design should be built rather than that of another architect. In 1952, Mortimer and his brother Raymond, both psychiatrists, had bought the Purdue pharmaceutical company and set it up in new offices on Christopher Street in lower Manhattan. As a result of selling such medicines as the laxative Senokot and the antiseptic Betadine, within 35 years the company's annual sales had increased from $22,000 to $100 million, enabling the London-based Mortimer to engage in philanthropy on a similar scale to his better-known elder brother, Dr Arthur M. Sackler.[10]

The result, known as the Sackler Library, is one of the largest classical projects to be undertaken in Britain in recent decades and Robert Adam's most important public building to date. It took ten years from the initial sketches made for fundraising purposes to its official opening on 24 September 2001, and cost a little over £9 million to build. For such a complex programme and convoluted site, both the concept and execution are remarkably lucid, mainly as a result of Adam's decision to break the programme into clearly defined parts arranged as though they were separate buildings around a courtyard. This imaginative approach, an extension of the methodology used at Nymans Gardens Visitor Centre, has also been used by Adam in his country house designs, such as the new house in Hampshire. As a technique for developing a *parti,* it is hardly found in classical architecture before 1800 but was a characteristic of picturesque domestic architecture of the early 19th century, such as the asymmetrical Italianate villas of John Nash and Karl Friedrich Schinkel. The Viennese architect Camillo Sitte compellingly argued for the adoption of irregular and organic layouts for cities in his influential treatise on town-planning, *Der Städtebau* of 1889. Sitte's approach to urban design, while out of favour during the heyday of Modernism, was championed again in the 1970s and 1980s by Leon Krier, a Luxembourgeois theorist and close contemporary of Robert Adam. Despite being a powerful polemicist in favour of classicism, Krier decried the redundant symmetries and rote formalism of the Palladian and Beaux-Arts traditions, arguing instead that the complex programmes of large buildings could be more successfully handled if distributed throughout smaller structures. The result would not only be clearer and more rational, but would also create interesting and lively spaces between the buildings. As we have already seen, Adam himself had come to appreciate the lively irregularity of the historic city as a result of his time spent in Rome and his studies of its diachronic development.

A circle has been imagined as an ideal form for a library since the Enlightenment. The impetus was, perhaps, the notion of housing universal, encyclopaedic knowledge in a microcosm of the universe, a domed rotunda. Following Dr Radcliffe's immense bequest to the University of Oxford for a new library in 1714, Hawksmoor proposed just such a building, though it was ultimately only realised by James Gibbs over two decades later.

9   Some of these drawings, which included an exquisite watercolour rendering by Chris Draper of a proposed new cast gallery in the form of a half-Pantheon, were exhibited at The Prince of Wales's Institute of Architecture in 1995: see Jeremy Musson, 'Adding to Ashmole', *Country Life*, 19 October 1995.

10  Ian Zack, 'Pain in the Asset', *Forbes*, 5 February 2001, p. 57.

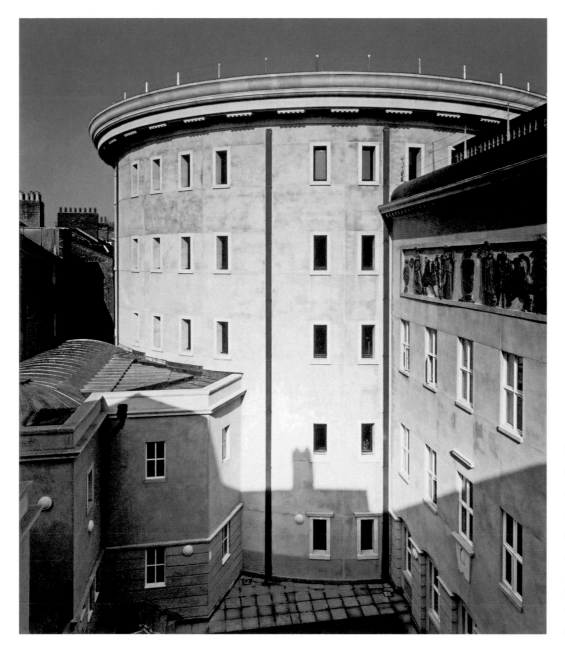

*Opposite: Sackler Library, Oxford. The entrance is through a small circular pavilion with full classical details that introduces the larger but simpler circular main library behind. The columns have a harder stone on the lower part to protect the decoration against incidental damage.*

*Left: The main library building can only be seen at its full height for a small segment of its circumference within an inner court*

In 1835, Benjamin Delessert, the *homme d'affaires* and botanist, proposed a circular library with radiating stacks for the Place du Carrousel, the area between the palaces of the Louvre and the Tuileries in Paris.[11] His proposal was the likely inspiration for Sidney Smirke's addition of a round reading room to the British Museum in the 1850s, though authorship of the idea was fought over publicly by the Chief Librarian Antonio Panizzi and William Hosking, the first professor of architecture at King's College, London.[12] The circular form continued to exert an influence over library designers up until the Second World War, including the austere Stockholm Public Library (1928) by Gunnar Asplund and, in marked stylistic contrast, the pompous Central Library for Manchester (1934) by Vincent Harris. In designing the main rotunda of the Sackler, Adam was particularly influenced by the pared-down Scandinavian classicism of the Stockholm library, which suited

11   See Benjamin Delessert, *Mémoire sur la Bibliothèque royale, ou l'on indique les mesures à prendre pour la transférer dans un batiment circulaire, d'une forme nouvelle, qui serait construit au centre de la place du Carrousel … Avec deux planches*, Paris 1835.

12   See William Hosking, *Some observations upon the recent addition of the Reading-room to the British Museum; with plans, sections and other illustrative documents*, London 1858.

**Opposite, clockwise from top left:** *The Griffith Institute, a special collection of Egyptological references, is housed in a separate building attached to the main library. The top floor contains the new Sands Gallery, accessible from the Ashmolean Museum and top lit. The blind elevation contains a bronze frieze by Alexander Stoddart, shown in detail below. A figure representing the city library presents a figure of William Blake's Newton – a reference to the sculpture in the forecourt of the British Library. A putto offers a drink to a griffon in the foreground.*

*Entrance to Sackler Library. The glass roof light was the largest structural glass roof at the time of construction.*

*The Ashmolean Museum Sands Gallery was built on the top floor of the Griffith Institute but accessed independently from the rear. The simple gallery interior is top lit with the entrance door as its only significant architectural feature. The windowless exterior created the opportunity for the external bronze frieze by Alexander Stoddart.*

**Above:** *Interior of Sackler Library showing the square library stacks inside the circular walls*

both the available budget and his desire that the building should not appear too dominant or bulky. Its cylindrical form helps dispel the sense of mass, as its smooth stucco walls continuously curve away from the viewer. The Sackler does differ, though, in one major respect from its illustrious antecedents: the external circular form is not celebrated in a domed reading room within, as it was in all the historical examples.

Professional librarians today condemn a radial or circumferential arrangement of bookshelves as one that is 'usually more costly and results in less usable space' than an orthogonal layout.[13] So, according to their wishes, the bookstacks are set out in a square in the centre of each of the five floors, framed quite logically by the main structural columns, with the reading desks and ancillary functions disposed around the perimeter. Special study rooms, such as the one housing the Edgar Wind collection of rare books, lead off to the sides.[14] From a functional point of view, this arrangement works extremely well for a research library. The study areas are well illuminated with natural light, offer interesting views out of the building, and are divided up in a way that minimises visual and aural distractions. The resulting geometry of a circumscribed square has, of course, its own multiple resonances in architectural history and theory, going back via the iconic interpretation of the so-called Vitruvian Man by Leonardo da Vinci to Vitruvius himself.

Adam placed the main library rotunda at the north end of the site, so that it backs onto the rear alleyway, Pusey Place, for service access and emergency egress. The primary entrance is through a much smaller stone tholos set in a gap at the end of the terrace of houses in St John Street. Though of very different scales, these two circular buildings are clearly related in both their geometries and details. Both are Doric, though the large rotunda is astylar and only betrays its order through the giant mutules of its cornice. In Adam's initial sketches of the early 1990s, he had been encouraged to include in his scheme a projected later phase that would have extended the complex to the east, running behind Cockerell's museum all the way to St Giles. In these drawings, Adam had used the full gamut of the Greek orders – Doric, Ionic and Corinthian – to distinguish the various parts of the building, and in particular to identify the three different entrances from Pusey Place, St Giles and St John Street. Following Cockerell's lead, the Greek orders he used were specifically based on those of the temple of Apollo Bassitas, so that, where juxtaposed, the new fabric would complement the old. Sadly, the projected later phases were never followed through, and, as it developed, the design for what was in fact constructed was simplified for budgetary reasons. This explains why the building as executed uses the Doric throughout and so lacks the variety of the orders that had made Iktinos' temple of Apollo so unusual. Both the interiors of the entrance tholos and of the library rotunda are Doric like their exteriors, though the extent to which the order is expressed is reversed in each case: the exterior of the tholos features columns and entablature, while the interior has only a mutulary cornice; for the rotunda it is vice versa. This uniformity of treatment creates some felicitous juxtapositions: seeing the mutules of the entrance pavilion, of either its exterior or interior cornices, with the much larger ones of the rotunda in the background creates a powerful sense of their connection, even though they are diagonally separated by the catalogue hall and inner vestibule.

13   Joseph Wheeler as quoted by Michael Dewe in his *Planning Public Library Buildings: Concepts and Issues for the Librarian*, London 2006, p. 92.

14   The Edgar Wind collection of rare books was the subject of an exhibition at the Ashmolean Museum in 1994 curated by the present author. For more information see the exhibition catalogue: Richard John and Monique Kornell, *The Vitruvian Path*, Oxford 1994.

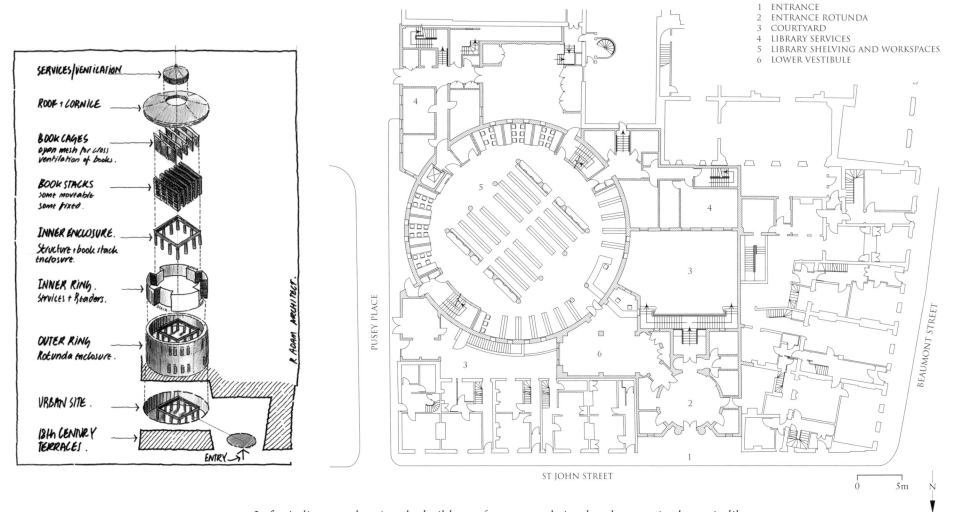

SERVICES/VENTILATION

ROOF + CORNICE

BOOK CAGES
open mesh for cross
ventilation of books.

BOOK STACKS
some moveable
some fixed.

INNER ENCLOSURE.
Structure + book stack
enclosure.

INNER RING.
Services + Readers.

OUTER RING
Rotunda enclosure.

URBAN SITE.

18th CENTURY
TERRACES.

ENTRY

R. ADAM ARCHITECT.

1 ENTRANCE
2 ENTRANCE ROTUNDA
3 COURTYARD
4 LIBRARY SERVICES
5 LIBRARY SHELVING AND WORKSPACES
6 LOWER VESTIBULE

PUSEY PLACE

BEAUMONT STREET

ST JOHN STREET

0       5m

N

*Left:* A diagram showing the build up of square and circular elements in the main library

*Right:* Sackler Library, ground floor plan

Such nuanced handling of classical details is evident everywhere in the Sackler. The cornice above the architrave of the main doorway disappears into the two columns *in antis* which flank the entrance, but then it reappears a short distance away as a cap moulding to the two rusticated wings connecting the tholos to the houses on either side. The two columns flanking the entrance so closely follow their models, those of the peristyle of the Bassai temple, that like them they lack the one refinement typically found in examples of the Greek Doric: entasis. Adam wisely adapted them for their position at the entrance by specifying a harder stone for the lower third of the column and, just as one finds in Hellenistic secular buildings such as stoas, the arrises on this vulnerable portion of the shaft are protected by filling the flutes.[15] The round form of the entrance pavilion gives the visitor a premonition of the rotunda that lies ahead, but the exquisite restraint of its exterior means that little warning is given for the drama of the vestibule within. Striped polychromatic walls rise from a star-patterned floor to a deep interior cornice. The colours, pink and yellow to represent porphyry and stone, are rendered with particular intensity by the natural light which

---

15   On this practice, and the designation 'filled fluting', see J.L. Benson, 'Spirally Fluted Columns in Greece', *Hesperia* vol. 28 (1959), no. 4, pp. 253–272, especially p. 255, note 8.

floods through the structural glass roof. This impressive expanse of glazing, supported only by a series of converging fins of clear glass, was, when it was built, the most ambitious roof of its kind. Like the Millennium Garden Pavilion in Hampshire, it indicates Adam's strongly held belief that the classical tradition can incorporate cutting-edge technology today in just the same way as it has in the past. As with many of the office's major projects, Paul Hanvey was 'the link between Robert Adam and the technical drawing and contract process.'[16]

Once inside the vestibule, the radiating pattern of the floor redirects the visitor to the left, to pass first through a vaulted, apsidal catalogue room that is lit by a thermal window, and then on into the library proper. If the cues are ignored and instead a route directly through the entrance pavilion is followed, the visitor will emerge at the top of a flight of steps that leads down into the courtyard in front of the Griffith Institute. From the vantage point offered by this staircase, the visitor can now best see the major sculptural ornament of the project: a bronze frieze by the Paisley-based sculptor Alexander Stoddart. The 5-tonne frieze, 36 feet long and 6 feet high, was cast at the Morris Singer foundry in Hampshire. Its iconography, which a university 'committee of taste' had tried to suppress, is a commentary on the history of libraries.[17] Four female figures, echoing the statues on the façade of Cockerell's Taylorian Institute, represent the four different kinds of libraries: the public, the private, the ancient and the modern state. The identification of the last is confirmed by the easily recognisable model of Sir Eduardo Paolozzi's 'Blake's Newton', the huge bronze sculpture that sits in front of the new British Library in St Pancras.[18] The central figures in the composition are framed by two griffins, male and female, the latter being a covert reference to one of the more obstructive dons on the so-called 'committee of taste'. At the focal point of the frieze's composition stands a tall vase. According to the artist, this vessel is in fact empty so as to represent the vacuity of modern aesthetic thought.

The organic compositional approach adopted by Adam for his intervention within an historic city block is markedly different from the way in which a neo-Modernist architect might handle the situation. In conclusion, let us consider, for example, the contemporaneous Ondaatje Wing at the National Portrait Gallery. Here, just as at the Sackler, a new building has been inserted within an urban block, though with a rather more generous lottery-funded budget. The architects Sir Jeremy Dixon and Edward Jones completely filled the area between the historic buildings with a vast amorphous space, one side of which is dominated by a giant escalator that takes increasingly confused visitors up two storeys at once, past a balcony gallery filled with pictures at which one longs to stop and look more closely. Here the lack of programmatic clarity could not be more evident and the results, blandly lacking colour and ornament, recall the undifferentiated circulation spaces of an American-style shopping mall rather than a noble public building. By contrast, at the Sackler Adam creates a beautifully orchestrated sequence of façades and interior spaces, which together carefully choreograph the progress of a visitor from the street into the heart of the library.

---

16  Paul Hanvey, project description, undated MS.

17  For this committee and its actions, see Robert Adam, 'The Sackler Library: Ancient and Modern', in Donna Kurtz (ed.), *Reception of Classical Art. An Introduction*, Oxford 2004, p. 88.

18  To anyone with even a passing familiarity with William Blake's art and thought, the choice and placement of Paolozzi's sculpture seems incomprehensible in view of his extreme opposition to what he saw as Newton's mechanistic and reductive view of the universe.

*Millennium Gate, Atlanta, designed by Hugh Petter*

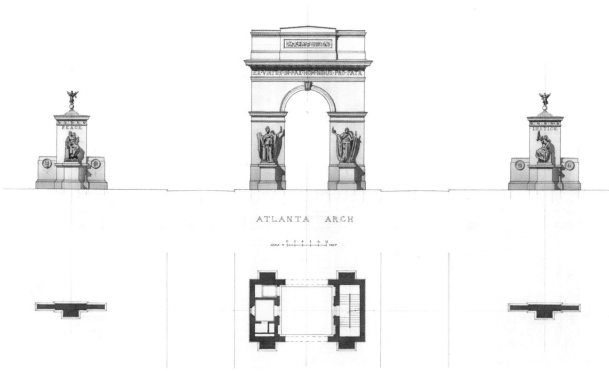

*Above: Millennium Gate, Atlanta. New monumental arch designed by Hugh Petter. Four large pedestals on each pier of the arch will each support a goddess figure, designed by the sculptor Alexander Stoddart. Each figure will represent an epoch of 500 years. The inscription in the main entablature celebrates 2000 years of peaceful endeavour. Original design drawing showing the two peripheral sculpture groups representing the civilizing virtues of peace and justice returned to the city. The executive architects were Collins Cooper Carussi.*

*Right: Peace, one of two peripheral sculpture groups designed to sit alongside the Millennium Gate, Atlanta. The Greek goddess of peace, Eirene, places a calming hand on the young and impetuous Plutus, the personification of wealth. Sculpture by Alexander Stoddart.*

## MILLENNIUM GATE, ATLANTA, USA

In 1998, at a meeting of traditional architects and educators at the Newington-Cropsey Museum in Hastings-on-Hudson, an Atlanta designer and developer, Rodney Mims Cook Jr., proposed a competition for a monument to be built in Washington, DC, to mark the Millennium. Cook, a trustee of the Prince of Wales's charitable foundation in the US had previously played a key role in arranging for a classical monument marking the centenary of the modern Olympic movement to be built in Atlanta with the foundation's sponsorship. The Millennium project for Washington did not go quite so smoothly. An impressive raft of supporters was gathered including two senators and the mayor of DC, and a prominent site was identified: Barney Circle, marking the point at which Pennsylvania Avenue begins its crossing of the Anacostia river over the John Philip Sousa Bridge.[19] The competition was won by Daniel Parolek of Opticos Design, Berkeley, but the $50-million proposal ultimately failed to garner enough support in Washington to go forward.

---

19   Benjamin Forgey, 'Backward To the Future; Millennial Memorial Designs: Anchored In the Classical Past – Or Mired There?',
      *The Washington Post*, 16 July 2000, p. G01.

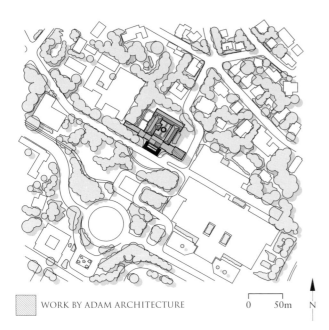

WORK BY ADAM ARCHITECTURE      0    50m    N

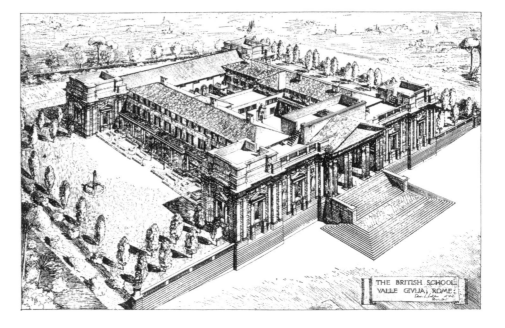

THE BRITISH SCHOOL, VALLE GIVLIA, ROME

A few years later, Cook had found a new location for his Millennium monument, this time in his hometown of Atlanta. A massive 138-acre brownfield site – the former Atlantic Steel Mills – was to be redeveloped to provide 6 million square feet of offices, 2 million square feet of retail space, 1000 hotel rooms and 5000 homes. Cook persuaded the developers that the central feature of the 11 acres of public parks should be a 73-foot-tall arch designed by Hugh Petter with sculpture by Alexander Stoddart. The new, smaller site in Atlanta required Petter to simplify and downscale the competition scheme. The aspirations of some donors resulted in further subtle modifications to the original design. The intention, however, was to retain the spirit of the competition design, which had taken its inspiration from the antique Arch of Titus in Rome. When complete, the Millennium message will be conveyed by four huge female goddess figures, one for each pier of the arch, each of which will represent an epoch of 500 years: Antiquity, The Middle Ages, The Renaissance and The Modern Age. The main frieze of the Corinthian order is embellished with an inscription in Latin celebrating 2000 years of peaceful endeavour. Two further seated figures on pylons on either side of the main monument represent the civilising values of peace and justice, represented by the Greek Goddesses Irene and Dike respectively as a tribute to the regeneration of this significant mid-town site with a dense, mixed use walkable development.

While public building is directed by committees and competitions, the current dominance of the genre by mainstream and modernist architects is set to continue. In the absence of a positive direction, committees will always tend to the safe option of the architectural establishment – which is modernist through and through. Architectural competitions are frequently judged by establishment architects and, when entry is limited, the same list of well-known mainstream architects comes up on each occasion. The major public projects by ADAM Architecture have been led by the vision of individuals: Gerard Vaughan and Mortimer Sackler on the Sackler Library and Rodney Mims Cook on the Atlanta Arch. Bordon Library belonged to a rare moment of deliberate eclecticism in architecture in the 1980s – now extinguished. Nymans Gardens was commissioned specifically to be a continuation of the work of Philip Jebb, then recently deceased.

As an increasing number of the new public buildings of the last decade fail spectacularly, such as the Scottish Parliament in Edinburgh and the new Spa building in the city of Bath, the robustness and appropriateness of traditional public buildings may become more apparent. The role of ADAM Architecture's public buildings and those of their fellow traditionalists will be of the utmost importance in offering examples of the highest quality traditional design available for comparison.

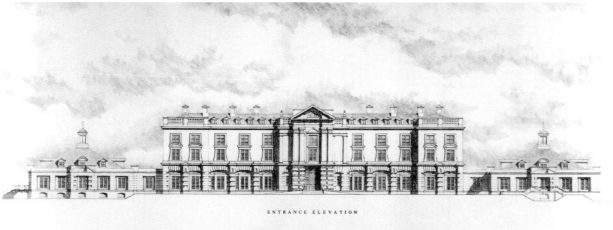

ENTRANCE ELEVATION

*Opposite left:* New Packard Library wing for The British School at Rome, designed by Hugh Petter. Site plan.

*Opposite right:* Aerial perspective by Sir Edwin Lutyens showing his original design for the British School at Rome

*Above:* The design for the original building, by Sir Edwin Lutyens, included a colonnaded verandah along the west elevation which was not built. Hugh Petter adapted this design to create a new reading room for the library.

*Right:* New golf club, West Wratting, Cambridgeshire. Entrance elevation. Unbuilt.

*Left:* New Sainsbury lecture theatre and art gallery, The British School at Rome, designed by Hugh Petter. The original building, by Sir Edwin Lutyens was designed as the British pavilion for the 1911 exhibition in Rome. Robert Adam and Hugh Petter developed a phased masterplan to restore the original building. Hugh Petter then developed designs for the Sainsbury lecture theatre and gallery and the Packard library wing, which were realised in partnership with the Italian architects, Studio di Architettura.

*Right:* The original British School at Rome building, by Sir Edwin Lutyens, was modelled on St Paul's Cathedral by Sir Christopher Wren. Petter's design similarly draws inspiration from St Paul's.

*Opposite top:* Perspective by Edwin Venn showing the new club building designed by Hugh Petter for Stocks Golf Club. The building takes inspiration from the simple barn buildings of the Chiltern Downs with weather-boarded walls and a clay tile roof. Inspired by the early work in Hertfordshire by Sir Edwin Lutyens.

*Opposite bottom:* Rhodes House, new wings. A competition-winning design for two new wings to Rhodes House, the headquarters of the Rhodes Trust by Sir Herbert Baker. The project was later abandoned.

PROPOSED NEW WINGS FOR RHODES HOUSE OXFORD        ROBERT ADAM, WINCHESTER DESIGN [ARCHITECTS] LTD    1995

# CHAPTER 9
# FURNITURE AND ORNAMENT

*'I have been black and blue in some spot, somewhere, almost all my life from too-intimate contacts with my own furniture.'*

Frank Lloyd Wright, *The Future of Architecture*, 1953

Since historic pieces of furniture are often unsigned, their designers generally have remained anonymous. Even when we know who made an individual piece, through surviving accounts or cabinetmakers' labels, there is little guarantee that the fabricator was also responsible for the design, which might just as likely have been copied from another maker or taken from a pattern book. During the Middle Ages, the designs of architects clearly influenced the form of religious furniture such as lecterns and stalls, but it was only in 17th-century France that architects began to exercise complete control over every aspect of an interior. A notable exponent of this all-encompassing approach to design was the Huguenot architect Daniel Marot, whose influence was soon felt in England, partly through his publications and but also because of his work for William III at various royal residences.[1] In the first half of the 18th century there were plenty of examples of occasional pieces designed by architects, including ones by such distinguished practitioners as James Gibbs and William Kent. During the third quarter of the century, our subject's namesake, Robert Adam, adopted Marot's approach wholeheartedly and effected a revolution in interior design by taking far greater responsibility for the details of a scheme than his predecessors. In fact in two or three projects, the 18th-century Robert Adam had the freedom to design every last detail of an interior, including carpets and door hardware. In many other schemes his control was not absolute, but still included seating, commodes, bookcases, pier glasses and side tables. His approach was to design them *en suite* with the architectural ornament of chimneypieces, pilasters, doorcases and niches, so that together they produced a unified composition. It is therefore not surprising to discover that, as Jill Lever has lamented, 'a great deal is lost when Adam's furniture is divorced from the interiors for which it was designed'.[2]

The level of integration between freestanding furniture and its architectural setting which Robert Adam introduced to Augustan England came to be particularly valued by Modernists in the 20th century with examples of *Gesamtkunstwerken* ('total works of art') being created by Frank Lloyd Wright, Le Corbusier and Mies van der Rohe. At the height of the modern movement even second-rate architects could aspire to control all aspects of a project: one notable instance was that of Arne Jacobson at St Catherine's College, Oxford, where he designed every last object even down to the awkward and barely functional cutlery used for meals in the Senior Common Room. Innovative furniture design was not, however, the exclusive preserve

---

1  Jill Lever, *Architects' Designs for Furniture*, London 1982, p. 13.

2  ibid., p. 19.

*Left: Book stacks, Sackler Library, Oxford. Book cases contained in a square area inside a circular library space. The structural columns are Doric and picked out in pink with bronze capitals. The book cases are oak.*

*Centre: Library chair, Sackler Library. A design derived from the Ancient Greek klimos. The chair is anatomically proportioned with a tilted seat and lumbar support. The joints are carried through and expressed as decoration.*

*Right: Wind room, Sackler Library, Oxford. Bookcases designed to complement the Edgar Wind collection of books on renaissance art. The bookcases are in oak with rustication and details picked out in ebony.*

of Modernist architects in the 20th century; Sir Edwin Lutyens, for instance, designed highly distinctive chairs and benches, reproductions of which remain popular today.

Turning to our subject, we find that, in general, Robert Adam's designs for furniture have been for stand-alone pieces or matching suites in buildings not designed by him. He was, however, given the opportunity to design both furniture and its setting at the Sackler Library in Oxford. Here, in addition to the handsome bookcases, Adam provided readers throughout all the reading rooms with sturdy chairs based on Ancient Greek and Roman models of the Klismos type. Their forms are known from vase paintings, relief sculpture and from the surviving stone seats modelled after lost wooden prototypes, such as those set aside for the Archons at the Theatre of Dionysius in Athens. They first influenced Western European furniture design at the end of the 18th century, when elegantly curving front legs were introduced to chair design. Despite the obvious structural disadvantages of this form in wooden chairs – the outward curvature of the legs means that they have a natural tendency to collapse under the weight of the occupant – these so-called sabre legs were to become characteristic of Regency furniture. For the Sackler, Adam designed them to withstand institutional use, and thus gave them the solidity of the original stone representations. The methods of timber construction employed, including the mortise and tenon joints for the legs, are made subtly visible as decorative elements. The seats, covered in leather, are easily removable to allow for periodic reupholstering.

Another project in which Adam designed the furniture and architecture to complement one another is his own house, Crooked Pightle. Here the galleried Great Hall, a perfect cube that functions both as a dining

*Clockwise from above: Refectory table. Designed for the architect's own house in a renaissance style. The table is in English oak and can be dismantled for ease of transport.*

*Ceremonial chair. A presentation chair derived from renaissance examples.*

*Refectory table: foot and leg. The pegs and tenons that allow the table to be dismantled are expressed as decoration. The tapered octagonal leg has a spiral decoration of inlayed holly wood.*

room and the major reception room, is dominated at one side by an oak refectory table drawing on 17th-century models and the traditions of the Arts and Crafts movement. Yet again, here the construction is celebrated, in this case by wedges at either end, which can be removed to allow the table to be dismantled. The massive tapered columns, which support the top, are lightened by a spiral inlay of fruitwood that echoes the bay garlands wreathing the marbled columns of the entrance hall.

An early English inspiration can also be detected in the ceremonial chair designed for the Jerwood Foundation. This monumental oak throne was intended for the foundation's official visitor. The tradition of architects designing ceremonial chairs in Britain is a distinguished one: Sir William Chambers designed one for the President of the Royal Society of Arts and William Richard Lethaby for the Master of the Art Worker's Guild.[3] Given Adam's involvement with the latter institution, it is not surprising that one sees echoes of Lethaby's rather austere creation in the Jerwood chair, though perhaps wisely the 'honesty' of a hard wooden seat and back is foregone in favour of padded leather upholstery.

3   On this topic see Clare Graham, *Ceremonial and Commemorative Chairs in Great Britain*, London 1994.

In striking contrast to the solid Arts and Crafts feel of these oak pieces, Adam designed a suite of witty and elegant heraldic furniture for Lord Portsmouth. In the 1980s, Quentin Gerard Carew Wallop, the Tenth Earl of Portsmouth, was restoring Farleigh House, his family seat, as a residence after a long period of institutional use. Rather than attempt to locate an extensive set of suitable antique chairs for the dining room, he commissioned Adam to design a suite of furniture instead. Though traditional in their overall form, for instance the cabriole shape of the chair legs, Adam's designs are highly innovative both in their functionality and their ornament. The dining table is divided into three sections in order to be unusually flexible in its disposition. These sections can either be arranged together to form a conventional long dining table, or split up as smaller individual tables. The top of each section is supported by a carved pedestal in the form a mermaid who has raised her arms and put her hands behind her head, resulting in a most provocative pose, though one that is virtually invisible to diners because of the projection of the table's surface. However, the hinged tops of each section allow them to be placed against the wall with the tops tipped up if not in use with the table top to the wall; this allows the mermaid pedestals to be seen and framed by the underside of the table that has been decorated with elaborate nautically themed marquetry and an engraved brass hinge plate specifically for this purpose.

On the chairs, the ornament becomes even more specific to the patron: Lord Portsmouth's coat of arms is stylised in silhouette to create a splat, with his coronet fitted neatly under the top rail. In his drawings Adam indicated that surface of the wood at the knees should be carved in imitation of fish scales, and the armrests should curl around to form breaking waves at their ends.

*Left to right:* Heraldic dining room furniture for the Earl of Portsmouth; the table is in three parts. The top of each part can be folded back to reveal mermaid supports. The mermaid is the Earl of Portsmouth's crest. The chairs are of American cherry wood and have the Earl of Portsmouth's coat of arms set in the back. The legs are mermaid's tails and the scrolls on the arms are breaking waves.

*Opposite: Four seasons Pembroke table. A reinterpretation of a classic type. The legs are four stylised female figures, the four seasons, in the form of classical herms.*

*Left to right: Pews in St Bride's church, Fleet Street, London. Designed to create more seating for this very busy city-centre church designed by Sir Christopher Wren.*

*Pews in St Bride's church, detail*

*Chairs for St Bride's Church with hymn-book shelf below the seat*

The iconographic nature of this dining suite, with its maritime symbolism, is also characteristic of other pieces of neo-Georgian furniture by Adam. A new version of the Pembroke table, supposedly so called because the first one was ordered by the Countess of Pembroke in the mid-18th century, is named the 'Four Seasons' table. While it follows the familiar form of its prototype, with two flaps of the top folding down at either side to allow the table to be stored away easily, it departs from its models in having a rich symbolism. The slender legs are now recast as Herms, or anthropomorphic columns, each being topped by a female face carved in ebonised wood. These figures represent the four seasons and in appearance are derived from Sebastiano Serlio's treatise on architecture. This table was bought by the Victoria and Albert Museum in London and is on permanent public display as an exemplar of traditional late-20th-century furniture design.

Another type of twist on tradition which Adam takes great pleasure introducing to classical design is the integration of modern technology. A perfect example of this is to be found in his clock designs. Two of these feature radio-controlled movements from the German manufacturer Junghans which, to ensure absolute accuracy, are periodically synchronised with a central atomic clock. The simpler of the two, called the Obelisk Clock, is made from a blonde cherry wood with ebonised details, recalling the stark colour contrasts one finds in Biedermeier furniture. Its pyramidal form, though derived from Egyptian obelisks, also owes something to the familiar outline of a traditional metronome. The more elaborate radio-controlled clock symbolises its automated regulation through its gilded dome and aerial, which are set on top of a marbled pedestal housing a large, clearly marked clock face. Though the technology of these timepieces is impressive, undoubtedly Adam's most elegant creation in this field is his Temple Clock. This mystery clock takes the shape of a miniature Tuscan tholos made of hardwood with bronze mounts. Its form is loosely based on Bramante's Tempietto at San Pietro in Montorio in Rome though it also presages Adam's own Millennium Pavilion at Preston Candover. The Tuscan entablature supports a blue sphere into which are set two gilt chapter wheels; as these rotate the time can be told from the numerals framed by the antefixae above the colonnettes.

*Left to right:* Obelisk clock. A radio-controlled clock made as a limited edition.

*Radio controlled clock. Set in a case gilded and marbleised by the designer. The face is designed with the layout of a surveyor's measuring staff, similarly required to be read with accuracy from a distance.*

*Temple clock. The time is told as the rotating gilded rings pass by the bronze arrow; the hours in Roman numerals and the minutes in Arabic numerals. Set in an enamelled sphere these represent the sun circling the firmament. A relief representation of the sun is set in the centre of the base. The clock movement is inside the sphere.*

# ARCHITECTURAL ORNAMENT

From the earliest period mankind has enriched its artefacts with ornament. These embellishments have generally been based on geometrical patterns or motifs drawn from local flora and fauna. Sometimes an overt symbolism is evident, but often there is no apparent meaning, so that the ubiquity of ornament on man-made objects suggests that the desire to create it is a fundamental human characteristic. When the first monumental masonry architecture developed in Egypt during the third millennium BC, many of its details were modelled after the vegetation and animals of the fertile Nile valley. Thus at King Djoser's mortuary complex at Saqqara there are columns based on the lotus and the papyrus, and cornices featuring a pattern of repeating cobras. The explanation for other elements of architectural ornament in Djoser's complex lies in the concept of the skeuomorph. This occurs when forms originally realised in one material are translated into another medium, for instance from timber to stone, and the constructional details peculiar to the original material are copied in the new medium. So one finds stone columns carved to represent bundles of reeds, the supports used in everyday buildings, thus commemorating in permanent monumental form the ephemeral structures of mundane life in Ancient Egypt.

These same influences on the creation of ornament – local vegetation, geometric patterns and skeuomorphs – can be seen in the development of the Greek Classical orders during the archaic and classical periods. Though we are confident now that the Doric order was not actually a literal example of skeuomorphism, we can be certain that its inventors must have drawn on the techniques of timber construction for inspiration. In the case of the Ionic order the volutes of its capital utilise one of the oldest geometrical motifs used by man in patternmaking: the spiral. Finally, the Corinthian capital stylises a plant common throughout the Mediterranean, Bear's breeches, or the acanthus. In his book, *Classical Architecture: a comprehensive handbook to the tradition of classical style*, Robert Adam traces the origins of all these features and discusses the early ethnic associations of the Greek orders: the Doric and Ionic being used by the Dorian and Ionian tribes, and the Corinthian being, perhaps, a reference to the elaborate bronze work for which Corinth was famous. The way in which he discusses the rows of stylised acanthus leaves as 'applied like repeated [bronze] castings to a central core' betrays his insight as a designer who, as we have seen, has actually worked with these motifs and techniques in his built work.[4]

The transformation of the orders by the Romans, both in terms of their form and meaning, is of particular interest to Adam, since he has spent so much time studying the buildings of Rome. He observes the evolution of the Corinthian from being simply an alternative capital used with Ionic columns and entablatures, to a fully-fledged order with its own particular enrichments. He suggests that the only wholly Roman order, the Composite, as it came to be known in the Renaissance, was associated with victory, since it was used extensively on triumphal arches and buildings symbolising imperial power.

Adam did not intend that *Classical Architecture* should be an academic treatise, rather he wanted it to be a useful handbook that might sit within arm's reach of the draughting table. So instead of a continuous narrative organised into neat thematic chapters, he broke the content down into a series of single page essays – nearly 150 in all – each facing a page of elegant line drawings by Derek Brentnall. The main text is so carefully keyed to the illustrations that it almost plays the part of a commentary, a familiar idea in the history of successful architectural publications. It was a similar, though even more reductive approach that had made Vignola's treatise, the *Regola della cinque ordini dell'architettura,* the most popular treatise in the history of

---

4   Robert Adam, *Classical Architecture: a comprehensive handbook to the tradition of classical style,* London 1990, p. 90.

*Left: Illustration from* Classical Architecture: A Complete Handbook. *Classical buildings from the 1930s from Germany, Sweden and Britain.*

*Right: Illustration from* Classical Architecture: A Complete Handbook. *The Classical Orders gradually stripped away in an interior.*

architectural theory, with some 500 editions published from 1562 to the present day.[5] Practising architects, now as then, are much more likely to think visually or graphically than verbally, and so the appeal of a book that can be glanced at quickly to obtain specific pieces of information is strong. The buildings illustrated, all drawn to the same scale on each page, are carefully chosen to challenge preconceptions: for example, one finds Gunnar Asplund's Stockholm Library juxtaposed with Albert Speer's Reichs Chancellery to dispel the notion that classicism in the early 20th century was the preserve of totalitarian regimes.

5   See Branko Mitrovic's introduction to his edition and translation of Giacomo Barozzi da Vignola, *Canon of the Five Orders of Architecture*, New York 1999.

*Sketch study by the master carver Dick Reid for a swag to form part of the window surround for the English Baroque Country House in Berkshire, designed by Hugh Petter*

Another strength of the book, and one that reflects Adam's fundamental beliefs about classicism, is that it presents the tradition in all its richness, rather than trying to straitjacket it into a narrow vision of one particular stylistic manifestation. With the exception of a few so-called 'Parallels of the Orders' (that is, books comparing different authorities), almost all treatises on classicism have emphasised a single canonic interpretation of details and proportions. Adam not only draws in the Carolingian and Romanesque variations on the classical tradition, but he even presents the Gothic of the Middle Ages as its offshoot, describing it rather poetically as 'a style born of a clouded vision of Rome'.[6]

In his introductory essay on the Orders, Adam drew attention to the arguments, both *pro* and *contra*, for using a single recognised authority for the proportioning and detailing of columns and entablatures: 'Authors such as Palladio have provided a useful and authoritative basis for classical design where a lack of familiarity makes successful variation unlikely, but they can give the misleading impression that classical architecture is merely the application of old rules and devoid of creative potential.'[7] This is an important point, because the accusation that classicism consists of nothing more than the vacuous repetition of an academic canon continues to be mouthed by boosters of the so-called avant garde (and, like many of the philosophical fallacies of Modernism, was also trotted out by the Gothic Revivalists, their 19th-century intellectual predecessors). It is indeed true that much of the success of the classical tradition in providing a noble and handsome urban fabric in cities like Paris and London is a result of the reliability of the basic canon, a sort of 'default setting' that could easily be adopted by simple craftsmen lacking a profound education in design. But for singular statements such as civic structures, or important private residences, the kind of nuanced variations to which Adam is referring allow a building to stand out from the crowd, transcending its mundane surroundings, and communicating on an altogether higher level with the viewer. It is precisely this kind of subtlety in the handling of the orders that we have seen Adam himself employ at houses such as at the new Country House in Hampshire.

In addition to the fundamental elements of the five Orders, Adam also gives an account of a range of classical ornament. He discusses garlands and wreaths, in particular looking at the associations of the different plants used to make them. For instance laurel being used at the Pythian games at Delphi, because they were sacred to Apollo.[8]

---

6   ibid., p. 20.

7   ibid., p. 68.

8   ibid., p. 272.

**Clockwise from top left:** *Window mullion capital, new country house in Hampshire*

*An Ionic capital and entablature from the front door of a new Palladian villa in Berkshire, designed by George Saumarez Smith*

*Egg and dart bronze pilaster capital, new offices, Picadilly, London*

*Stainless steel capitals, Solar House in Sussex*

*Bronze capitals, Millennium Garden pavilion, Hampshire. The capitals are made of individually cast bronze leaves surrounding a stainless steel ball.*
*A steel finial is set in the centre of the ball and the roof rests on these finials. Steel cable bracing is also anchored into the balls.*

*Large column capital, new offices, Picadilly, London. Bronze pilaster capitals designed by sculptor Alexander Stoddart. These represent courage and are inscribed 'Audax'.*

*Clockwise from top left:* Principal column capital, new country house in Hampshire. An original stiff-leaf design.

Cast iron capitals for a pergola, riverside country house in Dorset

Doric capital to library stacks, Sackler Library, Oxford

Hart's tongue fern designs in terracotta developed with ceramic artist David Birch. Extension to a Manor House, Hampshire.

Small column capitals, *new offices, Picadilly, London. Bronze column capitals by sculptor Alexander Stoddart. These represent clemency and are inscribed 'Clemens'.*

Porch capitals, Bordon Library, Hampshire. Hart's tongue fern designs developed in terracotta with the ceramic artist David Birch.

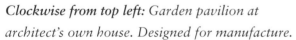

*Clockwise from top left:* Garden pavilion at
architect's own house. Designed for manufacture.

*Cabinet and display for relocated stained glass
window of Tydale, first translator of Bible into
English, on the occasion of his tercentenary,
at Hertford College Oxford*

*Rusticated obelisk on urn in cast stone, extension
to a Manor House, Hampshire*

*The richly carved and detailed Ionic entablature of
a new house in Surrey designed by Nigel Anderson*

A floral motif that predates even the acanthus in Greek architecture is the anthemion, perhaps derived from the honeysuckle family or from a stylised palmette, which forms the decoration for single elements, such as an acroterion, and also running friezes. Adam discusses the use of both zoomorphic and anthropomorphic forms, and, betraying his fascination with iconography and symbolism, emphasises the polyvalent nature of motifs: for instance, the eagle is associated with both the god Jupiter and the evangelist St Mark, and can also represent the United States of America.[9] While we no longer believe the maidens of the south porch of the so-called Erechtheion are figures representing the enslaved women of Caryae, Adam's account of the human form in ornament tackles the complex issue of the translation of the pagan genius into the Christian cherub.[10] Another essay is illustrated by a variety of waves and key patterns, the latter including the fret, the meander and the swastika, and their possible origin in textile weaving; even their associations with labyrinths and the myth of the Minotaur are mentioned. A further essay in the series on geometrical patterns is devoted to the guilloche, which is based on plaits or knot patterns, and is discussed in the context of other circular motifs and mosaic designs.

The kinds of historical observations that Adam makes about ornament in *Classical Architecture* clearly reflect his own beliefs and experiences as an architect. As we have seen, his own attitude towards ornament has developed and changed over time. In the 1980s he reacted to the banality and anomie of the neo-vernacular by developing meaningful ornament based on local flora, such as the hart's-tongue fern capitals used at Bordon library. In the 1990s, as he increasingly strove to demonstrate the progressive potential of classicism, he realised some of its most iconic elements in strikingly new materials, for instance the stainless steel capitals at the solar house in Sussex. Subsequently, the creative potential offered by the classical column capital has become a theme in Adam's design. These range from different versions of the stainless steel capital, to the unusual almost Greek capitals on the new Country House at Ashley in Hampshire, through the cast bronze open-topped capitals on the Millennium Pavilion, culminating in a tour de force on the Piccadilly offices with Alexander Stoddart. In the first decade of the 21st century, the larger canvas provided by country houses such as the new Country House at Ashley in Hampshire have allowed a layered and nuanced use of canonic ornament that has placed him fully in the great tradition stretching back to the Italian Renaissance: the rich and complex classicism that Lutyens so evocatively called 'the High Game'.

---

9   ibid., p. 276.

10   On the question of the porch of the maidens, see now Alexandra Lesk, 'A Diachronic Examination of the Erechtheion and its Reception', unpublished PhD thesis, University of Cincinnati, 2004.

# EPILOGUE

*'But after Q? What comes next? After Q there are a number of letters the last of which is scarcely visible to mortal eyes, but glimmers red in the distance. Z is only reached once by one man in a generation.'*
Virginia Woolf, *To The Lighthouse*, 1927

Robert Adam has called himself a 'Progressive Classicist.' Is this an appropriate label? Have contemporary practitioners succeeded in taking the tradition forward or are we still just catching up with the accomplished classicists of the early 20th century?

Human beings, when they have thought about it, have generally envisaged the path of history as following one or other of two forms: cyclical or linear.[1] The rhythmic alternation of Golden Ages with periods of darkness is a standard trope in the mythistory of ancient cultures. In the Italian Renaissance this historiographical framework was applied by Vasari to his account of the progress of painting, sculpture and architecture, so that the development of a style or artistic movement traced a trajectory like the lifecycle of an organism – birth, youth, maturity, and finally, decay. This circular vision of history bows out, however, at the beginning of the 20th century with Oswald Spengler's *Der Untergang des Abendlandes* (1918).[2] By then, a linear vision of progress was already being generally adopted, powered by the indefatigable twin engines of scientific positivism and historical determinism. As the 20th century unfolded, this approach, replete with such fallacies as the *Zeitgeist*, became so commonplace that by 1989 Francis Fukuyama could ponder if we had reached 'The End of History?'[3]

With such a world view predominating, it is not surprising that 20th-century historians of architecture interpreted the succession of styles and theories of the 18th and 19th centuries as simply so many steps up to the temple mount of Modernism. But the history of Western architecture, which is dominated by the classical tradition, is unquestionably cyclical. Not just the major Renaissance revival of the *all'antica* style – but also smaller cycles and eddies within the tradition – Andrea Palladio (1508–1580) looking back not only to antiquity but also to the work of Donato Bramante (1444–1514), and in turn, Palladio providing inspiration for Inigo Jones (1573–1652) , then Lord Burlington (1694–1753), and later, John Soane (1753–1837), C.R. Cockerell (1788–1863) and Raymond Erith (1904–1973) to name but a handful of 'progressive classicists'.

Stylistic progress is judged retrospectively by comparing individual works of art with the overall pattern of historical development to see if they appear innovative for their time or not. We can only just now begin this process with the current classical revival in architecture because scarcely 30 years have passed since its

---

1   Frank E. Manuel, *Shapes of Philosophical History*, Stanford 1965.

2   Translated as *The Decline of the West*, New York 1926–28.

3   Francis Fukuyama, 'The End of History?', *The National Interest*, vol. 16 (1989), pp. 3–18.

first stirrings in the late 1970s with designs and buildings by, among others, Thomas Gordon Smith and Allan Greenberg. In the case of Adam, the historian's job is further complicated by his extreme facility for designing in different idioms, ranging from Romanesque to Baroque, from Queen Anne to the Greek Revival, and from the Arts and Crafts to a classicising version of high-tech. Such an undogmatic approach to style confounds easy categorisation. One particular idiom, however, supports Adam's own claim to be a progressive classicist: the 'Trabeated Rationalism' first seen in its fully developed form in his proposal for 2B Paternoster Square, and later employed with great vigour in several buildings including the Solar House, the new house at Ashley, and 198–202 Piccadilly. Whatever reactionaries may wish, we cannot unthink the Modern Movement and Adam is not alone among contemporary architects in attempting to introduce some of the aesthetic qualities of Modernism into classical architecture.[4] In each of its past phases, from Ancient Greece to the American Beaux-Arts, classicism has constantly evolved as a living thing, with its best practitioners always drawing on what has gone before but, at the same time, reinventing the tradition anew. Over his career Robert Adam has transformed the profile of traditional architecture so that it continues to flourish and advance. This is a legacy he enthusiastically entrusts to his fellow directors.

4  As seen, for instance, in Thomas Beeby's Daniel F. and Ada L. Rice Building for the Art Institute of Chicago (1988), Demetri Porphyrios' Pavilion at Battery Park City (1990) and Robert A.M. Stern's Nashville Public Library (2001).

# SELECTED BIBLIOGRAPHY

Adam, R., 2009. 'Create your own instant classic'. *Homebuilding & Renovating*, August 2009, pp. 74–80.

Adam, R., 2008. 'Manufacturing Consent', *Building Magazine*, 1 August, 2008.

Adam, R., 2008. 'Dinosaur Modern', *RIBA Journal*, May 2008, pp. 42–44.

Adam, R., 2008. 'Globalisation and Architecture', *Architectural Review*, February 2008, pp. 74/2–77/2.

Adam, R., 2006. 'The Culture of Conservation', *Planning in London*, issue 56.

Adam, R., 2004. 'Save the Gummer Clause', *Country Life*, vol. 198, no. 22, pp. 50–53.

Adam, R., 1998. 'Het andere moderne: traditie in architectuur en matschappij = The other modern: tradition in architecture and society', *Archis*, no. 5, pp. 40–45.

Adam, R., 1998. 'The other modern: tradition in architecture and society', *Classicist*, no. 5, pp. 42–45.

Adam, R., 1995. 'Comment [opinion]', *Perspectives on Architecture*, vol. 2, no. 15, p. 7.

Adam, R., 1995. 'The new Library, Classics Center, and Cast Gallery at the Ashmolean Museum, Oxford, England', *Classicist*, no. 2, pp. 58–67.

Adam, R., 1995. 'The oral history of modern architecture [by] John Peter', *Perspectives on Architecture*, vol. 2, no. 9, p. 19.

Adam, R., 1995. *Buildings: How they Work*. New York: Sterling Pub. Co.

Adam, R., 1994. 'A genuine addition to Palladian scholarship', *Architects' Journal*, vol. 200, no. 5, p. 42.

Adam, R., 1994. 'Obeying orders', *Perspectives on Architecture*, vol. 1, no. 4, pp. 34–37.

Adam, R., 1994. 'Space station', *Perspectives on Architecture*, vol. 1, no. 1, pp. 44–45.

Adam, R., 1994. 'Analysis of a pioneer Renaissance man', *Architects' Journal*, vol. 199, no. 19, p. 51.

Adam, R., 1993. 'Shaping up: Terry Farrell at Vauxhall Cross', *Architecture Today*, no. 38, p. 24.

Adam, R., 1992. 'The built, the unbuilt and the unbuildable: in pursuit of architectural meaning [by] Robert Harbison', *Royal Society of Arts (Great Britain) RSA Journal*, vol. 140, no. 5430, pp. 469–470.

Adam, R., 1992. 'Diverse drawings', *Royal Society of Arts (Great Britain) RSA Journal*, vol. 140, no. 5430, pp. 470–471.

Adam, R., 1992. 'The legacy of Modernism in New Classicism', *Architectural Design*, vol. 62, no. 5, pp. 60–61.

Adam, R., 1990. *Classical Design in the Late Twentieth Century: Recent Work of Robert Adam*. London: Royal Institute of British Architects, Heinz Gallery.

Adam, R., 1990. *Classical Architecture: A Complete Handbook*. London: Viking.

Adam, R., 1989. 'Oriental charm: The origins of the Romanesque, by V. T. [sic] Atroshenko and Judith Collins', *Architects' Journal*, vol. 190, no. 24, p. 77.

Adam, R., 1989. 'Personal columns', *Building Design*, no. 946, pp. 18–19.

Adam, R., 1989. 'Tin Gods: technology and contemporary architecture', *Architectural Design*, vol. 59, no. 9, pp. viii–xvi.

Adam, R., 1988. 'Holding the tiller steady [neo-vernacular architecture]', *Building Design*, no. 899, p. 9.

Adam, R., 1988. 'Drawing lessons: English cathedrals drawn by Dennis Creffield', *Architects' Journal*, vol. 187, no. 12, p. 81.

Adam, R., 1988. 'Spurious linkage: does the development of technology impose a duty to produce an architecture which reflects this process?' *Building Design*, no. 875, pp. 32–33.

Adam, R., 1988. 'The paradox of imitation and originality', *Architectural Design*, vol. 58, no. 9, pp. 18–19.

Adam, R., 1988. 'Visions of Britain and the Academy Forum at the Tate', *Architectural Design*, vol. 58, no. 11, pp. 6–17.

Adam, R., 1985. 'Classic views', *Architects' Journal*, vol. 181, no. 30, p. 18.

Allen, I., 1997. 'News in pictures: Adam's addition to Oxford's Ashmolean', *Architects' Journal*, vol. 205, no. 8, pp. 10–11.

Aslet, C., 2003. 'In praise of Poundbury', *Country Life*, vol. 197, no. 26, pp. 84–89.

Aslet, C, 2001. 'The pursuit of houses' [editorial], *Country Life*, vol. 195, no. 6, pp. 53.

Cadji, M., 2000. 'Show and tell', *RIBA Journal*, vol. 107, no. 12, pp. 12–[15].

Churchill, P., 2005. 'Keeping the faith: two new developments have more claim than most to the description "divine"', *Country Life*, vol. 199, no. 48, pp. 94–95.

Cruickshank, D., 1994. 'Modern masters', *Perspectives on Architecture*, vol. 1, no. 4, pp 38–41.

Cruickshank, D., 1986. 'Good bookkeeping' [Bordon Library], *Architects' Journal*, vol. 184, no. 32, pp. 4–5.

Dowling, E. M., 2004. *New Classicism: The Rebirth of Traditional Architecture*, New York: Rizzoli.

Hall, M., 1999. 'Seated in tradition', *Country Life*, vol. 193, no. 7, pp. 42–43.

Kahn, E. M., 2004. 'Classical globetrotters' [Robert Adam Architects], *Clem Labine's Traditional Building*, vol. 17, no. 1, p. 6.

McDonald, M., 2002. 'Sackler Library [Oxford University, U.K.] turns a page in classical library design', *Clem Labine's Traditional Building*, vol. 15, no. 5, p. 12.

Melvin, J., 2002. 'Classical education: Sackler Library, University of Oxford', *RIBA Journal*, vol. 109, no. 1, pp. 38–42.

Melvin, J., 1988. 'Technology transfer: Robert Adam in his RIBA lecture this week on technology and contemporary architecture', *Building Design*, no. 872, p. 2.

Melvin, J., 1990. 'Fearful symmetry', *Building Design*, no. 1015, pp. 14–15.

Musson, J., 1995. 'Adding to Ashmole', *Country Life*, vol. 189, no. 42, p. 73.

Papadakis, A., and Powell, K., 1992. 'Paternoster Square', *Architectural Design*, vol. 62, no. 5, pp. 6–59.

Pawley, M., 1990. 'Robert Adam: too much genius for his own clients?' *Building*, vol. 255, no. 24, p. 33.

Pawley, M., 1988. 'Attenzione, arrivano gli "skeuomorphs"', *Casabella*, vol. 52, no. 546, p. 39.

Pearce, D., 1986. 'Profile: Robert Adam', *RIBA Journal*, vol. 93, no. 3, pp. 5–8.

Powers, A., 2005. 'Holistic houses', *Country Life*, vol. 199, no. 27, pp. 62–65.

Powers, A., 1998. 'The write stuff', *RIBA Journal*, vol. 105, no. 2, p. 21.

Powers, A., 1990. 'Battle on unreal terms: Robert Adam exhibition', *Country Life*, vol. 184, no. 49, p. 202.

Robinson, J. M., 1990. 'Classical quartet: new country houses', *Country Life*, vol. 184, no. 35, pp. 74–77.

Stamp, G., 1993. 'New buildings in historic contexts', *RIBA Journal*, vol. 100, no. 2, pp. 24–40.

Watkin, D., 2006. 'The rise of the house of Adam', *Country Life*, vol. 200, no. 8, pp. 76–81.

Watkin, D., 2001. 'Wakeham, West Sussex: a residence of Mr. and Mrs. Harold Carter', *Country Life*, vol. 195, no. 25, pp. 174–177.

White, C., 1997. 'The Ashmolean Museum today', *Apollo*, vol. 145, no. 423, pp. 4–20.

White, R., 1990. 'Home counties child: Classical design in the late twentieth century: the recent work of Robert Adam', *Architects' Journal*, vol. 192, no. 24, pp. 54–55.

Woodward, A., 1995. 'Such stuff as dreams are made on', *Perspectives on Architecture*, vol. 2, no. 13, pp. 50–51.

# PHOTOGRAPHY AND DRAWING CREDITS

**198–202 Piccadilly, London**
Photography: Morley von Sternberg (51–55)

**An Ionic capital and entablature, a new Palladian villa, Berkshire**
Photography: John Critchley (248 top row, centre)

**Apollo Tower**
Drawing: Robert Adam (25)

**Arts & Crafts farmstead**
Drawing: Chris Draper (111 top)

**Avenel in Kilmacolm, Scotland**
Photography: Douglas Martin (181 top);
Alan Dimmock (181 bottom)

**Blue Ball Hill, Winchester**
Drawing: Chris Draper (180)

**Book stacks, Sackler Library, Oxford**
Photography: Morley von Sternberg (239 left)

**Bronze capitals, Millennium garden pavilion, Hampshire**
Photography: Carlos Dominguez (248 bottom row, centre)

**Bust of Robert Adam**
Photography: John Critchley (8)

**Cabinet and display, Hertford College Oxford**
Photography: John Critchley (250 top right)

**Cast iron capitals for a pergola, Riverside country house, Dorset**
Photography: John Critchley (249 top row, centre)

**Chairs for St Bride's Church**
Photography: John Critchley (243 right)

**Competition submission for Worcester College, Oxford**
Drawing: Robert Adam (188 bottom)

**Cottage Ornée restoration, Yorkshire**
Drawing: Chris Draper (85 bottom)

**Country house, Cheshire**
Drawings: Chris Draper (148–149); Robert Adam (151)

**Crooked Pightle House, Robert Adam's own house, Hampshire**
Photography: John Critchley (58, 59, 60, 61)

**Directors of ADAM Architecture**
Photography: Tiddy Maitland-Titterton (6)

**Dogmersfield Park**
Photography: John Critchley (41)
Drawing: Robert Adam (42)

**Doric capital to library stacks, Sackler Library, Oxford**
Photography: Morley von Sternberg (249 top row, right)

**Douai Abbey, Berkshire**
Drawing and photography: courtesy Bewley Homes plc (178–179)

**Egg and dart bronze pilaster capital, new offices, Piccadilly, London**
Photography: Morley von Sternberg (248 top row, right)

**Extension to a manor house, Hampshire**
Photography: Joe Low (74, 75)
Drawing: Robert Adam (75)

**Extensions to farmhouse, Oxfordshire**
Photography: John Critchley (80–83)

**Field Farm, Shepton Mallet: an urban extension**
Photography: John Critchley (192–193)

**Garden Pavilion at architect's own house**
Photography: John Critchley (250 top left)

**Georgian country house, Hertfordshire**
Photography: John Critchley (157)

**Georgian house extension, Hampshire**
Photography: John Critchley (69 top, 70 top);
June Buck (70 bottom)
Drawing: George Saumarez Smith (69 bottom)

**Georgian villa restoration, London**
Photography: Seb Bone (111 bottom right)

**Gothic cottage renovation, Hampshire**
Photography: John Critchley (85 top left)

**Hart's tongue fern designs, extension to a manor house, Hampshire**
Photography: Joe Low (249 bottom row, right)

**Houses adjacent to Minster, Wimbourne, Dorset**
Photography: courtesy Hampshire Chronicle (167)

**Houses in Weybridge, Surrey**
Photography: Joe Low (169)

**Hyde Church Path, Hampshire**
Photography: John Critchley (165)

**Industrial workshop conversion, North Hampshire**
Photography: John Critchley (109 bottom)

**Kitcombe Folly, East Hampshire**
Photography: John Critchley (175)

**Large column capital, new offices, Piccadilly, London**
Photography: Morley von Sternberg (248 bottom row, left)

**Library at Bordon, Hampshire**
Photography: John Critchley (215, 216)

**Library chair, Sackler Library**
Photography: Morley von Sternberg (239 centre)

**Lower East Side redevelopment, New York**
Photography: courtesy City Journal (34)

**Millennium garden pavilion, Hampshire**
Photography: Carlos Dominguez (31)

**Millennium Gate, Atlanta**
Photography: Hugh Petter (232, 233 top left and right)

**Modern classical villa, Cheltenham**
Photography: John Critchley (92–95)

**New Colonial house, Paradise Island, The Bahamas**
Photography: Scott Frances (86–87, 89–91)

# ACKNOWLEDGEMENTS

This book has been many years in the making and has involved a number of people whom I would like to thank.

First of all a special thank you to the author Richard John for his dedication, fortitude and perseverance in researching and writing this book. It captures a big part of my work over the past 30 years and some important projects from my fellow Directors whom I would also like to thank for their part in the book: Nigel Anderson, Paul Hanvey, Hugh Petter and George Saumarez Smith.

I would like to sincerely thank all the clients, without whom these projects would obviously not have been possible; Mr & Mrs R Abrahams, Hon J P Allsopp, Amdahl Corporation, Mr Andreae, Mr & Mrs J Anderson, R Aroskin, Mr & Mrs A Atha, Sir James A Bart, J Barroll Brown, Barwood, Ed Bellhouse, Bendall Developments, Mr & Mrs M Bickford-Smith, G Bingham, M Brown, R Brisbane, British School at Rome, Bewley Homes plc, The Hon Brenda Carter & Harold Carter, Castillian Town & Country Ltd, M A Cherrington Ltd, Mr & Mrs H Clarke, Crown Point Estate, H D'Abo, Mr D Dadral, F Dagher, D Daymond, N Diab, Donfield Homes, Mr & Mrs Douglas, Duchy of Cornwall, East Street Borough, Edward Ware Homes, Mr & Mrs T Everett, B C Fairchild, Forth Property Developments Ltd, P Fowler Esq MBE, N Gabie, Mr & Mrs P Gadsby, Grace & Sons, Griffon Land & Estates, Mr A Haig, P Hall, Hampshire County Council, Mr P Harris, Lord & Lady Hay, Hertford College Oxford, Mr & Mrs C Hopton, Ideal Homes, IHG, Ingliston Developments Ltd, N Johnston, Hon & Mrs R Lloyd-George, Lockhard Ltd, Mr & Mrs J Maclean, Mr L Masters, McKay Securities, Mr & Mrs N Measham, Mountleigh Estates, Myron Magnet, National Monuments Foundation, National Trust, Oxford University, Mr & Mrs Pain, Prince's Foundation, Mr & Mrs T Roberts, Mr & Mrs G Rolls, Mr & Mrs R Rout, Richmond Borough Council, JB Richmond-Dodd, Lord Sainsbury, Sarum Development Ltd, Scops Development Ltd, RJ Smith, St Bride's Church, Standard Life, Mr F Stockdale, Mr & Mrs T Stockdale, M Tasos, The Rhodes Trust, Tower Court Ltd, Townsend, Mr & Mrs M Weaver, Mr & Mrs Williams, Working Group, 8CU.

The staff at the Practice have continued to show an interest in the book over the years and have helped in various ways, for this I thank them. I would particularly like to thank Trudy Coutts and Becky Sykes without whom my working life would have been impossible. I would like to thank the photographers and artists who have granted permission to include their illustrations this book. I hope you agree that they have captured the particular quality of each and every property.

I hope you enjoy reading this book as much as I have enjoyed developing tradition in architecture and urban design, trying to ensure that this remains active and relevant in modern society.

Robert Adam

# INDEX

# ABOUT THE AUTHOR

Professor Richard John is a scholar of Peterhouse, Cambridge, and a former fellow of Merton College, Oxford, where he taught Medieval and Renaissance Italian history. In 1995 he was appointed Director of The Prince of Wales's Institute of Architecture, London. He has been a faculty member at the University of Miami since 1999 and served as the Harrison Design Scholar at the Georgia Institute of Technology in 2007–08. His books include *Thomas Gordon Smith and the Rebirth of Classical Architecture* (London, 2001) and *John Simpson: The Queen's Gallery Buckingham Palace and Other Works* (London, 2002). He is the Editor of *The Classicist*, the award-winning, peer-reviewed journal of the Institute of Classical Architecture and Classical America.

Every effort has been made to trace the original source of copyright material contained in this book. The publishers would be pleased to hear from copyright holders to rectify any errors or omissions.

The information and illustrations in this publication have been prepared and supplied by ADAM Architecture. While all reasonable efforts have been made to ensure accuracy, the publishers do not, under any circumstances, accept responsibility for errors, omissions and representations express or implied.

DISCARL